Maya History

Tatiana Proskouriakoff

MAYA HISTORY

Edited by Rosemary A. Joyce
Foreword by Gordon R. Willey
Biographical Sketch by Ian Graham

Illustrations by Barbara C. Page

 UNIVERSITY OF TEXAS PRESS, AUSTIN

Requests for permission to reproduce material from this work should be sent to
Permissions, University of Texas Press, Box 7819, Austin, TX 78713-7819.

⊗The paper used in this publication meets the minimum requirements of
American National Standard for Information Sciences—Permanence of Paper
for Printed Library Materials, ANSI Z39.48-1984.

LIBRARY OF CONGRESS CATALOGING-IN-PUBLICATION DATA

Proskouriakoff, Tatiana, 1909–
     Maya history / by Tatiana Proskouriakoff ; edited by Rosemary A. Joyce ;
foreword by Gordon R. Willey ; biographical sketch by Ian Graham ;
illustrations by Barbara C. Page. — 1st ed.
        p.   cm.
     Includes bibliographical references and index.
     ISBN 0-292-75085-4
     1. Mayas—History.   I. Joyce, Rosemary A., date   . II. Title.
F1435.P76   1993   92-9387
972.81′016—dc20   CIP

Contents

Acknowledgments

THE PRODUCTION OF THIS BOOK, THE LAST WORK OF a great Maya scholar, owes much to the efforts of a number of interested people. During the final composition of the manuscript, Tatiana Proskouriakoff consulted with the staff of the Peabody Museum Press, particularly Robyn Sweesy and Donna Dickerson, who supervised the initial copy-editing of the manuscript. As Proskouriakoff's health faded, Peter Mathews agreed to help advance the project. He selected the individual glyphs to be illustrated within the text to complement the larger figures which Proskouriakoff had chosen. He supervised the drawings done by Barbara C. Page and indicated the location for in-text placement of glyphs. Peter Mathews also consulted with Peabody Museum staff in the initial stages of preparation of the manuscript.

In the production of the final version of the manuscript, we have worked from the revised version produced by Peabody Press staff in consultation with Proskouriakoff. This version of the manuscript lacked citations of published literature and a bibliography. John G. Fox compiled the initial bibliography for the manuscript, which has been corrected and augmented by Rosemary Joyce. The current bibliography incorporates all sources referred to by all contributors to this volume.

Emeritus Professor Gordon R. Willey kindly agreed to provide his impressions of Tatiana Proskouriakoff, and Ian Graham contributed a biographical sketch previously published in *American Antiquity*. Both scholars have also provided valuable assistance with the final production of illustrations for the book, and have been a source of guidance to Rosemary Joyce as she edited the manuscript.

Foreword

TATIANA PROSKOURIAKOFF WILL SURELY BE remembered as one of the outstanding Mayanists of all time. She brought to her work great love and dedication, and this shows in all of her writings—as well as in her superb drawings of Maya architectural reconstructions. While not trained as an ethnologist, she was highly sensitive to and empathetic with peoples from cultures other than her own. I can explain it in no other way except to say that she had an intuitive perception in such matters.

Tatiana, or Tania, was born in Czarist Russia, and she was with her family in the United States—her father was a purchasing agent for the Czar's government during World War I—at the time of the Russian Revolution. They remained in the States, and Tania never went back to Russia until much later in life, and then only for short visit. She attended Pennsylvania State College and the University of Pennsylvania as an architectural student, and she was drawn into Maya archaeology as an architectural draftsperson with the Carnegie Institution's Maya staff in the Depression years. Although I never spoke with her about it, I can imagine that she became intrigued early on with the imagination of the ancient Maya architects. Here on this American hemisphere were Precolumbian architectural masterpieces that rivaled those of the Old World. She went on to become a leading authority in the subject.

When I first met Tania, in 1950, she was also recognized as an authority in Maya art, the author of *A Study of Classic Maya Sculpture,* which had just been published in that year, the first major work on that subject since Herbert J. Spinden's *magnum opus* of almost forty years before (1913). In my early conversations with her, I don't think I was aware of the range and depth of her interests. I suppose they were there all along, but I remember Tania as a person who, much more than most, continued to develop intellectually throughout her entire life. In the early and middle 1960s she published three important short papers on Maya hieroglyphic texts (1960; 1963; 1964). As Rosemary Joyce has stated in her Introduction, these papers "changed the basic premise of Maya scholarship." Maya hieroglyphic texts, as carved on monuments and buildings, were read, for the first time, as applying to actual historic human events rather than being considered as only ritual and priestly lore. Proskouriakoff had done this very much in the contexts of the Maya portrait art and the Maya calendrical dates which were associated with the texts. Archaeology, in its most meaningful sense, is a study of contexts, and Tania's archaeology was always very contextual.

At the same time that she was writing these pathbreaking papers on Maya glyphs, Tania was analyzing the many humble artifacts from Mayapan, which she was to publish upon in 1962, and she went from all of this to her very detailed and scholarly examination of the big jade collection from the Sacred Cenote of Chichen Itza. The jades, which had been brought from the murky waters of that well by E. H. Thompson more than a half-century before, were mostly the fragmentary pieces of hundreds of beautifully carved heirloom ornaments dating back to earlier Classic Period Maya times. These had been thrown into the Cenote, along with other sacrifices, by the Postclassic inheritors of these treasured pieces. Tania and her assistants spent years painstakingly fitting all of these back together so they could be properly described in her monograph, *Jades from the Cenote of Sacrifice, Chichen Itza, Yucatan,* which was published in 1974.

That academic year of 1974–1975 Tania was kind enough to collaborate with me in a seminar on Maya art and the interpretations of Maya iconography. I look back on it as an outstanding learning experience for our students and, especially, for me. In the seminar she constantly surprised me with the "anthropological" approach she brought to the subject. I was always hesitant to tell her this; somehow I didn't think that she would appreciate it. I had the impression that she always thought of herself as an art historian—and she was, I am sure, by the most professional definitions of that term. Above all, though, she was a great humanistic scholar, but one who disciplined humanistic appreciation with a strong critical intelligence.

During that year, and later, Tania spoke of her desire to bring together her vision of the Maya past into a history that would transcend the somewhat bleak, skeletonized, and fragmented chronicles which normally characterize archaeology. She saw this as her last work. It would draw upon all of the Maya past, as this could be recreated in the context of art, monuments, land, and peoples, and it would be given its narrative force by an understanding of events as these could be interpreted from the ancient texts in this setting. It was to be *Maya History.*

G.R.W.
November 1990

IAN GRAHAM

Tatiana Proskouriakoff

1909 – 1985

TATIANA PROSKOURIAKOFF WAS ACTIVE FOR FIFTY years in the field of Mesoamerican archaeology, and will always be remembered for the important contributions that she made, most notably in her studies of Maya art, architecture, and hieroglyphic writing.

She was born in Tomsk, Siberia, where her grandfather taught natural science (and wrote articles on Siberian archaeology) and where her father, Avenir Proskouriakoff, a chemist and engineer, also worked. Tatiana's mother, Alla Nekrassova, the daughter of a general, had met him in Moscow and eloped with him to Tomsk. She was a physician, who had graduated from the first class in any Russian medical school to accept women.

At the entry of Russia into World War I, her father found himself unable to enlist because of a weak heart; instead he was appointed inspector of ordnance, and late in 1915 was sent on a mission to the United States to supervise the manufacture of arms for his country. The Proskouriakoffs and their two daughters took ship from Archangel but had gone only a short way when ice closed in. While in this ship, stuck fast in the ice, the two girls contracted scarlet fever and diphtheria—Tatiana's sister also came down with measles—and they had to be carried back across the ice. Eventually the family was reunited in Pennsylvania the following spring, and there, after the Russian Revolution had occurred, they elected to stay. Her mother resumed her career as a physician in her adopted country, and her father taught chemistry.

At Lansdowne High School Tatiana—or Tania, as later she was universally known among her colleagues—acquired the nickname "Duchess," by no means bestowed for hauteur or pretensions, but for the Rolls-Royce quality of her mind, and by this name her sister and friends from those days continued to call her. After graduation,

Reproduced by permission of the Society for American Archaeology from *American Antiquity* 55(1), 1990.

Proskouriakoff enrolled in the School of Architecture of Pennsylvania State College, though one academic year was spent at the University of Pennsylvania. Upon graduation in 1930 she found that because of the Depression, building was practically at a standstill, and some dismal years were spent job hunting. For a time she worked at Wanamaker's store. Then she took on a small job which involved copying drawings at a scale suitable for needlepoint, and for this purpose was given access to the University Museum. Having met one of the curators, she volunteered to make drawings for him— mostly to stave off boredom, she later said—and was accepted. The pay was poor, but at least she could use the library.

Soon after, Linton Satterthwaite, impressed by the quality of her work, invited her to join the 1936 expedition to Piedras Negras, with travel and expenses paid but no salary. On the way to the site they visited Palenque, and there, on seeing the elegant Temple of the Sun, Proskouriakoff knew she had found her vocation.

Unfortunately, the Depression showed no signs of letting up, and after another season at Piedras Negras, Satterthwaite was threatening to fire her (as he put it) because he could not agree to go on employing her without salary. Just then Sylvanus Morley, on a visit to the museum, was shown a drawing she had done as a pastime, one showing the Piedras Negras acropolis as it might have looked in its heyday. Morley immediately encouraged her to do a series of such drawings; in addition he secured funds to send her in 1939 to work with the Carnegie Institution team at Copan, and later at Chichen Itza.

Proskouriakoff traveled alone to Copan, and once there, found life at the staff camp distinctly wild. Having been brought up in a very proper European household, she was surprised considerably by the battery of bottles displayed on a table in the camp *sala,* and more so on finding how much the consumption of their contents enlivened the nightly games of poker, especially on Saturdays. One Sunday morning, annoyed with the men for sleeping so late, she opened the door of Gustav Stromsvik's room and let his parrot in. Soon there was a duet of squawking, the parrot having gotten Stromsvik by the mustache.

Proskouriakoff continued working on the series of reconstruction drawings in her spare time, and it was published by the Carnegie Institution as *An Album of Maya Architecture* (1946). It was Morley again who provided the stimulus for her next major work, even though this time it arose out of a friendly disagreement they had over the dating of a certain monument. Stimulated as ever by disagreement, she started on a bold attempt to establish a method of dating monuments on the basis, not of aesthetic values (on which Morley tended to rely) but of morphology and sculptural style. Through her systematic and laborious analysis of the known body of Maya monuments datable by their own inscriptions, she was able to provide a method of dating any monument lacking an inscribed date to within twenty or thirty years. Since this important work, *A Study of Classic Maya Sculpture* (1950), was compiled, a large number of new monuments has been found, and a new edition incorporating them is needed.

In 1943 Proskouriakoff had been promoted by A. V. Kidder, then head of the Carnegie's Division of Historical Research, from draftsman and illustrator to staff member, and it was as a surveyor and excavator that she took part in the Institution's last archaeological work, at Mayapan (1950–1955). At its end, all staff members were to be retired. Kidder, however, managed to persuade the Institution to retain on a permanent basis the three youngest members of the staff, of whom Proskouriakoff was one, at a reduced salary.

Now free of all assigned duties and established as a research associate in the Peabody Museum of Harvard University (where ultimately she was named honorary curator of Maya art), Proskouriakoff could turn to the study of Maya hieroglyphic writing. From the beginning this had fascinated her and it had been the subject of her first published contribution (1944). Within a very short time she was to produce a paper, modest in presentation but of surpassing importance, entitled "Historical Implications of a Pattern of Dates at Piedras Negras, Guatemala" (1960). At one blow, this short paper freed the study of Maya writing from lengthy stagnation, which largely was due to the generally accepted idea that monumental inscriptions contained exclusively calendrical and astronomical matter. Proskouriakoff's demonstration that they contained instead records of the principal events in the lives of historical personages was truly liberating. In 1962 it won for her the fifth A. V. Kidder Medal (she herself had been designer of the medal), and it continues to underlie much of today's greatly increased epigraphic activity.

Proskouriakoff's next major undertaking, if less remarkable for originality, was notable for the great perseverance it called forth. This was preparation of *Jades from the Cenote of Sacrifice* (1974), an illustrated and descriptive catalog of nearly one thousand complete or restorable jade pieces (besides innumerable other fragments) that had lain nearly seventy years in the Peabody Museum. Identifying and sorting the shattered components of incomplete plaques, and then to the best of her ability supplying the missing portions of the designs in modeled plaster presented a tremendous challenge—one that exploited to the full her visual memory and unrivaled knowledge of iconography.

That task occupied a good part of her time for fifteen years. During some of that time she also was engaged in an analysis of design motifs found on pottery. This project must be counted as her one failure. Having amassed a large amount of data, she came to realize that little of value could be extracted from it. In her brief description of this work (1968) she still expressed hopes of completing a monograph; in fact she abandoned work on it at about that time.

Early in 1973, with work on the jades completed, Proskouriakoff began her last major work, a review of historical material in Classic Maya inscriptions tentatively titled *Maya History*. Characteristically she had chosen an extremely difficult and time-consuming study. The dynastic histories and intersite relations for most of the larger sites had to be pored over, and hieroglyphic passages copied onto working sheets. Though her eyesight and energy began to fail, she battled on and was able to complete the work in its essentials before the onset of her final illness.

According to family anecdotes Tania's independent spirit and high intelligence were evident in early childhood. As she grew up, a facet of that independence grew into a dislike of arbitrary rules, one of which she became aware of soon after arriving in New York. When her mother lit a cigarette in a restaurant she was immediately informed that smoking by women in public places was prohibited. "But," the eight-year-old asked her mother, "isn't the United States a free country?"—and on turning sixteen she did not forget to take up smoking!

As an adult, this tendency to swim against the current settled into the healthy skepticism that underlay her scholarly judgment. Sometimes it came to the surface as a propensity for lightly but almost automatically contradicting her colleagues, a habit that most of them regarded more with amused indulgence than irritation. A lively example of this slight contrariness and disdain for the expected response is found in her reply to a questionnaire concerning the suitability of the term "primitive" in the expression "Primitive Art." In her short comment (1965) Proskouriakoff had nothing to say about "primitive," but attacked "art" as a really ambiguous and poorly defined term, listing five of its connotations.

As friends and old Carnegie hands have described her, and on the evidence of photographs, Tania as a young woman was distinctly attractive, and quite feminine—there was nothing of the tweedy bluestocking about her. Decided in her opinions she may have been, even at times a little formidable in conversation, yet socially she was shy and retiring; but here again there was a contradiction in that she enjoyed giving parties and had a way of making them go. In the field, she has been described as good company and quite unperturbed by the horrible accommodations she sometimes had to endure. Friends she had, and a few of her close friendships meant enough to have stirred occasional yearnings for a more social or companionable existence, as against the cloistered life of the scholar.

Later in middle age, she began to feel a certain alienation not only from a world imbued with violence and greed (her heroes had been Gandhi and Franklin Delano Roosevelt), but also from the newer trends in archaeology. As a scholar who was self-taught and preferred to work alone, she had a romantic streak appropriate to the lone adventurer. It seldom showed, but it was this side that felt the appeal of boats and steamships, and the novels of Joseph Conrad, which she read and reread, partly for the sake of improving her style (and she did write very well). There also is a hint of that side in a note to the editors that accompanied her contribution to the *Codex Wauchope* (1978): "If you read between the lines [of my contribution], you will probably see it as a nostalgic retreat from contemporary methodologies, and a plea for old-fashioned hit or miss logic, which is more fun, and once in a good while pays off."

"Hits that paid off" she undoubtedly scored in her life's work, and she had some fun. Her achievements gained her, in addition to the Kidder Medal, Pennsylvania State University's nomination as their Woman of the Year for 1971; an honorary Doctorate of Laws from Tulane University in 1977; and in 1984 the Guatemalan Order of the Quetzal. For her successes she always was ready to pay tribute to her early mentors, especially Satterthwaite, Morley, Kidder, and Tozzer; it was her hope that she might pass on to the next generation something of their tradition. Through her work, at once adventurous and meticulous, that ambition has abundantly been fulfilled, and through her friendship, example, and scholarly counsel, she left a small band of students and many others forever indebted to her.

I.G.

ROSEMARY A. JOYCE

Introduction

DAVID KELLEY, VOICING A WIDELY SHARED OPINION, credits Tatiana Proskouriakoff with one of the four most important breakthroughs in the modern study of Maya inscriptions (1976:5). Yet this achievement was embodied in a mere handful of articles limited almost entirely to comments on two little-known peripheral sites (Proskouriakoff 1960; 1961a; 1963; 1964). These few pages literally changed the basic premise of Maya scholarship. Maya monuments, Proskouriakoff demonstrated, far from presenting only gods and priests, record the deeds of human beings and form the basis for a Maya history.

The history that Proskouriakoff envisioned was her final life work. In scope, it incorporates the entire Classic Maya area. The basic sources of information are the iconography and themes of monuments which can be placed in chronological succession. Proskouriakoff puts less reliance on interpretations of texts, since she remained skeptical of the ability of scholars to read what the Maya recorded. As she reconstructs it, Maya history is the sketchy story of the spread from the central Peten, and above all from Tikal, of institutions of government. Warfare and intermarriage are the common ground she detects for the city-states of the Classic Maya Lowlands. The Classic Maya collapse is mirrored in the decadence of Maya art, a gradual infiltration of foreign elements which signaled the entry of outsiders into the Maya lowlands and the rise of secular authority and a mercantile class.

Since Proskouriakoff wrote, the volume of scholarship on Maya inscriptions has increased dramatically. Much of this work has been accomplished by researchers who accept the methodology of phonetic decipherment, about which Proskouriakoff expressed great reservations. New excavations have resulted in the addition of new documents unavailable for her analysis. Many suggestions made in this book have been independently elaborated by other scholars. Proskouriakoff's unpublished ideas about Tikal's Early Classic history informed the discussions of other scholars with whom she shared her insights. Still other points raised in her analysis have not as yet been adequately addressed, and provide a challenge for future scholarship.

THE SCOPE OF *MAYA HISTORY*

Underlying this work is the belief that a global review of the Maya world is necessary to understand the developments reflected in the erection of monuments, changes in themes depicted in art, and the events recorded in texts. Proskouriakoff limits herself to an examination of carved stone monuments, primarily those visible to the public, such as stelae, altars, and hieroglyphic stairs. Her goal can be seen as a study of the processes which spread the use of carved stone monuments from a relatively small area in the Central Peten in the fourth century to a broad arc extending from Mexico to Honduras in the eighth century. Her discussion of the gradual contraction of this sphere through the tenth century, and in particular her exclusion of Palenque from the historical record (a separate chapter on the site was left unfinished at her death), illustrate how central the spread of public stone monuments is in this work. It is clear that Proskouriakoff sees this spread simultaneously as evidence of political events, such as conquest, intermarriage, and alliance, and as evidence for the existence of a pan-Maya "ethnic" identity expressed in the form of a shared art style.

Tikal is central to her analysis, and the rise and fall in the fortunes of this site provide the structure for the presentation (see Jones, Coe, and Haviland 1981 for a discussion of Tikal archaeology). Early Classic Tikal established the themes which are found throughout the Classic Maya world. Military conflict with Uaxactun is reflected in the monuments at both sites. Tikal's hegemony in the central Peten begins a long history of military raids as a primary means to establish polities. Equally important in Early Classic Tikal were alliances cemented through marriage, reflected in paired depictions of male and female figures like those of Stelae 23 and 25. Proskouriakoff detects possible reflections of a complex system of elite succession integrating three matrilineages with the ruling patriline on Tikal Stela 26. From the very beginning, political power was based on a balance between conflict and alliance.

Carved monuments and the political system they represented spread from Tikal. Sites along the Río San Pedro prior to 9.10.0.0.0 are interpreted as stages on a trade route important to the central Peten power. Little is made of the preexisting centers in which large-scale architecture, ornamented by stucco sculpture, predominated and freestanding stone sculpture was not used (such as Cerros, Belize; see Friedel 1985). Tikal and Uaxactun, themselves examples of this Late Preclassic tradition, were not alone in the early Maya world, but the roots of the distinctive Peten developments are unexplored.

As the Tikal polity extended its ties out from the central Peten, images of male-female pairs became widespread. Proskouriakoff interprets this pattern as an indication that elite intermarriage was a key to the expansion of Maya polities (compare Marcus 1976; 1987; Molloy and Rathje 1974). Equally widespread are indications of warfare, marked by male figures dressed for battle and taking prisoners. The Maya world, with Tikal at its center, quickly reaches its maximum southern, northern, and western peripheries. In this expanding world, however, internal strains between the elite and a middle class are detected. The succession at Tikal is disrupted, and a hiatus in monument building occurs. The hiatus at Tikal marks the removal of the ruling lineage to the Petexbatun region, where a court is established at Dos Pilas.

The fragmentation of the Maya world is not complete, and through military power and marital alliance, Tikal's lineage is re-established in the Late Classic. The conservative style of monuments and grand scale of the site suggest to Proskouriakoff a status as a pilgrimage center for the entire Maya world. As that world shrinks, the Maya of Tikal continue to perpetuate traditional ways. The end of the Classic Maya tradition comes as foreigners conquer Chichen Itza, foreign elements enter the monumental art of the western fringe, and the secular concerns of the trading class predominate.

Revolving around this central story of the waxing and waning of Tikal are subordinate plots in which sites initially touched by Tikal themselves practice Maya statecraft of warfare and marriage alliance. Caracol in Belize, initially founded by Tikal, becomes deeply involved in affairs of Naranjo. Pusilha in Belize plays a part in the founding of Quirigua, which in turn is related to Copan. War captains at Yaxchilan, legitimated by their marriage with the royal line, play roles in the political stabilization of Piedras Negras. The effects of developments in each site on its neighbors and allies are constantly reviewed. The world of *Maya History* is a world of intimate interconnections reflected in the public monumental record.

TRAILS BLAZED AND PATHS FOLLOWED

Proskouriakoff constantly restrains her speculation and calls for more research. Despite this restraint, she makes several intriguing points which have not been pursued by other researchers. Other conclusions have been independently discovered or elaborated by later scholars. Some studies based on methodological assumptions which Proskouriakoff does not share are not incorporated in her discussion. Others postdate the completion of her manuscript.

Proskouriakoff recognizes the importance of Teotihuacan as the source for iconography which was particularly prevalent in the Usumacinta river drainage. She notes the use of goggle-eyed Tlaloc faces on shields and in headdresses, and the trapezoidal "year sign" motif in headdresses. The significance of Teotihuacan iconography in the Maya lowlands has been the topic of much debate, with scenarios ranging from invasion and conquest (Coggins 1975; 1979; 1983) to the independent adoption of the foreign style to symbolize warfare and sacrifice (Schele 1984a). Exploration of such highland-lowland interaction has clarified considerably the conditions of culture contact and their potential reflection in the archaeological record (A. Miller, ed., 1983, especially Ball 1983). Nonetheless, no consensus has been reached about the precise nature of the iconographic relations which Proskouriakoff describes.

An equally lively debate continues about the nature of relationships between Copan and Quirigua, the southernmost Classic Maya centers. Proskouriakoff discusses stylistic relations in monumental sculpture between the sites and tentatively supports glyphic evidence of connections between the sites. Recent studies have capitalized on decipherments of texts at Quirigua and Copan to describe relations surrounding the apparent defeat in battle of "Eighteen Rabbit" of Copan by the ruler of Quirigua (Jones and Sharer 1986; Riese 1986; 1988). Analysis of the site plans of the two centers confirms their close relationship (Ashmore 1986). Divergent traditions at Quirigua and Copan are evident in other studies, such as ceramic analyses (e.g., Bishop et al. 1986). These ceramic analyses also support Proskouriakoff's association of Pusilha with the southeastern Maya sites, although specific relations seem stronger with Copan than with Quirigua.

Issues such as these, phrased as they are in the idiom of great events and wide-ranging processes, are naturally part of *Maya History*. But contained within the narrative of history are an extraordinary number of rich suggestions about the relationship between particular sculptural formats and programs and social, geographic, and religious forces. These suggestions recall the contributions made by Proskouriakoff's short topical articles (1961b; 1968; 1973). Many of these ideas have been independently investigated by later researchers.

Among observations of this kind, Proskouriakoff notes the association of depictions of ballgame players with hieroglyphic stairs (see M. E. Miller and Houston 1987). While summarizing the waning years of the Classic Maya world, she identifies and traces out what she calls the "cloud-rider" motif in sites near Tikal (compare D. Stuart 1984). At Yaxchilan and Bonampak, Proskouriakoff notes a glyphic compound she calls the "moon-comb" title of subordinates (compare Houston 1989:55–56, based on D. Stuart 1986). She briefly discusses names and titles of royal women on shells from a burial at Piedras Negras (see D. Stuart 1985). She notes the apparent association at Yaxchilan between a particular form of staff with cut-out flaps and solstice dates (compare Tate 1992).

Results from New Excavations

The breadth of Proskouriakoff's work allowed her to identify a wide range of patterns which have become obvious to later researchers through more detailed analyses of single sites and single themes. Researchers studying Caracol (Beetz and Satterthwaite 1981; Chase and Chase 1987; Stone, Reents, and Coffman 1985) and the Petexbatun region (Houston and Mathews 1985; Johnston 1985) have begun to trace the effects of warfare recorded in the texts of the two areas. Tonina, a site barely touched on by Proskouriakoff, has been thoroughly investigated (Becquelin and Baudez 1979–1982) and its monuments discussed from both epigraphic (Mathews 1983) and thematic (Baudez and Mathews 1979) points of view.

Continuing excavations at Tikal have produced new Early Classic monuments, especially in the Mundo Perdido zone (Fahsen 1987; 1988; Fialko 1987; 1988; Laporte and Vega de Zea 1987). These give further weight to Proskouriakoff's speculations about an intimate relationship with Uaxactun, suggestions which underlie other published discussions of Early Classic Tikal (e.g., Coggins 1975; Jones and Satterthwaite 1982; Marcus 1976; Mathews 1985). Newly discovered texts from Caracol suggest the rulers of this site defeated Tikal in battle, and the timing of this defeat may be related to the Tikal hiatus. Continuing debate revolves around the relationship of Tikal and Dos Pilas, in particular about the meaning of the shared Emblem Glyph of the two sites (Houston and Mathews 1985).

The continuation of archaeological investigations at Copan has produced carved monuments from both early and late in the occupation of the site. Proskouriakoff rejected the designation of the Copan village area as the center of Early Classic development, drawing attention to the fact that early monuments there were fragmentary and could have been moved from the Main Group. The many fragments of Early Classic monuments recently recovered in the area of the Great Plaza (Riese 1983) amply support her view, as does detailed stratigraphic evidence for the construction of the Great Plaza beginning in the Early Classic (Cheek 1986). Recent dramatic discoveries of intact Early Classic monuments under the Hieroglyphic Stairway of Temple 26 provide final confirmation that the Main Group was the earliest, and longest occupied, zone of elite activity at Copan (G. Stuart 1989). Late Classic carved benches and other texts excavated in the elite residential zones (e.g., Webster, ed., 1989) reinforce Proskouriakoff's suggestion that stelae scattered throughout the valley may document political grants to subordinates by the ruler of Copan. Contemporary events at Quirigua have been clarified by a project of excavations and investigation of inscriptions (Sharer 1978).

Results of recent excavations at Copan and Quirigua dramatically illustrate that new excavations have disproportionately affected knowledge of the Early Classic period. A fragmentary stela depicting a human figure holding a serpent-bar discovered at Copan (Baudez 1986) challenges Proskouriakoff's characterization of the early monuments at the site as exclusively glyphic. A deeply buried Early Classic monument with both figural carving and inscription from Quirigua provides a similar challenge (Jones 1983; Jones and Sharer 1986). As excavators uncover fragments of early monuments at other Maya sites (e.g., Lamanai, Belize; Closs 1988), the sketch Proskouriakoff draws of a tightly integrated Early Classic Maya world is greatly altered.

New Analyses of Existing Evidence

While new excavations have been the most dramatic source of new information, reanalysis of known monuments has also been a rich area of investigation since the completion of *Maya History*. The assumption that Chichen Itza was occupied by Mexican invaders after an initial Maya occupation has been questioned on archaeological grounds (Ball 1979; Lincoln 1986). Studies of the inscriptions of Chichen Itza, Uxmal, and other Puuc sites have begun to document political relations of what now appear to be contemporary sites (Kelley 1982; Kowalski 1985; Love 1989, Wren, Schmidt, and Krochok 1989).

Art historical analysis of the zoomorphic sculptures from Quirigua (Stone 1985) addresses a gap which Proskouriakoff identified in the understanding of this site. A thorough analysis of the construction of Yaxchilan as a sacred center (Tate 1992) complements Proskouriakoff's research on the Late Classic dynasty (1963; 1964). The demonstration of important astronomical alignments at the site, independently confirming a suggestion by Proskouriakoff, is typical of the growing interest in archaeoastronomy in Maya studies (compare Aveni 1980; Lounsbury 1982; 1988).

The Bonampak murals have been given detailed attention in a study which integrates epigraphy and iconographic analysis (M. E. Miller 1986) and complements research on the carved stone monuments from the site (Mathews 1980). The inscriptions of many centers have begun to receive attention as scholars increasingly turn to the detailed study of single sites (e.g., Fahsen 1984; Pahl 1977; Reents 1986). The monuments of Naranjo and Calakmul, discussed in great detail by Proskouriakoff, have drawn renewed attention from recent scholars (Closs 1984; 1985; Marcus 1987). Perhaps the greatest body of new analyses not discussed in *Maya History* concerns the western

Maya center Palenque (e.g., Lounsbury 1974; 1985; 1988; Mathews and Schele 1974; Schele 1979; 1984b). The emphasis of much recent work has been the refinement of royal histories from individual sites, complementing the broader thematic perspective which Proskouriakoff brought to *Maya History*.

Themes for Future Consideration

Several themes represented in *Maya History* have received only limited attention by other researchers. The most obvious of these is the investigation of the role of women in Maya art. Proskouriakoff was the first to establish the identifying characteristics of women in Maya art (1961b), and, perhaps predictably, she devotes considerable attention to discussing this theme (see also Bruhns 1988; Marcus 1976; 1987; Stone 1988). Her analysis is straightforward. She regards paired stelae of male and female figures as evidence of intermarriage. She detects the pattern first at Tikal, and she attributes its spread from that center to growing webs of alliance. She draws attention to the depiction of women as lineage founders at a number of sites, such as Yaxchilan and Naranjo. Her interest in this pattern leads her to call for renewed attention to suggestions of matrilineal or double descent, perhaps manifest in some instances of double Emblem Glyphs (compare Fox and Justeson 1986).

Proskouriakoff also highlights the importance of tripartite divisions of rulership in Classic Maya art. She draws attention to structures like the Palenque Group of the Cross, where three temples document three complementary aspects of rulership (compare Schele 1979). She points to Postclassic Quiche traditions in which one of four founding ancestors dies, leaving three ancestral lines. Equally applicable are Postclassic Yucatec documents which speak of "three-part rule" (e.g., Edmonson 1982:45).

A third neglected theme is the divinatory significance of particular dates. Proskouriakoff, in a conservative reflection of the traditional assumption that Maya monuments were concerned with time and its ritual significance, often alludes to the character of particular dates. She describes dates which fall on the day sign Men as times of evil omen. Recent scholarship has emphasized the historical content of Classic Maya inscriptions to the exclusion of the divinatory significance of intervals of time (but compare Coggins 1979). Investigation of the potential significance of time intervals, in light of sixteenth-century descriptions and modern survivals of the use of the 260-day calendar, might prove fruitful.

Contemporary research on Maya inscriptions represents an almost total rejection of the assumptions of traditional scholarship represented by J. Eric S. Thompson (1950). Instead of portrayals of priests and records of the intricacies of time, Maya monuments are now seen as portraits of rulers, and Maya inscriptions as the literal chronicle of their actual deeds. Proskouriakoff's cautious approach lies somewhere between the two extremes. Her methodology avoids the excesses of both schools of interpretation.

METHODOLOGY IN THE INTERPRETATION OF MAYA MONUMENTS

Proskouriakoff's contributions to Maya archaeology include the elaboration of a chronological sequence for Maya sculpture based on details of style (1950). This chronology forms the background for her historical interpretation, indicated clearly by her discussions of her disagreements with dates applied to particular monuments on the basis of their texts. Stylistic seriation not only provides chronological control over the order in which monuments were carved and erected; it also directly documents the spread from place to place of Classic Maya culture. Contradictions between the apparent stylistic date and the dates carved on monuments are usually resolved in favor of the style dating.

As style provides the preferred method of constructing chronology, thematic analysis of motifs provides the preferred means of describing the content of the monuments. Proskouriakoff's hypothesis that Maya monuments record events in the lives of Maya rulers was based on matching visual patterns with the order of events in the chronology of individual lives (1960; 1961a; 1963; 1964). The procedure of visual pattern matching, on which her sculptural chronology and breakthroughs in studying particular sites were based, is the basic methodology of _Maya History_.

The repetition of visual themes at Classic Maya sites allows the specification of a small number of actions as the subject matter of carved stone monuments. Men dressed for battle and shown capturing prisoners form one such set. The surface meaning is clear, and Proskouriakoff interprets these monuments as evidence for battles which form a major part of the history she describes. Paired male and female figures form another large set. These are taken as evidence of intermarriage between Maya sites. Figures shown scattering droplets or streams form a third set, which she describes as divination scenes. Bloodletting is recognized in other scenes. Less open to surface interpretation are depictions of figures holding staffs, scepters, and other regalia. Nonetheless, Proskouriakoff suggests the association of the flap-staff at Yaxchilan with solstices, and of the holding of the serpent-bar with posthumous scenes. The interpretation of the meaning of the scenes is based on assumptions about universals of human behavior or specifics about Mesoamerican practices recorded in the sixteenth century.

Inscriptions do not carry the weight of interpretation in this approach, but they are not excluded from consideration. Proskouriakoff was an early supporter of the work of Yurii Knorosov (1967).

She proposed connections between specific glyphs and actions (1968; 1973). However, she remained dubious about the prospects for modern scholars to accurately translate Classic Maya texts. The relatively few readings she suggests herself follow the model of Thompson's rebus-writing principle rather than the syllabic phonetic approach articulated by Knorosov. Phonetic translation has become increasingly accepted in recent years and forms the working hypothesis of many active researchers (see Bricker 1986; Houston 1989; Justeson and Campbell, eds., 1984; Kelley 1976; Korbjuhn 1989; Schele 1982).

Proskouriakoff pays most attention to the detection of the names of individuals and the Emblem Glyphs which indicate the site, lineage, or polity from which individuals come. Her interpretation of the relationships between people named is based primarily on the actions represented in visual form. She uses texts as an adjunct, primarily a source of potential information about social and political status embodied in titles. Her approach to reading texts is well illustrated by the interpretation of the compound which she labels *u ahaulil*. As she notes, other researchers interpreted this as the term for the relationship between father and child (Jones 1977; Schele, Mathews, and Lounsbury 1977). Proskouriakoff's interpretation is based on the use of the frontal face that distinguishes the day sign Ahau, or "Lord." The compound is interpreted as identifying the named individual as ruler. Her proposed reading, incorporating a possessive prefix (*u-*) and a derivational suffix (*-lil*), is almost irrelevant to her interpretation, which rests on the pictographic part of the compound. Consequently, the accuracy of her interpretation is independent of any changes in the phonetic reading of the prefix and suffix, but rests on the interpretation of the *Ahau* image itself.

Proskouriakoff's approach to interpretation was ultimately iconographic, not epigraphic, part of the study of Maya art, not Maya writing. In that study, Tatiana Proskouriakoff held a secure place supported by her overwhelming familiarity with the breadth of Maya art, reflected in her vision of *Maya History*.

Abbreviations Used

Sites

AGT	Aguateca
ALS	Altar de Sacrificios
BJC	Bejucal
BPK	Bonampak
CNK	Chinikiha
CRC	Caracol
CPN	Copan
DPL	Dos Pilas
FLD	La Florida
IXK	Ixkun
IXZ	Ixtutz
LAC	Kuna-Lacanha
MQL	Machaquila
MTL	Motul de San José
NAR	Naranjo
PNG	Piedras Negras
PSD	La Pasadita
PUS	Pusilha
QRG	Quirigua
SBL	Seibal
TIK	Tikal
UAX	Uaxactun
YAX	Yaxchilan
ZAP	El Zapote

Other

Alt	Altar
DO	Dumbarton Oaks
HS	Hieroglyphic Stairway
IS	Initial Series
L	Lintel
LP	Leyden Plate
Mon	Monument
MT	Miscellaneous Text
Sc Pan	Sculptured Panel
Sh Pl	Shell Plaque
St	Stela
Sup	Support
T	Temple
Thr	Throne

CHAPTER ONE

The Earliest Records

8.12.10.0.0 − 8.15.0.0.0

A.D. 288 − 337

THE EARLIEST MONUMENTS OF CENTRAL PETEN DO
not record ends of periods, but we assume that they were erected
soon after the date of their Initial Series to commemorate the event
recorded. Only two monuments are definitely dated in this fifty-year
interval: Stela 29 at Tikal, 8.12.14.8.15 13 (Men 3 Zip), with only the
Initial Series surviving; and Stela 9 at Uaxactun, 8.14.10.13.15 8 Men
8 Kayab, with a longer but badly eroded text. It is curious and perhaps significant that both these dates, thirty-six years apart, fall on
the day Men, considered to be a day of evil portent. On both monuments, the figure holds a serpent-bar diagonally across its chest,
suggesting reference to legendary ancestry and noble birth. Although most of the later monuments seem to have been erected during the lifetime of the persons portrayed, these early stelae, featuring
the ceremonial bar, may have been posthumous, possibly indicating
apotheosis of deceased kings. The details of the Uaxactun figure are
obscured by erosion, but on the figure from Tikal we can make out
the standard Emblem of Tikal on a mask worn on the belt of that
figure. This sign attests to the antiquity of Tikal as a capital city of
its province, as no other Emblem Glyphs have been found in the
texts of this early period.

The Leyden Plate, with its date, 8.14.3.1.12 1 Eb 0 (seating of)
Yaxkin, is stylistically linked to somewhat later monuments and was
probably a funerary offering carved some years later. Although
Sylvanus G. Morley (1937−1938:1:296) makes a good case for its having been made at Tikal, the Emblem of Tikal does not appear in its
design or in the text. After the date there is a second seating glyph
(T772), implying appointment to office(?). This, in turn, is followed
by a bird compound. I am not certain whether this glyph refers to
an individual or to an office, but the same glyph occurs in a different
context at D6 on Stela 31 at Tikal, where it is preceded by a skull

Tikal Emblem Glyph
(TIK St 29, front)

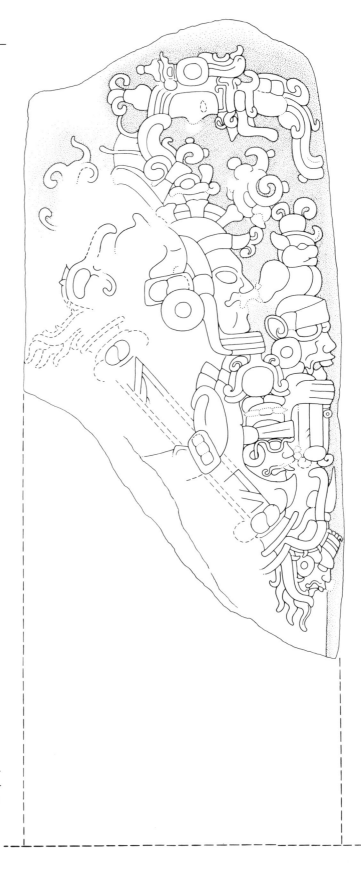

Tikal Stela 29, front: An early Maya
ruler holds the serpent bar. (© Copyright by University Museum, University of Pennsylvania, 33rd and Spruce
Streets, Philadelphia, PA 19104.
Not to be reproduced without
permission.)

compound. The beginning of the clause is missing and its meaning here is not clear. Nor, to my knowledge, is the name of the person depicted on the Leyden Plate found at Tikal, and I am inclined to think that it comes from some other site in the vicinity.

These are the only certain dates of this period that are known, but a number of broken and eroded monuments at Uaxactun, Yaxha, and El Zapote may have been erected before 8.15.0.0.0. At Uaxactun, Stelae 15, 16, and 17 are very probably of this period, and Stela 10 is undoubtedly so, for it was reshaped to serve as an altar to Stela 9. Originally it was carved on both faces with figures, and the striding position of these figures and the round form of the scrolls that can be seen on both sides suggest that it may be the oldest monument yet discovered in this region.

In the lowland regions surrounding central Peten, we have so far no monuments to which we can ascribe dates of comparable or greater antiquity, with the possible exceptions of Mirador in north-central Peten, Tres Islas on the Pasión River, and possibly some sites in southern Belize.

seating glyph
(LP, B10)

bird compound
(LP, A11)

CHAPTER TWO

The Arrival of Strangers

8.15.0.0.0 – 8.17.10.0.0

A.D. 337 – 386

STELAE 18 AND 19 AT UAXACTUN ARE THE FIRST KNOWN stelae whose Initial Series record period endings. Both are dated by these series at 8.16.0.0.0, but the end of the inscription on Stela 18 is a glyph with the coefficient 17, followed by another with the coefficient 1. It is possible that this stela records Katun 1 Ahau, 8.17.0.0.0. Both monuments are broken and in very poor condition, but on Stela 19, one can make out the striding pose of the figure, so characteristic of this period, and on both monuments the enormous, deeply hollowed earplugs worn at this time. The figures wear elaborate high headdresses, but there is as yet no trace of featherwork in their design.

The best source on the events of this period is the remarkable text of Stela 31 at Tikal. This monument was found removed from its original location, broken, and later set up and buried in an ancient temple. Its butt and the lower part of the eight-column inscription on the back are missing, so that the text is interrupted in three places and lacks the final date, but what remains is perfectly preserved. The Initial Series date, 9.0.10.0.0 7 Ahau 3 Yax, is assumed to be the dedication date of the monument, for the text follows the usual pattern of stepping back in time and then progressing forward. A later dedicatory date, originally proposed by Linton Satterthwaite, not only would be inconsistent with the style of this monument but would place it with monuments of another reign.

After a rather unusual Supplementary Series is the record of lahuntun (A13), 1 katun (B13), the latter resembling a baktun sign, a rather unusual but not unknown form. The next passage contains a group of "godmasks," introduced by glyphs of the sky and the earth, recalling the frequent allusions in the Books of Chilam Balam and the Popol Vuh to "Heaven and Earth," sometimes "the Heart of Heaven, the Heart of the Earth," which seems to have been the cen-

Tikal Stela 31, back: The history of events leading to the reign of Stormy Sky.(© Copyright by University Museum, University of Pennsylvania, 33rd and Spruce Streets, Philadelphia, PA 19104. Not to be reproduced without permission.)

tral concept of ancient Maya religion. The mask that follows is the jaguar-eared mask with a fillet under the eye, twisted over the nose, sometimes regarded as the midnight sun, or the Jaguar God of the interior of the Earth, and used to denote the numeral 7. The second mask I do not recognize, but the third is the mask for the numeral 3. Two more masks and an unknown glyph follow, and then the mask for 13 with a prefix 1. The meaning of this passage is obscure; it may be merely a liturgical introduction to what is to follow. It ends with a *hel* compound with the coefficient 9. After this come the title and names of the ruling king of Tikal, introduced by a compound *u caban*. *Cab* can mean "region," town," or "tribe," and probably makes reference to the land or to the people under the command of the lord. His first appellative is a mask with a long, tapering element hanging from the forehead. It appears to be a title used with other names, and I give it the designation of the Early Title Glyph. The second element is a mask with a dotted prefix, a variable form of uncertain meaning, possibly also a title, and the third is the name of the king who has been called Stormy Sky, followed immediately by the Emblem Glyph of Tikal.

The next passage (B21) begins with *u ahaulil* (in the reign of) and the sky and *ich-ben* compounds, perhaps referring to the highlanders who had taken the city. There follow two statements each beginning with a hand glyph, extended with its thumb up. The first hand glyph holds an element of unknown meaning, somewhat like the main element of Glyph G8 of the Supplementary Series, and refers to a ruler whom we call Curlsnout, a predecessor of the ruler portrayed on Stela 31, Stormy Sky. The second hand glyph holds a "hook-scroll" (T19), associated with death expressions, and refers to a rare *ahau* compound such as that inscribed on a vessel from the Tzakol III burial 22 at Uaxactun (R. E. Smith 1955:2:Fig. 7). The text continues with two mask glyphs, the second sometimes identified as the jaguar-eared mask of the "midnight sun," and ends with an *ich-ben* tun variant, vaguely connoting death and funeral services.

Here the inscription breaks off, and the first five glyphs at the beginning of the next two columns are of unknown meaning. After a *hel* glyph, which seems to introduce a new subject, we read *u caban* (the land of people of) Jaguar Baby. The jaguar baby can be seen on top of an animal mask attached to the belt of Stormy Sky, who is pictured on the front of the monument. It is one of three glyphs analogous to the three "gods" defined by Heinrich Berlin at Palenque, and I believe it may refer to one of three Maya matrilineages (a point I will return to again).

Next comes the record of 7 Ahau, the end of Katun 14, and, after two glyphs, *u hel, u caban*, and the name Great Paw. This name consists of three glyphs: a sky glyph prefixed by an S-scroll in a cartouche, an eyeless mask, which is used with names of deceased persons and may indicate an ancestor, and a Chaac sign (T1030) with three dotted scrolls above and an animal paw beneath. At Tikal, in later times, the prefixed sky glyph is the identifying element in names of kings, and Great Paw may be a sobriquet, but in a later passage that is how he is referred to. The end of Katun 17 is then declared, and soon after, a Secondary Series 1.4.12 leads to 11 Eb (15 Mac). Its month position is not given, but it was a very important date in Maya history and was remembered at Uaxactun for more than a century. What happened on this date we can only conjecture. The event is represented by a hand glyph followed by two very unusual face glyphs, with incised rather than modeled detail, as if the artist was not altogether sure of the required forms. Then two statements follow, each introduced by a glyph with a peculiar hand prefix, a hand that looks as if it is holding a bludgeon. In the first instance the main

Uaxactun Stela 5, front: A foreigner, possibly conqueror of Tikal? (Ian Graham, *Corpus of Maya Hieroglyphic Inscriptions, Volume 5, Part 3: Uaxactun,* Peabody Museum of Archaeology and Ethnology. Copyright 1986 by the President and Fellows of Harvard College.)

glyph is a *kin* sign; in the second, the *imix* sign. The first refers to a Frog Scroll, a name (?) that occurs also on Stela 4 of Uaxactun. The second refers to Great Paw. Since the *imix* sign is often found with names of captives, I suspect these phrases document a confrontation or even a battle, in which Frog Scroll is victor. Moreover, Frog Scroll is mentioned again in the inscription; Great Paw is not.

The day 11 Eb had a special importance at Uaxactun. It is recorded on Stela 22 (erected in 9.3.10.0.0) and, as at Tikal, its month position is not given. It is counted from Katun 3.0.0.0, and the Secondary Series reads 6.1.4.12. This, however, does not reach the day 11 Eb, which is given in the text, and Morley (1937–1938:1:195), who could not have known the Tikal record, changes its coefficient to 13. If, instead, we add only 1.4.12 to Katun 3, we reach the sixth katun anniversary of 8.17.1.4.12 11 Eb: 9.3.1.4.12. That, I believe, is what was intended here, and the celebration of a date after almost 120 years raises the suspicion that Uaxactun, either in league with foreigners or using the foreigners as mercenaries, was responsible for the incident that led to the demise of Great Paw. The date 8.17.1.4.12 may also be the correct reading for 11 Eb in the Initial Series of Stela 5 at Uaxactun. It is a badly eroded text, with incised numbers, and Morley's reading, 8.16.1.0.12, is, by his own admission, questionable. The carving on the front is well preserved, and the figure is equipped and dressed in a fashion foreign to the Maya of this period. He holds an atlatl (dart-thrower) and a club set with flint knives, and feathers are conspicuous in his costume. There can be little question that he is a foreigner. His name, if it appears in the text, is undecipherable, but the last glyph on the Initial Series side is clearly the Emblem of Tikal, without its prefixes, suggesting that he may be described here as its conqueror.

Stela 5 was centered on the stairway of a small temple, B-VIII, containing an unusual group burial of two women and three children in a tomb, approached by a vertical shaft (A. L. Smith 1950: 101), that contained Tzakol II pottery. Stela 4 was later erected beside it, and Morley's date for it, 8.18.0.0.0, is very probably correct, though most of the Initial Series is missing. The next to the last glyph of the second column is the Frog Scroll that has been noted on Tikal's Stela 31. Near the end of the inscription is the Early Title Glyph followed by a complex animal or bird head compound, but if the last glyph is an Emblem, it is drawn without prefixes, like the Tikal sign on Stela 5.

Many questions remain unresolved in regard to this crucial incident of Maya history. Who were these strangers who appeared at this time in the Peten, bringing with them weapons originating in the Mexican highlands? How long had they been in the country, and from what direction did they come? Were any other Maya sites involved in the conflict that appears to have been instigated by Uaxactun? What really happened on this day to perpetuate it in the memory of the Uaxactun rulers? We are not yet equipped to answer

Tikal Emblem
(UAX St 5, C9)

such questions, for the undeciphered inscriptions give us only the barest of hints that something momentous was happening at this time, which can only be clarified by combined efforts of future archaeologists and epigraphers.

To return to the inscription on Stela 31 of Tikal, the next notation is a Secondary Series of somewhat uncertain reading: 12 or 17.10.12 (?), probably to be counted back in time to reach a date in Katun 16 of Cycle 8, does not lead to any event now known, and the phrase that follows it is interrupted, so we do not know its origin. At the top of the next two columns is a stepped glyph that may indicate a temple, followed by six glyphs, one of which may be the name Curlsnout. The date that follows appears to be in error. It reads 10 Caban G4 10 Yaxkin, but this date cannot occur between 8.17.0.0.0 and 8.18.0.0.0, the next katun recorded, and aided by the text on Stela 4, we can correct it with reasonable confidence to 5 Caban G4 10 Yaxkin, 8.17.2.16.17.

Tikal Stela 4: The accession monument of Curlsnout. (© Copyright by University Museum, University of Pennsylvania, 33rd and Spruce Streets, Philadelphia, PA 19104. Not to be reproduced without permission.)

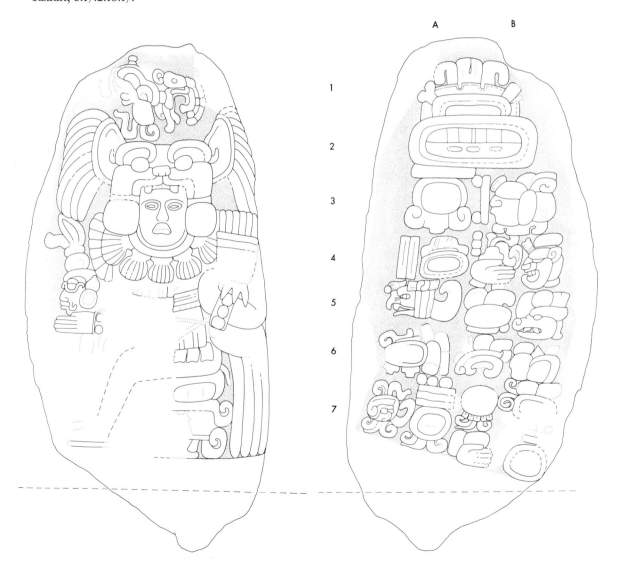

inaugural glyph
(TIK St 4, A5)

Stelae 4 and 18 are low, squat monuments, presenting the figure seated, with legs in profile and feet on the ground but with the head and torso in full front view, a pose not usually seen on Maya monuments. On Stela 4, the ruler is shown wearing a headdress with "wings" of feathers attached. The design is an innovation, as is the collar of pecten shells, both typical elements of costume at Teotihaucan. On Stela 18, the ruler wears a mask under his chin in the Maya style, but on his lap he holds a device designed in the Teotihuacan style. The conclusion is inescapable that if the lord was not himself a foreigner, he had consorted closely with highland people.

Stela 4 records the king's accession with the inaugural glyph commonly used at Piedras Negras, but the "bundle" element of this glyph contains a vulture head, implying that he was a conqueror and not a legitimate successor to the throne. The date of his accession is given here as 5 (Caban?) G4 10 Yaxkin (8.17.2.16.17). The day coefficient is written here with a very broad bar, and the later scribe of Stela 31 probably copied it incorrectly. Stormy Sky, his successor, does not acknowledge his kingship and merely gives him the military title of vulture (general of the army or viceroy?). Moreover, the Early Title Glyph that follows refers not to Tikal but to an *ich-ben cauac* glyph, possibly designating highlanders, or referring to Tlaloc, their god of war and storm. Thus Curlsnout is not here acknowledged as a legitimate king of Tikal. An explanatory clause follows: a hand glyph, thumb up, holding an *ahau* declares that he received lordship (?), but the next two glyphs are of unknown meaning. These, however, are followed by the *u caban* expression and the Frog Scroll glyph, suggesting that he may have been declared a king by the victorious people of Uaxactun. A *hel* glyph then leads to the declaration of Katun 18.

At least three other sites may eventually provide us with additional dates of this period: Yaxha and El Zapote, southeast of Tikal, which have some very early monuments, and on the upper reaches of the Pasión River, the site of Tres Islas, whose early monuments clearly exhibit highland traits. The discussion of the monuments of these sites will be deferred to the end of the next chapter.

CHAPTER THREE

The Maya Regain Tikal

8.17.10.0.0 – 9.0.0.0.0

A.D. 386 – 435

THE TEXT OF TIKAL STELA 31 CONTINUES WITH THE
record of 8.18.0.0.0, recorded also on Stela 18. On Stela 31, this date
is followed by the standard *caban* compound, *ich-ben* katun, and the
name Curlsnout, perhaps indicating that this was the first katun of
his reign. A Distance Number, 1.5.2.5, which follows, seems to have
no point of origin and possibly makes references to his age when he
took the throne. Soon after that is recorded the lahuntun 8.18.10.0.0
and another Distance Number, ?.5.11.0, at the break in the stone.
Presumably, the end of his reign is recorded on the missing butt of
the stela, for the lahuntun 8.19.10.0.0, near the top of the last two
columns, is associated with the name Stormy Sky. The date 9.0.0.0.0
follows in the form of an Initial Series and a period ending. This was
8 Ahau, a fateful katun for the Itza in Postclassic times. The name
Stormy Sky is repeated after a *caban* glyph, and in the phrases that
follow, we find first a Jaguar Baby glyph (the matriclan of the king?)
and further in the clause the atlatl-*cauac* glyph, apparently designating the foreigners. The statement ends with the sign of Tikal, and a
Secondary Series leads to the date 9.0.3.9.18 12 Etz'nab, followed by
a quincunx with a hand-holding-bludgeon prefix (T218, lower) and
a compound of the *cauac* shield. Although the rest of the inscription
is all but destroyed, the implication of the last statement seems to be
that after the death of the foreign king (Curlsnout), his army capitu-
lated to the new monarch (Stormy Sky). Whatever the event, this
date seems to have been of great importance, for 13 katuns later, its
anniversary was marked by special rites of sacrifice (see Chapter 9).

The last Secondary Series is partially destroyed by the break in the
stone, and the record of any subsequent events is lost, but on the
sides of the monument are brief texts that refer to figures of foreign
soldiers. The foreigners hold atlatls and rectangular shields. The face
of the shield on the right side is exposed and shows a goggle-eyed

Curlsnout
(TIK St 31, N2)

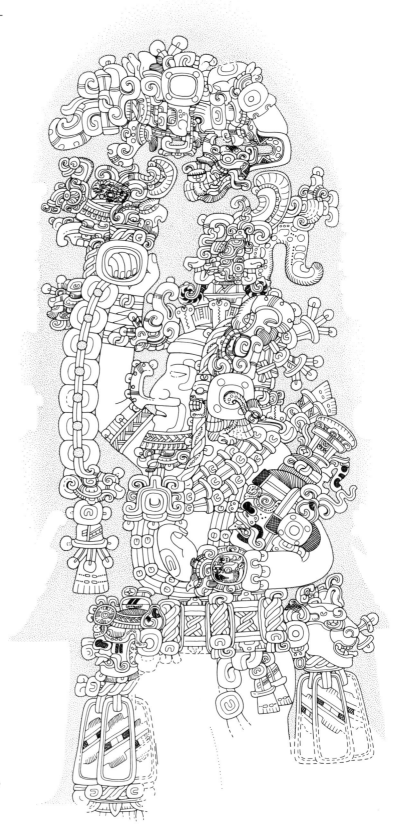

Tikal Stela 31, front: Portrait of Stormy Sky, who restored the Maya dynasty at Tikal. (© Copyright by University Museum, University of Pennsylvania, 33rd and Spruce Streets, Philadelphia, PA 19104. Not to be reproduced without permission.)

Teotihuacan icon. Both figures wear headdresses adorned with feathers and necklaces with pecten shells. Although Curlsnout is mentioned in both texts, the presence in both texts of the atlatl-*cauac* shield glyph suggests that the principal subject is not the former king but his army, which after his death remained in the service of his successor, Stormy Sky.

There is a possibility that, during the reign of Curlsnout, Stormy Sky lived at Uolantun, and that he or one of his close relatives is pictured there on Stela 1, which records the date 8.18.13.5.11. No name can be discerned in the badly weathered text, but the carving on the front of the stela shows an ancestor in the sky wearing on his head the Tikal Emblem, and it may appear also near the end of the text. The device on the loincloth of the figure, moreover, is a dragon head with three protruding knives or spearheads and a long upturned nose in the form of a huge jaguar paw, an intimation that he may have been a descendant of Great Paw, intent upon his vindication. The date on this monument falls just at the time or shortly before Stormy Sky must have been seated on the throne of Tikal.

Whether Stela 32 of Tikal belongs in the reign of Curlsnout is hard to say. This monument is almost a replica of the device on the shield of the figure on the right side of Stela 31 and has no text. It was found mutilated and discarded and may have been merely an icon set up before the headquarters of the foreign army.

atlatl + *cauac* shield
(TIK St 31, N3)

Another such monument carved in the Teotihuacan style, with the figure posed rigidly in full front view, is Stela 11 at Yaxha. Its huge round earplugs, with deep indentations, suggest a Cycle 8 date. Stelae 1 and 5 of Yaxha also look very early and may precede the reign of Curlsnout, but the dates of Early Classic stelae at Yaxha are difficult to judge, since their style combines very early traits with elements that were introduced elsewhere only after the turn of the cycle; in any case there can be no doubt that this site also experienced an invasion from the highlands. Stelae 1, 5, and 10 are mutilated fragments and may have been deliberately broken by the invading highlanders. Stelae 2, 4, and 6 are better preserved. The figures on all these stelae are shown in side view. There are no plumes in their headdresses, and their sandals are of the earliest variety, with a strap below the ankle passing through a loop attached to the sole. The headdresses are very elaborate and frame the face, with a mask under the chin, and their bodies are obscured by ornament. The draftsmanship, especially in depicting arms and legs, is crude. Nevertheless, some or even all of these monuments could have been carved as late as or even later than 9.2.10.0.0.

The reign of Curlsnout seems hardly to affect the normal sequences of monuments at other sites in the Peten. At Uaxactun, Stelae 15, 16, and 17 were probably erected near the end of Baktun 8. To the north, Balakbal Stela 5 cites two dates in the lahuntun 8.18.10.0.0, and Stela 12 at Xultun, though it has no text, can almost surely be placed in the last years of the cycle. Traits such as the wearing of

cauac shield
(ZAP St 1, B10a)

Jaguar Baby
(ZAP St 5, back)

plumes in the headdress and the full frontal position of the figure were only gradually assimilated by the Maya culture, probably as a result of increased trade with the highlands, and there is a hint of growing prosperity and pomp in the introduction of jade-netted skirts in the costume of women.

Six previously unknown monuments recorded by Ian Graham at the site of El Zapote, southeast of Tikal, may provide an illustration of this development. I have seen only preliminary sketches of the inscriptions and am not certain of the readings of the dates, but the style of the monuments is illuminating. Stela 1 is a very unusual monument, showing a masked figure with spindly, curiously bent legs, carrying in his hand a head with a coefficient of 8 or 9. It gives the impression of a shaman or sorcerer rather than of a prince or potentate, and his character hints of a troubled time and recourse to supernatural aid. The inscription is of particular interest because it contains the *cauac* shield glyph with a prefix that could be the same atlatl sign that it has on Stela 31 of Tikal. The Initial Series is ambiguous but probably falls in Katun 19 of Cycle 8. On Stela 4, the Initial Series reads best as 8.17.2.5.3 5 Akbal 1 Kankin, a date that falls less than a year before the accession of Curlsnout. The figure on this stela is a woman, depicted stiffly and with no refinement of detail. It is possible that Stela 6 is its companion monument, for the male figure on this stela looks in the opposite direction, and the two may have been facing each other. On Stela 7, we find another female figure, which is similar to that on Stela 4 but of somewhat more natural proportions. It bears a date in Katun 18 and may be associated with the figure on Stela 3, which has at its feet a mask with a headdress that resembles the Emblem Glyph of Tikal. The inscription on this monument is presented in round panels and reveals no dates. On Stela 5, with the date 9.0.0.0.0, we can observe a distinct change. On the front of this stela is carved a figure of a man; on the back is a figure of a woman. This woman wears a cape and skirt covered with a net of jade beads, a costume that implies trade with the highlands and a growing opulence of the aristocracy. She holds in her hand a rectangular frame with the device of the Jaguar Baby, which links her with the family of Stormy Sky. The establishment of kin affiliations by intercity marriages may have been one way of ensuring peaceful relations without disturbing the rules of succession of local princes. It was again resorted to in 9.9.0.0.0, after a long period of disturbances in outlying regions.

Two very interesting monuments at the site of Tres Islas, far to the south of Tikal, recently recorded by Ian Graham, deserve mention here, although their dates are unknown and their style is unique. The figure on Stela 1 carries a bag in his left hand and three darts in his right. His sandals are provided with ankle guards, and his helmet has a long chin guard projecting forward, like that of the figure on the right side of Stela 31 of Tikal. The inscription began with an Initial Series Introducing Glyph, but there seems to have been no

Initial Series. Mentioned in the text are 12 Ahau, 10 Ahau, 6 Ahau, and possibly 4 Ahau (8.18, 8.19, 9.1, 9.2?). Following the 4 Ahau is the *caban* compound, the Early Title Glyph, and other more badly eroded glyphs, apparently recording a name that we cannot read. Stela 2 tells us little more. It has a very unusual composition, showing a standing figure of a man holding a double-headed serpent-bar across his chest in the usual Maya manner and below him a seated woman wearing a netted jade skirt. Most of her figure is gone, but one can see the heads of the horizontal serpent-bar she was holding. She is seated with her feet on the ground in a cruciform aperture surrounded by masks and scrolls, suggesting an ancestral tomb. The Initial Series on this monument seems to have recorded the end of a katun, but the coefficient of the Ahau is destroyed and no month position is visible. There is a record of the completion of a tun and a name introduced by the Early Title Glyph. This text ends on 4 Ahau and, like the text of Stela 1, mentions at least two other Ahau dates, one of which is 6 Ahau. These texts require further study before their nature can be grasped.

At the site of Bejucal, recently discovered by Ian Graham, an early monument, Stela 2, records the date 8.17.17.0.0 11 (Ahau) 3 Zec. The event and the name that follow are obscure, but the name is clearly preceded by the Early Title Glyph and ends with a turtle carapace. There is also a cartouche of a glyph with the coefficient of 12, but if it is a day glyph, it does not seem to be accompanied by its month position. This day could be Ben, and one might consider the possibility that it is the day following the date 8.17.1.4.12 11 Eb that was recorded at Tikal, the last day association with Jaguar Paw, about a year and a half before the accession of Curlsnout.

The location of Tres Islas on the upper Pasión suggests that the infiltration of foreigners at this time was stemming from the Guatemalan highlands rather than directly from Teotihuacan, but the dates of these monuments, being very uncertain, do not permit a definite conclusion on this point. With the possible exception of these monuments, we have no indication that Classic Maya monuments were being erected in the lowlands except in central Peten in Cycle 8, though occasionally we find very early dates being mentioned in texts, some of which may be historical.

turtle carapace
(BJC St 2, B6, lower right)

CHAPTER FOUR

Some Ragged Pages

9.0.0.0.0 — 9.2.10.0.0

A.D. 435 — 485

hatchet manikin
(TIK St 1, Az3)

AT TIKAL, THE REIGN OF STORMY SKY SPANNED THE change of the cycle, but we do not know how much longer it lasted. Burial 48, with the date 9.1.1.10.10 painted on the wall, may be his, but his name is not mentioned there. One other monument, Stela 1, records his name, and Stelae 2 and 28 are so similar that they may have been carved by the same sculptor. These three monuments are very different in style from Stela 31. They exhibit many new features that later become standard in Maya art. Feathers adorn their head-dresses, and the serpent-bar is held horizontally. Stela 2 shows a mask headdress with the *kin* and Triadic Symbol, and there are masks with coefficients 7 and 9, which are widely used later and occur also on early stelae of Yaxha. On Stela 1, we see the hatchet manikin, with a snake leg, that later becomes the manikin scepter, and the design of the apron over the loincloth is flanked by abbreviated serpent heads with upturned noses that later become frets. The compositions flow around the stelae, and on each side there are serpent heads on the ground. The figure on Stela 28 stands on a prone captive.

The glyphs on the back of Stela 1 have lost all detail, but some signs can be recognized by their overall forms. The first complete glyph in the left column is the hatchet manikin head, which replaces the Early Title Glyph, though it is usually the last, rather than the first, glyph of a name. Two glyphs below, we see the atlatl sign above an oval that could be the *cauac* shield. The next glyph, to the right, contains a completion sign and is followed by "second katun(?)" and what is almost surely the Stormy Sky glyph with an unidentified prefix. The two glyphs that follow are not clear, and the inscription ends with the Tikal Emblem and the *imix*-comb-*imix* glyph that so often stands at the end of a text.

Although the passage is ambiguous, the mention of Stormy Sky so near the end of the inscription constrains us to place this monument in his reign, especially since the figure on the front wears the Jaguar Baby symbol on his belt as does Stormy Sky on Stela 31. The old-fashioned attire on the latter monument may have been assumed deliberately in impersonation of his ancestors, since the theme there is the restoration of an early dynasty.

At Uaxactun, Stela 26, erected at the same time as Stela 31 of Tikal, shows the assimilation of new traits in the full-face presentation of the figure. Before being buried within a shrine, the sculpture was almost entirely effaced, but its general outlines are still visible, and the inscription is in a good state of preservation. The last two glyphs, however, which are preceded by a *caban* compound and very probably named the ruler, are damaged and do not appear clearly in photographs. Stela 20, another full-face presentation at Uaxactun, may belong to the same reign, and Morley's date 9.3.0.0.0 seems somewhat late for it. Stela 23, dated by Morley 9.2.0.0.0, is only a fragment, and little can be gleaned from the portion of text preserved. (See Morley 1937–1938:1:188–191).

It was at this time that cities to the south and to the east of central Peten began to record their histories on monuments. The earliest stelae at Altar de Sacrificios and at Copan had only texts, no sculptured figures. At Altar de Sacrificios, Stelae 10 and 11 are dated 9.1.0.0.0 and 9.2.0.0.0, respectively (J. A. Graham 1972). Their texts are illegible, but the last two glyphs on Stela 11, a mask with three dotted scrolls above and an *ich-ben* plus Muluc-variant glyph, although much more carefully squared and executed than the glyphs of the 9.2.0.0.0–9.4.0.0.0 period at Tikal, are somewhat similar to their forms. The angular cartouche on Stela 10 recalls the angular cartouche containing the Jaguar Baby motif on Stela 5 of El Zapote.

At Copan, Morley (1920) suggests the date 9.1.10.0.0 for Stela 20 and 9.2.10.0.0 for Stelae 24 and 25. All three are small fragments located at Group 9, on the outskirts of the village of Copan, and about 2 kilometers from the Main Group of ruins. This could have been the original center of Copan, but it seems more likely that most or all the monuments collected here had been removed from the Main Group and gathered here during one or another of the periodic alterations at the center. In view of the massive destruction of the Main Group by the encroaching river, one must also consider the possibility that these stones were picked up along the river shore during times when the waters temporarily receded and were carried by later residents of Copan to their village. Together with these fragments and four later stelae are fragments of four sculptured altars.

From the outset, the hieroglyphs of Copan are elaborate and contain many masks and zoomorphs that are difficult to identify. Initial Series periods on Stela 24 (9.2.10.0.0) are represented by bird heads, and the uinal glyph is a full-figure frog. For a century and a half, this elaborate script shows little change, and the subject matter of

birth?
(CPN Alt Y, A2)

stela texts seems to be more concerned with ritual than with historical events. History is more often recorded on altars, and even in this
early period we find what may be a birth notation on Altar Y, and a
shield glyph on Altar X. As at Altar de Sacrificios, no figure sculpture of this period is known from Copan.

We have only a single retrospective date in this period from the
Usumacinta. It is carved on a late lintel of Structure 22 of Yaxchilan,
where it was assembled with earlier lintels. The date reads 9.0.19.2.4,
but it was carved more than a century later, and I am somewhat
uncertain of its historical accuracy. Moreover, it is related in subject
matter to another set of lintels in Structure 12, and I prefer to discuss the two together in Chapter 5, for the dates cannot be readily
reconciled.

CHAPTER FIVE

Expansion of the Maya Tradition

9.2.10.0.0 – 9.5.0.0.0

A.D. 485 – 534

A GROUP OF EIGHT STELAE ERECTED AT TIKAL AT about this time is different from all earlier monuments. Only four of these stelae record Initial Series: Stela 3, 9.2.13.0.0; Stelae 15 and 27, 9.3.0.0.0; Stela 6, 9.4.0.0.0. Joyce Waddell Bailey, in her dissertation (1972) ascribes the simple iconography of the sculptures to "a change of policy and attitude of official art." This is an overly cautious statement. Changes far more profound seem to be indicated. Nothing less than a revolution in the power structure of the state can adequately account for them. Gone is the double-headed serpent-bar, symbol of royal, possibly even divine, descent. Gone is the Early Title Glyph and the sky sign that accompanied the names of ruling lords. There is no longer an ancestor up in the sky or earthly symbols such as the base mask. All the regal trappings are gone, including the numerous glyphs and signs that adorned and identified the personages portrayed. What is more remarkable is that the representations are so uniform. The figures are all shown in profile view, holding a segmented staff. Only the figures on Stelae 9 and 13 are distinguished by capes and by staffs of simpler design.

The inscriptions also undergo a change. The fine incised detail of earlier texts disappears. The glyphs are irregular in form, and most of the texts are arranged in single columns on the sides of the stelae, often with irregular spacing. All but one of the dates recorded are period endings, and masks play the major role in the texts. The Tikal Emblem Glyph occurs on three of the monuments, but only on Stela 9 is it at the end of the text, where it is preceded by a porcine animal head, its eye covered with a *kan*-cross sign. This animal glyph is peculiar to Tikal (the examples from other sites given in J. Eric S. Thompson's catalog [1962:T754] are questionable), and it is almost certainly the name of the current ruler, whom we may call Kan Boar. His glyph occurs also on Stelae 3, 7, and 13; on Stela 13 it is contained

Kan Boar
(TIK St 13, B5)

u ahaulil
(TIK St 13, B7)

T126.670[535]
(TIK St 13, B4a)

in a phrase with the *u ahaulil* expression, which normally refers to events in a former ruler's reign but here may indicate that the recorded event refers to another personage. This event is marked by a familiar glyph, T126.670 [535], which I interpret as an award of privilege or achievement of lordship. It seems that more than one personage is represented on these monuments, but without the familiar title glyphs, names are difficult to identify.

It is possible that the monuments were paired, each pair representing Kan Boar and another person, and that the inscriptions were continued from one monument to another. On Stela 27, the text ends after two mask glyphs, which immediately follow the Initial Series. The text of Stela 7 begins with a glyph that has a peculiar fretlike form, and the second glyph down contains the Tikal Emblem Glyph. After two more masks, there is a "completion" sign and a date. On Stela 15, the fret glyph is the third glyph down from the Initial Series, and again the Tikal Emblem follows. After two more mask glyphs, however, the inscription breaks off, apparently incomplete. If we pair Stela 27 with Stela 7 and Stela 15 with Stela 9, the sequence of statements, with minor variations, will be identical: the fret glyph, the Tikal Emblem Glyph, god masks, and the period ending. (The stelae, however, face opposite directions.)

Morley reads the date on Stela 9 as "end of Katun 2, 4 Ahau" but is unable to connect it with the day 1 (?) at the end of the column. If the date recorded is not 4 Ahau but the end of Katun 3, 2 Ahau, then the Distance Number 5.5 after the Ahau date counted back in time will lead to 9.2.19.12.15 1 Men, which I believe is the day intended.

Stelae 3 and 6 seem to have complete inscriptions, but Stela 13, which has no date at all, may have been paired with Stela 8, since both have a peculiar bird glyph that could be a name. The pattern, in any case, is not altogether regular and admits of different interpretations. One conclusion, however, seems to be justified: the earlier pattern of monarchical succession was interrupted. The rest is a matter for speculation. We might, for example, surmise that the merchant class, enriched by foreign trade in the reign of Curlsnout, now staged a revolt against the traditional aristocracy, establishing a four-part division of the town in accord with a Mexican custom. Clemency Coggins (1979:43) has suggested a dual rule of aristocracy and merchants at this time. Another possibility is that the chiefs of the four quarters of the city may have been ruling under a chosen leader who had no regal pretensions. It is notable that although no other Peten site shows a similar trend, there seems to have been a certain interruption in the sequence of recorded dates at many sites during and immediately preceding the reign of Kan Boar. The object of the new regime at Tikal may have been to establish regional capitals in distant provinces and to grant them autonomy and the right to establish independent kingdoms. We have, of course, the merest intimation of such events, but the expansion of Maya rule at this time is suggested by the fact that the more distant cities began to erect stelae almost simultaneously at the end of the rule of Kan Boar at Tikal. Caracol, Calakmul, and Yaxchilan erected their first stelae in 9.4.0.0.0. Recently a stela has been discovered in the vicinity of Quirigua, which was dated to approximately this period (Sharer 1978). The earlier stelae of Copan do not show portraits of rulers, and the origin of their tradition is obscure. The fact that the date 9.4.0.0.0 fell on 13 Ahau may have had something to do with the sudden expansion of the Classic tradition of stela erection, as Coggins has suggested (1975), as well as with the fact that histories recorded on later temples, such as that on the back of Temple VI at Tikal and that in the Temple of the Inscriptions at Palenque, begin their historical accounts with the date 9.4.0.0.0.

Some of the older cities of the Peten seem to have been relatively unaffected by these events. Uaxactun celebrated the sixtieth anniversary of the arrival of the highlanders on Stela 22, erected in 9.3.10.0.0. The figure is so badly damaged that it is difficult to make out its composition, but in the upper right corner is preserved a long row of plumes, depicted on a flat surface with fine, incised parallel lines, in the manner of the plumes we see on painted murals of Teotihuacan. Stela 3, erected in 9.3.13.0.0, shows the traditional Maya composition of a figure holding a ceremonial bar, with a sky figure at the upper left.

The date of Stela 6 at Xultun is uncertain, but the katun number of the Initial Series is clearly 3. It apparently represents a figure seated on a jaguar throne, but the design is far from clear. Stela 11, also of uncertain date, depicts a standing profile figure wearing a high headdress with a long row of plumes, similar to that of Stela 22 at Uaxactun but carved in relief. (The fragment of "Stela 13," which Morley [1937–1938:1:219–223] believed to be late, shows only the feet of a profile figure and the lower end of a staff. Eric von Euw [1978:42] has shown that this fragment is a part of Stela 11.) Stelae 12, 18, and 20 all exhibit very early features.

To the southeast, the figure on Stela 6 at Yaxha carries a segmented staff, like those of Tikal, but preserves a local style, omitting plumes and placing the figure on a base panel depicting an earth monster. Morley's (1937–1938:3:472–475) placement of this monument in the "Middle Period" is probably incorrect. Stela 10 has a similar panel, but only the legs of the figure are preserved. Neither Stela 6 nor 10 has a legible date, and both may be even earlier than I have provisionally placed them. The fragment of Stela 7, however, could be later, judging by its carefully squared glyphs. In any case, these incomplete and badly eroded texts of Yaxha provide us no historical information.

To the east of central Peten, Caracol had erected its first stela at 9.4.0.0.0, just as the reign of Kan Boar at Tikal was about to end. The sculpture and the inscription on Stela 13 of Caracol are all but

bird glyph
(TIK St 13, A7)

erased. Stela 15, a monument with a small sculptured panel at the top and a longer but damaged inscription below, records the Initial Series as 9.4.16.13.3 4 Akbal 16 Pop, but no further reading is possible. Stela 16 (9.5.0.0.0), however, still retains its figure and some of its text. The design of the figure has much in common with that of Stelae 1, 2, and 28 at Tikal, and one is inclined to wonder if, during the reign of Kan Boar and his associates, some of the aristocrats of Tikal did not emigrate and take over the rule of Caracol. The horizontal serpent-bar, the serpent heads at the feet of the figure, the prone prisoner on whom it stands, and the elaborate mask with small figures below are all shared with Tikal compositions, which were apparently designed some eighty years earlier, though we are not at all sure of their date.

At A13 on Caracol Stela 16 is a God C compound followed by the Triad Glyph that, at Palenque, introduces three names that some identify with three gods. If a similar triad is named here, it is a different one. Five glyphs follow this statement before the next glyph signifying an event occurs, but the first four may be read as two pairs. The first pair may name one person, the second pair a second person, and the lone fifth glyph the third member of this triad. The first pair of glyphs consist of a vulture glyph with a uinal infix (T-1036b) followed by a *kin-ben* prefix over an unknown sign. This vulture glyph follows an Early Title Glyph on a stela from Tres Islas and the "blind-god" ancestral title on the early Lintel 12 of Piedras Negras. The vulture glyph appears to be a military title, perhaps indicating a governor of a subject town. On Tikal Stela 31, it appears to be associated with the atlatl-*cauac* shield glyph, which stands for the foreign warriors, which is consistent with my proposal that the vulture (without the infix) serves as a military title. Thus, if the vulture plus a uinal form functions at Caracol as one of three expressions, it is probably in combination with the following glyph, an animal head with some resemblance to the main sign of Curlsnout's name, with a *kin-ben* prefix. The second pair of glyphs consists of the "night sun" followed by a compound of *ich-* (or *kin-*) and sky. The third name is a jaguar head with an unknown prefix. The record of the end of a tun follows this glyph. It is, of course, possible that only the first three glyphs pertain to the "god-triad." This entire clause may be repeated on Stela 14, probably erected on the next katun ending.

At least two and possibly three individuals are mentioned on Stela 16. The first name mentioned may be that of the figure portrayed. It is followed by a thumb-up hand glyph, but the next glyphs are erased. Near the end of the inscription are two clauses containing the "blind-god" title, which I suspect refers to ancestors. The nature of these clauses is unknown, but one may speculate that they refer to chiefs or founders of the three divisions indicated at the beginning of the text. The presence of the rare glyph T571, the only other occurrences of which have been noted on Stela 31 of Tikal, is perhaps

God C compound
(CRC St 16, A13)

Triad Glyph
(CRC St 16, B13)

vulture glyph with uinal infix
(CRC St 16, A14)

kin-ben over ?
(CRC St 16, B14)

worth mentioning here, as well as the presence of the "rain bat" which is the main sign of the Emblem of Copan.

By 9.4.0.0.0, cities to the north, with access to the Río Candelaria drainage, began to erect stelae of their own. Karl Ruppert and John H. Dennison (1943:135) date Stela 23 at Naachtun at 9.3.10.0.0 (9.4.10.0.0 according to Morley 1937–1938:3:326–329) and Stela 3 at 9.5.0.0.0. The latter has a very strange composition, but both monuments are very badly eroded. Calakmul erects its first monument, Stela 43, at 9.4.0.0.0, and it shows a typical Early Classic figure in side view with a diagonal serpent-bar on its arm. The practice of setting up stelae may even have spread at this time to northeastern Yucatan, where Stelae 13 and 17 at Coba were judged to be "archaic" by Jean Charlot (J. E. S. Thompson, Pollack, and Charlot 1932), though I would prefer to give them a date somewhat later. In the northwest, a lintel at Oxkintok, with an Initial Series 9.2.?.?.? suggests an early settlement of the southern Maya there.

Looking south to Altar de Sacrificios, Stela 13(?) (9.3.0.0.0), a glyphic panel with a divided field, continues the early tradition of all-glyphic monuments and a tendency to use rectangular cartouches. Some of the glyphs are legible, but the sense of the inscription escapes me. Stela 18 (9.4.0.0.0), later recarved and set up in the south plaza, probably once stood with other early monuments in front of Structure B1 (J. A. Graham 1972:67, Fig. 2). It is the first monument here carved with a human figure, and its date corresponds to the end of the reign of Kan Boar at Tikal and the simultaneous erection of stelae for the first time at distant sites. The pose is essentially in profile, but the torso appears to be facing front, though considerably narrowed.

The next monument, Stela 12, set up in 9.4.10.0.0, is a full-profile figure, not unlike those of Tikal in this period, with only a small tuft of plumes on its headdress. Morley (1937–1938:2:314–317) gives no explanation of "4 Ahau" and "4 winged-Cauac" glyphs which he noted. I suspect that they are not calendrical glyphs and that they refer, perhaps in an indirect way, to the governmental structure under Kan Boar. The Initial Series date ends with B8, and for the next three glyphs I do not venture an explanation. B10, however, can be read as *u ahaulil* (in the reign of), which is followed by a mask not unlike the Early Title Glyph used at Tikal under the rule of Stormy Sky. At B12 is the "scroll-god" title usually applied to deceased persons, suggesting that the subject matter of the text deals with the past. The left side of the monument begins with an *u* "jog" glyph (an interesting variant of the *u* prefix, something between the "bracket" form and T204, confirming their semantic identity). The next glyph seems to be an unusual compound of the sky title so often used at Tikal, and this is followed by the "scroll-god" title compounded with the leg of a bird. The V-shaped cut in the main sign of the next glyph reminds us somewhat of the name of Stormy Sky, but it is probably some other deceased person to whom this and possibly the next

"blind-god" title
(CRC St 16, C16)

rain bat
(CRC St 16, C18)

"scroll-god" title
(ALS St 12, B12)

u "jog"
(ALS St 12, C1)

sky title
(ALS St 12, C2)

4 Ahau
(ALS St 12, D6)

4 winged-*cauac*
(ALS St 12, D7)

Yaxchilan Emblem Glyph
(YAX St 27, last glyph)

glyph refer. Then there are two pairs of glyphs: the first of each pair, an animal compound of unknown meaning; the second, a glyph with the coefficient 4. The glyph Morley reads as "4 Ahau" is a profile face enclosed in a plain cartouche, without the usual day suffix. It could be read perhaps as "4 lords." The winged *cauac* is also peculiar in that it seems to lack the "cloud element," though this may not be significant. The final glyph is also one of a pair, and its coefficient is also 4 (or possibly 3). It has an *ich-ben* superfix, and it somewhat resembles the glyph for "three gods" (or three divisions, as I prefer to call them—see discussion of Tikal Stela 26 in Chapter 7). What I want to suggest here is that this text may deal with that change in Maya society or government which introduced a fourfold division in place of the ancient three. Admittedly, this is a highly speculative course of reasoning, but I believe that the inscriptions contain material beyond the mere life histories of kings, and that if we turn our attention to such as yet undeciphered phrases, we may discover in the texts a wealth of information about Maya society that is still untapped.

The earliest known monument at Yaxchilan is Stela 27, erected in 9.4.0.0.0. It is rather thin for a stela, and rectangular in form, and may have been a panel rather than a freestanding monument. Its figure is the first known example of the "scattering gesture," which I believe connotes divination, since the corresponding hieroglyph is often associated with ends of periods or, more rarely, with dates of birth or accession to rulership, which begin important stages in the lives of monarchs. In some instances it may be related to the 819-day periods affixed to Initial Series, which may serve as bases for divination for the dates. Most of the text on Stela 27 is destroyed, but at the very end is the Emblem Glyph of Yaxchilan, so that we can assume that at this time the city was already established as an important center of a province.

Stela 14 is an even thinner slab than Stela 27, and also rectangular. It presents a figure holding a serpent-bar in the diagonal position typical of the early period. The date recorded is 9.4.8.8.15 13 Men 13 Kayab. At Yaxchilan, the serpent-bar is never again pictured with a principal figure on a stela, but instead is often held by figures in the sky. This fact, and the fact that the day Men, a day of evil omen associated with the West and with death, often occurs with serpent-bar figures in early times, suggests that the bar may have been originally a mortuary motif.

Structures 22 and 12 at Yaxchilan contain some very early lintels, which were apparently reset in later buildings. On Lintel 18 of Structure 22, which possibly is not a lintel at all, the hieroglyphs are lightly incised. There is no date. The text begins with a glyph of a bearded animal, possibly a variant of the dog glyph 237.752. This is followed by a glyph that Thompson lists as 116:126:129? and by three names, each followed by the "rodent-bone" glyph 748:110, which is probably equivalent to (110)758. The first name, T782, is unique but may

Yaxchilan Stela 27, front: The earliest
known depiction of scattering.
(Drawing courtesy of Ian Graham.)

bearded animal
(YAX L 18, A1)

"rodent-bone" glyph
(YAX L 18, B2)

headless jaguar
(YAX L 47, D3)

numbered glyph
(YAX L 49, C4)

"crouching legs"
(YAX L 49, D4)

sun mask
(YAX L 49, A8)

be a variant of T1005a. The second is a skull glyph with a double prefix, and the third is T126.756:116, a bat that sometimes seems to substitute for the "Bird" of the great Bird Jaguar, who probably assembled these lintels. The cursive and somewhat archaic script on this lintel is unusual, and at the present time I can suggest no meaning for the remainder of the text. The beginning, however, may imply a chief and his three sons, or, perhaps more likely, a tribal name and its three divisions or lineages. A "bird-dog" glyph occurs also at Copan on Stela 2 and on Altar K, and at Palenque on Ruz Tablet 1. In every case, however, the contexts are obscure.

On Lintel 22 of Structure 22, which is carved in relief, the "bird-dog" glyph is preceded by an *ahau* compound, which may be an early form of the *u ahaulil* (in the reign of) glyph, suggesting the above interpretation that it is a name referring to ancestral origins, but we are not equipped yet to handle such early texts.

Unfortunately little remains of Lintels 19 and 20 of this building. Lintel 19 matched Lintel 18, but preserves only the last two glyphs of its text. Lintel 20, carved in relief, like Lintel 22, once had an Initial Series, now almost completely gone. The central lintel, although it was carved early in the seventeenth katun, gives us a date three centuries earlier in its Initial Series, which records 9.0.19.2.4 2 Kan 2 Yax, a time when Stormy Sky was ruling at Tikal, and before any known stelae were erected outside of central Peten. The name mentioned in connection with this date appears nowhere on Structure 22, whose inscriptions may deal with even earlier, and perhaps legendary, history, but it does appear on a lintel from Structure 12.

The central lintel of this building shows the outlines of a human figure holding a ceremonial bar diagonally in the early manner. No hieroglyphs survive, though the figure was accompanied by a brief inscription. Lintel 48, to the left of the central door as one faces the building, records an Initial Series, which is continued on the next lintel (47) to the left. These inscriptions are executed in full relief, but beginning with Lintel 34 at the extreme left, and progressing with Lintel 49 (at the extreme right), and Lintels 37 and 35, the detail is little more than incising. The Initial Series reads best as 9.4.11.8.16 2 Cib 19 Pax. The text, which contains many mask glyphs, does not at present yield a meaning, but it may be worth noting that the fourth glyph after the Initial Series (repeated as the tenth) occurs also on Lintel 22 of Structure 22. Moreover, in the extreme right column of Lintel 47 there is a headless jaguar glyph (T832), which occurs also on Tikal Stela 3, and this is followed by a thumb-up hand glyph (T670) and T1030k, a mask holding an eccentric flint, another expression shared with Lintel 22.

Lintel 20 is only a small fragment, and it is not certain whether it belongs with the Initial Series lintels or the lintels on the right. The legible portion of the text begins on Lintel 49. It presents a series of passages, each introduced by a number glyph and T700, "crouching legs." Morley reads the numbered glyph as the day Oc, but it is surely not a day glyph at all. If we consider not the lines, but the spatial form, it resembles the Mexican sign *ilhuitl*—two hooklike elements placed back to back. The number of the first legible passage is destroyed, as is the glyph under it, but the "crouching legs" glyph shows that the pattern was already set, and that the number must have been 5. The missing glyph under it apparently recorded a name. The name in passage 6 is a sun mask and an animal skull with a double superfix. The Bird Jaguar glyph also appears in this passage. Number 7 is another skull glyph, and in the ensuing passage we see a turtle-carapace glyph and an *ich-ben* glyph with a leaf prefix that is somewhat similar to the Emblem Glyph of Piedras Negras. Number 8 (Lintel 37) is the name Bird Jaguar. In this passage the turtle-carapace glyph and the Emblem Glyph (?) are repeated, and the quincunx that characterizes the Piedras Negras Emblem Glyph appears at the lower right as a separate element. Number 9 is the name Trophy-head Jaguar—a jaguar head with a knot through its empty eye. The long passage that follows this name contains the date 1 Cauac 7 Yaxkin and ends with a death mask and the normal Tikal Emblem Glyph without its usual prefix. The mask appears to be identical to that which is cited on Stela 26 at Tikal, first after the name of Stormy Sky and again at the end of the text on the other side. One can also discern it there on Stela 3 (at D1), on Stela 7 (at B5), and on Stela 15 (at B7), all erected during the reign of Kan Boar (9.2.13.0.0–9.4.0.0.0). Some investigators consider this mask to be a personal name, and refer to it as Paw Skull. I suspect, however,

animal skull
(YAX L 49, B8)

Bird Jaguar
(YAX L 49, C2)

skull
(YAX L 49, C5)

turtle carapace
(YAX L 49, D6)

leaf + *ich-ben* + ?
(YAX L 49, C7)

Bird Jaguar
(YAX L 37, A2)

Piedras Negras Emblem Glyph
(YAX L 37, B6)

Trophy-head Jaguar
(YAX L 37, A8)

death mask
(YAX L 37, C8)

Tikal Emblem Glyph
(YAX L 37, D8)

skull
(YAX L 35, A2)

"Muluc variant"
(YAX L 35, B2)

4 bat
(YAX L 21, C6b)

sky glyph + scroll mask
(YAX L 21, C7)

that it denotes a lineage or some other kinship group, possibly claiming descent through Great Paw, who is mentioned on Stela 31. Number 10 (Lintel 35) names a skull with a double prefix T74.184, read by Floyd G. Lounsbury (1985) as Mahkina. Trophy-head Jaguar is mentioned again, and the date 1 Cimi 14 Muan.

The names listed here carry no titles or other honorifics, and the "crouching legs" glyphs that precede them as well as the "Muluc variant" glyphs that follow them suggest to me that they are not names of individuals, but names of the principal lineages or families that lived in the province, or even the names of its several towns. The Initial Series 9.4.11.8.16 follows the erection of Stela 14 (which I have suggested may record the death of the first king) by about three years and may or may not be the date when this list was compiled. The subsequent lack of stelae tends to suggest that the rule passed to a council of heads of lineages or chiefs of the several towns composing the province, and it may be pertinent that the Emblem of Yaxchilan does not appear in these inscriptions.

Two retrospective dates make reference to the names on this list. One, mentioned in the previous chapter, refers to name number 7 and links the date 9.0.19.2.4 to a date 9.16.1.0.9, just nine days after the accession of Bird Jaguar. I am somewhat skeptical of the very early date with which Bird Jaguar seems to be trying to document the antiquity of his ancestry, but I may be mistaking his motive. This inscription (Lintel 21) is very unusual and contains at least two glyphs that are not found elsewhere. One is a jaguar holding in its paw a *cauac* glyph; the other is a bat glyph with a coefficient 4 and the superfix T84. The latter introduces two parallel clauses, the first relating to the number 7 name, the other to the seventeenth-katun Bird Jaguar. In both instances, the title preceding the name is a sky-glyph followed by the scroll mask. This seems to be a very ancient title, first appearing on Tikal Stela 31 with the Great Paw ruler mentioned after the date 8.14.0.0.0. Possibly it refers to an ancestor or to a founder of a clan.

It is hazardous to speculate about the meaning of these early and little-understood inscriptions, but there seems to be an implication here that the Bird Jaguar lineage was an offshoot of the Skull lineage, number 7. If we place the dates associated with numbers 9 and 10 between the date 9.0.19.2.4 and the Initial Series date 9.4.11.8.16, these dates would be 9.1.0.17.19 1 Cauac 7 Yaxkin and 9.2.9.15.6 1 Cimi 14 Muan. If Coggins (1975) is correct in identifying Burial 48 at Tikal, which has the date 9.1.1.10.10 painted on the wall, as that of Stormy Sky, then the first date at Yaxchilan precedes his death by two years and is fifteen years after the very important date at Tikal which terminates its highland connection. The second date falls ten months and eleven days before his death, and the last almost twenty-eight years later, roughly three years before the first certain date of the Kan Boar set of stelae.

The reader must make what he can of this confused history. I can only say that if these Yaxchilan lintels record the history of the settlement of the site by the Maya of the Peten tradition, then it must have taken place just about the time of the transition from the traditional aristocratic government of Stormy Sky to what appears to be the more secular regime of Kan Boar. Just what role Yaxchilan played in this transition is not clear to me. One may wonder whether the intervention more than a century later of a king of Yaxchilan in the restoration of one of the Tikal rulers, which I discuss in Chapter 9, was somehow related to the fact that Tikal is mentioned in connection with Trophy-head Jaguar—the ninth name mentioned here. This name, in turn, is mentioned again with Shield Jaguar, who, I believe, may have been responsible for the restoration. In this connection, it may be of interest that in the tribal histories of the Quiche, both in the Popol Vuh and in the Títulos de los Señores de Totoñicapan, it is said that there were four "first men," but that one, called Iqi-Balam, had no descendants, and, according to the latter document, he was a bachelor. It is possible, therefore, that the early Maya also had a three-part division based, as I have suggested elsewhere (1978) on three matrilineages, and reflected in a three-part arrangement of some of the earliest temples.

Piedras Negras, before 9.5.0.0.0, must have been a frontier town, still struggling to dominate its province, since its earliest monument, a panel called Lintel 12, presents a martial motif. The lord, wearing a lavishly plumed headdress, stands before three kneeling figures whose hands appear to be bound. They were probably local chiefs, and they are identified by three groups of four glyphs each. Behind the chief is another kneeling figure, divested of clothing and with his hands tied behind his back, as if ready for sacrifice. His name probably appears in the panel above. The text contains four dates: 9.3.19.12.12, 9.4.0.0.0, 9.4.3.0.17, and 9.4.3.10.1. The character of the events that occurred on these dates is not clear, but near the end of the inscription are three glyphs that probably give the name of the main figure: T-1013, 1036, and an unidentified head glyph. There seems to be no emblem after the name. An even earlier date, 9.3.16.0.5, was suggested by Hermann Beyer (1939) for the 8 Chicchan 3 Ceh recorded on Lintel 2, which dates from 9.11.15.0.0, but the text on this lintel does not reveal its significance.

Stela 30, tentatively dated 9.5.0.0.0, seems to be the first erected at Piedras Negras, and one may infer that the events recorded on Lintel 12 led to the establishment of this city as a provincial capital. Only a small fragment of the inscription on Stela 30 is preserved. The rest of the monument is in very poor condition.

The next stela, Stela 29, is a glyphic panel that begins with the Initial Series 9.5.5.0.0. Morley (1937–1938:3:40–45) advanced its date to 9.6.0.0.0, but with insufficient reason. He was unable to connect the Secondary Series 1.1.7.19 with any meaningful date, but if it is counted back from the Initial Series it reaches 9.4.3.10.1 7 Imix 19 Pop, the value that he himself proposed for the record of 19 Pop on Lintel 12. J. E. S. Thompson (1950:Fig. 47) read the Distance Number as 1.1.10.19 and reached a date 9 Cauac 7 Yax, but a forward count from the hotun date does not seem likely. The best readings for the next date, 8 Ix 7 Yax or Yaxkin, could be 9.6.5.10.14 or 9.4.0.14.14. Unfortunately, the glyphs that follow these notations are of unknown significance.

Copan, during this period, apparently continued to erect all-glyphic stelae and rectangular altars with symbolic motifs. Of the three stelae, 25, 16 and 15, ascribed by Morley (1920) to this period, only Stela 15 is dated with any confidence, at 9.4.10.0.0. Altar Q' was placed in this period by Morley, but with question marks. Neverthe-less, on Altar Y we find a clear record of the birth of an individual who may be mentioned on Stela P, erected in the Main Group in 9.9.0.0.0. Here the glyph appears in a phrase noting a bloodletting rite, possibly performed by a woman whose name appears above.

What happened at Tikal after the rule of Kan Boar and the estab-lishment of Maya kingdoms in the Classic tradition in distant prov-inces is a matter of speculation. It seems that for a second time there was a revival of aristocratic rule. From Stela 23, of unknown date, and found at some distance from the Main Group, we learn that on 9.3.9.13.3 8 Akbal 11 Mol, a woman was born at Tikal, who seems to have been the originator of a new dynasty. At the time of the next date mentioned, 9.3.16.8.4 11 Kan 17 Pop, she was only six years old. Here the inscription breaks off, for the stela was later broken and its butt has not been identified; so we do not know its original position. Stela 25, also found discarded at a distance from the principal plaza of Tikal, could conceivably have been its companion monument, for it had similar figures on the sides, depicting a young man and a young woman. It is also only an upper fragment of a stela, and badly eroded, but enough remains to suggest that it was a male figure. The inscription on the back of this stela has four columns of glyphs and begins with the Initial Series 9.4.3.0.0 1 Ahau (3 Yax). It is possible that Stela 14, which is only a butt, found in a different location, but which also had figures on its sides and an inscription on the back with four columns of glyphs, is the missing butt of Stela 25. It has no date, however, and no part of a figure on the front. Were the legs and feet of these figures better preserved, we might be in a better position to suggest a date for them. On later monuments, the figure stands with its feet pointing outward when the torso is shown in full front view, but we do not know when this transition takes place, since few monuments of this and the next period survive intact.

The inscription on Temple VI of Tikal records three dates in Tun 14 of the fifth katun: 9.4.13.4.16, 9.4.13.6.14, and 9.4.13.7.7. The first two dates are followed by short statements that may or may not be historical, but after the last date, another panel begins, whose text

Lady of Tikal
(TIK St 23, C4)

contains a combination of the *kan* cross and *cauac,* suggesting the title of a priest officiating at mortuary ceremonies, and serving in lieu of a king who had died. However, the order of reading is not entirely clear, and too much of this inscription has been destroyed to permit a definite interpretation of the events recorded. Nevertheless, it is not unlikely that the implied death is that of Kan Boar, and that the king portrayed on Stela 25 succeeded him in the neighborhood of 9.4.15.0.0. The woman whose birth is mentioned on Stela 23 was then about twenty-five years old.

The fact that virtually all known Maya histories that deal with more than a single reign begin with the date 9.4.0.0.0 13 Ahau 18 Yax, even when they record no events in the next five katuns, shows that the Maya, though they may have had no central government, nevertheless recognized the unity of their land and their people.

Expansion of the Maya Tradition

kan cross + *cauac*
(TIK T VI)

CHAPTER SIX

A Time of Troubles

9.5.0.0.0 – 9.7.10.0.0

A.D. 534 – 583

TIKAL, DURING THIS PERIOD AND THE NEXT, probably continued to erect stelae, but virtually all monuments of these periods are broken and no dates of their dedication now survive. Newly established peripheral capitals, such as Calakmul, Piedras Negras, and Yaxchilan, after erecting one or two stelae, were apparently too busy consolidating their frontiers at this time to continue their monumental activity, though sites on the eastern and southern frontiers seem unaffected. It is difficult to determine when the destruction of Tikal monuments took place. It could have been as early as 9.8.0.0.0 or as late as 9.12.0.0.0, and the monuments described here may have been spread over two periods. What they have in common is that in style they are all transitional between the Early and Late Classic periods. Some archaeologists call this transition the Middle Classic, but its chronological limits are not well defined.

None of the monuments mentioned here has a definite final date. Nor have Tikal Stelae 23 and 25, mentioned at the end of the previous chapter, though they may have been erected later, and the rule of this couple probably extended beyond 9.5.0.0.0. Moreover, the transition from the Early Classic period to the Late was apparently not a continuous and gradual process, but consisted of a series of radical transformations of styles that have no definite direction. It is particularly difficult to place Stelae 10 and 12 in the sequence because their style is different from all others in Tikal. The figures wear a short cape that just covers the shoulders, a very tight belt, and a short projecting skirt. The arms and legs of the figures are disproportionately long by Maya standards, though the placement of feathers high on the headdress is characteristic of this period. The position of the feet of the Stela 10 figure, however, is Late Classic, as is the figure of a prone captive behind the feet. Judging by the figures shown on these stelae, I would be inclined to place them in the neighborhood of 9.8.0.0.0 or even 9.10.0.0.0, but the irregular forms and spacing of the hieroglyphs on the sides and back of these monuments are not consistent with a Late Classic date, and the Initial Series on Stela 12, although largely damaged, reads best as 9.4.13.0.0 13 Ahau 13 Yaxkin. The inscription on Stela 10 is in poor condition, especially on the back. That on the left side begins with what may be an Initial Series glyph followed by a day 8 Manik and three unknown glyphs. Another introducing glyph is followed by a series of three periods above the baktun with coefficients 1.11.19, and finally by 9.3?.11.2.?. The day number and presumably the date should appear on the back, but most of the upper part of the back of this stela is virtually illegible. The only well-preserved Calendar Round date on this monument is near the end of the inscription on the right side: 7 or 12 Cib 14 Yax, but its position in the Long Count seems impossible to determine (9.5.4.5.16?).

The fact that Stela 10 was not broken and mutilated, as were all others of this period, and the fact that both of these strange stelae were found near the center of the large group of monuments in front of the North Acropolis require an explanation which I am not prepared to give. Perhaps, when all excavation reports have been published, they may shed some light on the matter.

Stela 17, which, like other monuments of this and the next period, is very badly battered, nevertheless retains parts of its inscription on one side and on the back, each beginning with an Initial Series. The series on the back reads: 9.5.3.(9?).15 (12?) Men 18 (Kankin?). There are some recognizable glyphs, as for instance what is probably the Tikal Emblem at B9, a shield glyph at G4, and the *u ahaulil* glyph at H7, but there is too much erosion to attempt a reading of this passage. The Initial Series on the one surviving side appears to record a katun anniversary of the Series on the back: 9.6.3.9.15 10 Men (18 Ch'en?). Beyond this the text is mostly illegible, though there seems to have been a Secondary Series of three or four periods ending with 7 uinals 5 days. The Men dates may suggest that the anniversary concerns the death of someone, but I do not venture to guess whose death it may have been. The figure on this monument is almost completely effaced, but there is a suggestion of a collar of large beads and upsweeping plumes that, in spite of the early character of the text, argues for an advanced stage of transition to the Late Classic period.

Tikal seems to be the only city in central Peten that was erecting stelae at this time, though it is possible that we are missing many monuments at sites less well explored. Uaxactun, Xultun, and Calakmul, however, all well-known sites, yielded no legible records of this time. Along the Usumacinta, only Stela 29 at Piedras Negras, erected in 9.5.5.0.0, can be ascribed to this period. At Naranjo, however, there seems to be a retrospective reference to this time on Stela 25, in the form of katun anniversaries of the date 9.5.12.0.4 6 Kan 2 Zip, ending with the three katun ten tun anniversary 9.9.2.0.4. The series

Triad Glyph
(CRC St 14, B8)

God C compound
(CRC St 14, A9)

two god heads
(CRC St 14, B9)

is perfectly regular if we read the first date on the left side as 4 Kan 7 Pax (9.6.12.0.4), instead of 2 Kan 7 Yax, as Morley did. What may be recorded here is the period when the royal family of Naranjo was not in residence, possibly having fled to the adjacent province of Caracol.

The inscriptions of Caracol that pertain to this period are of particular interest. We have already noted that early texts here are linked to those of Tikal, and that the base composition of Caracol Stela 16 is very similar to that of Tikal Stela 28. This composition is retained on Stelae 14, 6, and 5 of the transitional period, but is simplified and eventually disappears.

The earliest date noted in this group of stelae is 9.5.10.1.2 9 Ik 5 Uo, inscribed on Stela 14 and also on Stela 6. The event glyph after the date on Stela 14 is entirely erased, but on Stela 6 it looks as if it may be the "seating glyph." The seated position of the figure on Stela 14, moreover, suggests that it may commemorate an accession. The figure sits on a prone captive over a mask, and holds a serpent-bar horizontally on his chest. The remains of serpent heads can be seen also at the level of his knees, and in front of the mask are three seated figures, an arrangement identical to that on Stela 16. Two of these figures are almost certainly women, for their knees are covered. The central figure is indeterminate as to sex. Under the mask, inserted into the inscription is a *tau*-shaped panel containing a fourth seated figure lightly incised and shown in profile. The dress of this figure is ambiguous, but the name in the panel in front suggests that she is also a woman. The Initial Series of Stela 14 records Katun 6, and after three or four glyphs, we find the glyph which precedes the name of the triad at Palenque, at B8, followed by a God C compound. It is true that the number 3 which normally is prefixed to the Triad Glyph is not here apparent, but in view of the God C compound also associated with triad expressions elsewhere, I believe the Triad Glyph identity is unquestionable. Subsequent glyphs also support this identification, although I am uncertain of the meaning of glyphs at B9 and C4, which should form part of the names of the triad. The glyph at B9 may be composed of the same two god heads that follow the Triad Glyph at Naranjo on its hieroglyphic stairway (I. Graham 1978:108). The glyphs at D4, D5, and D6, which should form part of the names of the triad, are almost certainly related to the glyphs which appear at A14, A15, and A16 on Caracol Stela 16 after the Triad Glyph and God C compound. Although the glyphs at B9 to C4 on Stela 14 could represent another name, interpolations in similar phrases are quite common. I think the text on Stela 14 is best read as a reference to a triad.

The name of the ruler pictured on this stela is unknown, but vestiges of it on Stela 6 suggest that it was very similar to that of a later ruler, who may have been a grandson named after him. This may explain why the inscription on Stela 6 skips over Katuns 6, 7, and 8 without comment, and why the two figures portrayed on it are very different. The figure on the front on Stela 6 is in many ways similar to that on Stela 14 and retains many early traits. He stands on a prone captive, and his headdress closely encircles his face. The tie of his sandals is looped through a strap, and the heel is without an ankle guard. An innovation, however, is the small dwarf figure at his feet. This stela was erected in 9.8.10.0.0, and the figure on the front may have been posthumous.

The text on Stela 3, probably erected in 9.10.0.0.0, helps to fill the gap left in that of Stela 6, but it concerns the lives of later rulers and will be dealt with in Chapter 7. As almost everywhere in the Maya area, Katun 9.7.0.0.0 remains unmarked here. The reign of the un-named lord on Stela 14 may have lasted until 9.7.10.0.0, but, more likely, something happened even earlier to disrupt the regular prac-tice of erecting monuments, necessitating the retrospective refer-ences that we find on stelae erected after 9.9.0.0.0.

In the southeast, the hiatus in monuments is less evident. Pusilha dedicated a stela in 9.7.0.0.0: Stela O, its first monument except pos-sibly a small fragment recovered in debris. As everywhere else, there may have been a hiatus here, but if so, it came later, between 9.8.0.0.0 and 9.10.15.0.0, just when other sites were recovering from their troubles. Neither Stela O (9.7.0.0.0) nor Stela Q (9.8.0.0.0) has a carved figure or any noncalendrical text on the fragments remaining.

At Copan, Morley attributes four stelae to this period: Stela 17 (9.6.0.0.0?), a fragment of unknown provenience, Stela 9 (9.6.10.0.0), used as a foundation stone of a late monument, Stela 8, in the ceme-tery of the village, and Stela 18 (9.7.0.0.0), a small fragment from Group 9, described by Morley (1920) as having been sculptured with the earliest figure known from Copan. Group 9, located on the out-skirts of Copan village, has a large concentration of fragments of early stelae. It is possible that these monuments were originally lo-cated on the site of the village, before the group on the riverbank became the ceremonial center of Copan, but one can also conjecture that these monuments and fragments were moved to Group 9 from the Main Group at a time when it was being enlarged and rebuilt. The latest date at Group 9 is 9.9.0.0.0 (Stela 7), and the earliest at the Main Group is 9.9.5.0.0(?), though Morley suggests that this stela may also have stood originally in Group 9. The date is uncer-tain, appearing, as it does, on an altar, and not on the stela. In any case, if the monuments of Group 9 were actually moved from the Main Group, it could have been at any time after 9.9.0.0.0, for we have no indication of their original location.

It is not known whether Stela 9 (9.6.10.0.0) originally had a figure on the front, though the text survives, albeit somewhat damaged. Copan inscriptions of the early periods, however, are difficult to in-terpret, in part because they seldom record Secondary Series or in-termediate dates, and in part because the forms and expressions seem to differ from those of the Peten, suggesting a different dialect spo-

3? Caban
(CPN St 9, E3)

bloodletting glyph
(CPN St 9, E6)

Copan Emblem Glyph
(CPN St 9, F6)

u ahaulil
(CPN St 9, E7)

sacrifice glyph
(YAX HS 3, I, A3b)

ken here, or possibly merely different subject matter. The left side of Stela 9 is too damaged to yield a legible text, but on the right, two clauses are preserved with only minor flaws. The first is introduced by an unfamiliar compound of Caban possibly with the coefficient 3 (are they referring here to three divisions of the land?). The next glyph is a compound of God C, the mask tied vertically as in a "toothache glyph." The presence of God C and the coefficient 3 suggest that the three glyphs that follow may represent not the names or titles of a single personage, but the names of three titular gods of three lineages, clans, or offices. There follow an unknown glyph with a coefficient of 9 or 14, a glyph associated with the rite of blood-letting, and the Emblem Glyph of Copan. The next clause begins with the familiar *u ahaulil,* followed by two unfamiliar expressions, a katun sign without coefficient, and finally a first glyph preceding the jaguar glyph which was the last of the names above, a compound of glyph T541 or 542, and the Copan Emblem; two more glyphs are destroyed. Both the *ahaulil* glyph and the first suggest that the discourse is about ancestral and not about contemporary personages.

Far to the north, in the eastern sector, Stela 1 at Tulum is best dated at 9.6.10.0.0. This stela is sculptured on both faces. The best-preserved face shows a woman dressed in a jade skirt, holding on her arms a drooping serpent. The carving on the other face shows a man in profile view. Although there are other stelae on the East Coast, this is the only monument here that is carved in the Classic style. It is possible, however, that the two "archaic" stelae at Coba, mentioned previously, also belong to this unsettled period, when dispossessed families may have been migrating to distant parts, bringing with them the traditions of the Peten.

In the west, only at Tonina and at Lacanha are there stelae that may have been dedicated during this period. Tonina(?) Altar 6 was apparently set up in 9.6.0.0.0, and Stela 12 records the date 9.7.0.5.9, but at present no adequate records of the Tonina texts are available. At Yaxchilan, on the steps of Structure 44, is documented the career of Shield Jaguar, a later ruler of Yaxchilan, and one of the most notable characters in Maya history. The earliest date on the steps, 9.6.10.14.15 4 Men 3 Mac, refers to Trophy-head Jaguar, the ninth Jaguar name listed on Lintel 37. On Step I, the date 4 Men is followed by a long clause containing a sacrifice glyph and two bat heads. We have already noted the frequency of the day Men in the early period, suggesting the posthumous erection of stelae that depict the serpent-bar. Here we have a suggestion of an early sacrificed ruler, from whom the martial Shield Jaguar, hero of many conquests, is tracing his descent. The name Trophy-head Jaguar appears also on Lintel 46, where Shield Jaguar is shown with a captive.

CHAPTER SEVEN

Recovery on the Frontiers

9.7.10.0.0 − 9.10.0.0.0

A.D. 583 − 633

THERE ARE NO KNOWN STELAE OF THIS PERIOD AT Tikal, and my reasons for placing Stela 26 here are admittedly not decisive. The fragmentary inscription on Stela 26 has no date, and only the legs of the figure below the knees and a small fragment of a serpent head of a bar now remain. The feet of the figure point outward, in the Late Classic manner, but the heels of the sandals are of a transitional type, high and square, with a rectangular opening for the strap that ties them on the ankle, a type that occurs at Yaxha after 9.9.0.0.0, but here may appear earlier. On the other hand, the high ankle guards with feather ornaments flowing from them are shared with Stela 1, which also has no date, but which appears to be Early Classic. According to William R. Coe, Stela 26 was broken and buried in Structure 34 in a central altar "probably early in Late Classic times" (Jones and Satterthwaite 1982:57–58) and I may be placing it here too late, but its remarkable inscription, with its handsome glyphs, carefully organized and squared, does not fit with other Early Classic inscriptions at Tikal. If it once had an Initial Series or a period-ending date, no trace of it now survives. On the best-preserved side, however, we find two familiar names: Stormy Sky, followed by a compound of a death mask with its upper jaw ending in a jaguar paw, apparently referring to his ancestor Great Paw, and after three more masks, the name of Kan Boar, whose reign ended in 9.4.0.0.0. After this name is an elaborate compound of the *cauac* sign followed by the Triad Glyph attached to God C. This in turn is followed by three glyphs—the Jaguar Baby glyph which was worn by Stormy Sky, a masked figure holding an animal, and a sun mask (?) with a square of tied sticks—which I suspect name three matrilineages, since the last glyph is the head of a woman attached to the sign of Tikal without its usual prefixes.

Stormy Sky
(TIK St 26, zA4)

Great Paw
(TIK St 26, zB4)

Kan Boar
(TIK St 26, zB6)

Triad Glyph
(TIK St 26, zB7)

Jaguar Baby
(TIK St 26, zA8)

masked figure
(TIK St 26, zB8)

sun mask
(TIK St 26, zA9)

Lady of Tikal
(TIK St 26, zB9)

pyramid + *cauac*
(TIK St 26, yB2)

sky glyph + 6
(TIK St 26, yA3)

On the other side of this stela, the side that probably had an Initial Series, only the last three glyphs remain, but they are also of some interest. The first surviving glyph shows a pyramid and the sign *cauac*. The second is a "sky glyph" with the number 6 and a spotted face, and the third is the jaguar-paw mask. If one is permitted to speculate a little, one might wonder if this stela may have stood once in front of Structure 33 2nd, or one of the stairways that followed, and if the stela of Storm Sky, Stela 31, was placed there by the man pictured on Stela 26. Whether this is a viable suggestion I must leave to the archaeologists to determine, since the final reports on Tikal are not yet available. There seems to have been a long period at Tikal not documented by inscriptions, and when the story on monuments resumes, it begins not at Tikal, but far to the south in the region between the rivers Chixoy and Pasión, sometimes referred to as the Petexbatun region.

Before 9.9.0.0.0 there are no monuments with reliable dates of this period either at Tikal or in the surrounding sites. The fifty-year period between 9.6.10.0.0 and 9.9.0.0.0 is totally blank as to the history of what had once been the center of Classic Maya tradition. Morley (1937–1938) has partially filled this gap with dubious readings from badly eroded stelae, but where any sculpture remains, stylistic considerations do not support his readings. The monument from El Encanto is an Early Classic figure, without plumes on its headdress, with unsquared hieroglyphs, and seems altogether much earlier than the date in Katun 9 assigned to it. At Xultun, the figure on Stela 7 is completely eroded, but Stela 8 is certainly a much later monument. Even after 9.9.0.0.0, when stelae begin to appear at a number of sites, it is not in the vicinity of Tikal that activity is resumed, but at sites on the periphery of the Maya area. Stela 6 at Uaxactun is possibly an exception, but its date, too, is very uncertain. In general arrangement it recalls the stelae of Tikal in the rule of Kan Boar, but the staff held by the profile figure has a large circular plate in the middle, and angular projections from small segments of the staff, a design that persists in later times at several sites. So much of this sculpture is eroded that it is difficult to estimate its date.

To the north, at Uxul, Stelae 2, 3, and 4 were apparently erected soon after 9.9.0.0.0. The figure on Stela 2 is that of a woman in a jade skirt. She stands in a Late Classic pose, holding a slightly tilted serpent-bar on her arms, but the detail of her high headdress, with few or no plumes, is of early design. Dennison (Ruppert and Dennison 1943:147) suggests that Stela 3 may be a companion monument, but does not illustrate this stela or say whether it depicts a man or a woman. A male figure on Stela 4 is very similar in style to the female figure on Stela 2, and is probably also related to it. At Calakmul, Stelae 28 and 29, dated 9.9.10.0.0, are very clearly a pair. Their figures also stand in the Late Classic frontal position, their heads turned to face each other. Both are standing on crouching captives. This woman, too, is dressed in a jade skirt and wears a headdress with parallel plumes, no longer fastened under the chin in the Early Classic manner, but high on the head. The man has a similar headdress, his sandals are of Late Classic design, and a dwarf stands at his feet, as on the stelae of this period at Caracol. Naachtun Stela 1 (9.9.10.0.0) depicts a figure in profile, but details are eroded and the pose is ambiguous. A high plumed headdress with overlapping plumes and a back ornament of plumes are partially preserved. At Ichpaatun, on the Bay of Chetumal, Stela 1 is dated 9.8.0.0.0, and far to the north at Coba there are two monuments, Stelae 4 and 6, both probably erected in 9.9.10.0.0. J. E. S. Thompson (Thompson, Pollock and Charlot 1932:152) ascribes Stela 6 to the earlier of the two Initial Series dates on this monument, 9.9.0.0.0, but evidently does not take account of the fact that Stela 4, with the same lahuntun date, 9.9.10.0.0, portrays a woman. In addition to the lahuntun date, this stela records also 9.8.16.4.9 9 Muluc 7 Pop and 9.9.9.9.0 4 Ahau 18 Yax. The inscriptions on all these stelae are very badly eroded, and it is doubtful that even with the most careful recording we can extract from them any historical statements. Nonetheless, the incidence of a number of paired stelae in widely separated localities at this time suggests a series of alliances accomplished through intermarriages, a policy which may have been instrumental in reducing conflict between distant cities and making them independent of the central areas. Although the practice of portraying couples may have originated at Tikal itself with Stelae 23 and 25, monuments that apparently are later, Stelae 10, 12, and 17, show only masculine figures.

At Caracol, however, we have some indication of an alliance between Naranjo and Caracol, which may have been the result of a negotiated marriage. Stela 1 at Caracol was erected in 9.8.0.0.0 and appears to portray a woman holding a serpent-bar in her arms and wearing a sun symbol with a three-part superfix, which occurs in the Early Classic period at Tikal and is the principal symbol in the Temple of the Cross at Palenque. The woman on Stela 1 stands in the Early Classic position, her face and legs in profile, her torso in front view, and her sandals, anklets, and wristlets are of early design. A dwarf stands at her feet. Her name is not clear in the short inscription that accompanies her. At F1 is the hand-scattering (divination?) glyph, and the phrase that follows ends with what is probably a name introduced by a *kan* cross glyph: T33:281.23; 74:?:?. This may be the name of a priest or of the ruler pictured on Stela 14 and on Stela 6, who acceded in 9.5.19.1.2. Following that is a "1 shell" expression (T1:606) often associated with women (first son?), and possibly the figure's name, which, however, is not clear. At the end of the inscription is another Kan Cross name. This woman could have been the wife of the ruler pictured on Stela 14, but I am inclined to think that she was his daughter, who is later portrayed on Stela 3, though this stela was erected forty years later.

The inscription on Stela 3 records a birth on 5 Cib 14 Uo 9.6.12.4.16. It is not altogether clear whether it was the lady who was

hand scattering
(CRC St 1, F1)

kan cross
(CRC St 1, E3)

1 shell
(CRC St 1, F3b)

face with long lip
(CRC St 3, B15b)

ti-cab-kan
(CRC St 3, B17b)

hand glyph
(CRC St 3, C11b)

T351:774 [184:74]
(CRC St 3, C16a)

born on that date, or her husband, whose name appears only two glyphs removed from the statement of the event. The next event, on 8 Ahau 8 Mol 9.6.18.12.0, comes at the break of the monument, and we do not know its nature. Several times, however, about five years after the occurrence of a birth, we find another date recorded, which may refer to the naming of the child, or to the beginning of his training. Though the date recorded here is one year later, it may refer to a comparable ceremony. The next date I believe refers to the lady's husband, whose identifying glyph is a face with a long projecting lip and a Venus-like postfix. The event glyph here is not clear and could be either a *manik* hand compound or a seating glyph. Thus it could signify the lady's marriage or the investiture of her husband on 9 Lamat 16 Ch'en (9.7.10.16.8). Some three years later, on 3 Lamat 16 Uo (9.7.14.10.8), she bore a son. The first glyph of his name is unidentified in Thompson's catalog. It has the prefix *ti* and an unfamiliar sign with *caban* and *kan* cross infixes. I will refer to it as *ti-cab-kan*. It is later replaced by another sign. The name is completed by two more glyphs, the first of which is a *kan* cross compound. I have already mentioned the similarity of this name to that of the ruler who acceded on 9.5.19.1.2, and shall refer to him as Kan Cross II. Five years later, on 8 Eb 15 Zotz' (9.7.19.13.12), a bloodletting ceremony is recorded by a *caban* compound and 4 katuns. A large portion of the following text is eroded including a date we can reconstruct as 4 Lamat 6 Pax (9.9.5.13.8).

The first phrase after the eroded portion of the text begins with an *u caban* glyph, followed by a name that I do not recognize. A Secondary Series then leads to 3 Chicchan 3 Ceh (9.9.9.10.5), which is marked by the same glyph as was the earlier date 9.7.10.16.8. Here it is clear that this is a hand glyph, very similar to the lunar Glyph D, but without a coefficient. It introduces a long clause that contains the names of the long-lipped husband and of the son. This seems to be the last time the husband is mentioned, and it is possible that the transfer of power took place at this time. It is also apparently at this time that the first term of the son's name is changed to T351:774 [184:74]. After a mention of the lahuntun end there are two more dates, (9.9.13.4.4) 9 Kan 2 Zec and (9.9.14.3.5) 12 Chicchan 18 Zip.

The text is continued on the front of the monument. The first date is 9.9.18.16.3 7 Akbal 16 Muan. This date occurs also on the hieroglyphic stairway at Naranjo, and is associated with a venus compound prefixed to the Emblem Glyph of Naranjo. (I shall henceforth refer to all glyphs with this compound of Venus as prefix as the "star light glyph.") The precise meaning of the Venus compound I have not been able to determine, but, as we shall see, it seems to occur when two sites are in close interaction, and is often associated with a shield glyph and with the axe-*ca* prefix, both of which seem to connote conflict, although here these two glyphs are not evident. The text on Stela 3 of Caracol then mentions the end of Katun 10, and a date 8 Ahau 3 Zec, 4.7.0 later, from which it jumps back to

10 Ik o Pop (9.9.4.16.2), a date which is not visible in the inscription, but whose katun anniversary is recorded on the Naranjo stairway. This stairway and the fragmentary lintel of Naranjo together contain four dates that are also recorded on Stela 3 of Caracol, not counting the record of 1 Ahau 8 Kayab, the end of Katun 10. The first of these is the birthday of the king-to-be on 3 Lamat 16 Uo (9.7.14.10.8). The second is 10 Ik o Pop, when the king was thirty years old, a date that is cited at Naranjo by its first katun anniversary. The third is 12 Chicchan 18 Zip (9.9.14.3.5), for which I have no meaning to suggest, and finally, 7 Akbal 16 Muan 9.9.18.16.3, the date of the Venus compound also not yet very well understood.

Stela 6 at Caracol may offer a partial explanation of what occurred. Its inscription, crowded into rounded cartouches, is barely legible, and I can make out only two dates, but the contrast of the two figures that are presented on opposite faces of the monument is in itself significant. The text begins with the accession of Kan Cross I on 9.5.19.1.2, the date that was recorded on Stela 14. Stela 6 was probably erected in 9.8.10.0.0, and it is unlikely that he was still reigning. The inscription skips over the early events recorded on Stela 3, and the only date that can be clearly made out is 9.8.5.16.12 5 Eb 5 Xul. This falls in the time period which because of erosion is missing on Stela 3, and when the grandson was eleven years old, too young to take the throne. The boy is dressed differently from his grandfather. His headdress rests high on his head, in the new fashion. He wears a simple necklace of beads around his neck, and a cloak tied in a huge knot on his chest. His wristlets and anklets are cuff-shaped, and his sandals are provided with ankle guards in the Late Classic fashion. In his right hand he holds a three-pronged eccentric flint, and on his left arm rests a small serpent-bar, apparently with no heads in the serpent mouths.

In view of the similar names of the grandfather and the grandson, it seems to me reasonable to infer that the boy was named after his grandfather, and perhaps was even considered to be his reincarnation, thus acquiring a royal male line, although his father may have been a man of another province, and not entitled to rule. This raises the question of his father's identity, which still remains obscure. It is possible that the father is pictured on Stela 5, which features the dates 9.9.0.0.0 and 9.9.0.4.0, but the inscription is too fragmentary to identify him, and the detail of the figure so resembles that of Kan Cross I that I am reluctant to believe that he is someone from another town. Although the long-lipped head is nowhere mentioned at Naranjo, the mention there of the date of birth of Kan Cross II suggests that the father may have been a nobleman from that city.

What is more important than the problem of the king's paternity is the significance of the Venus-compound expression and its association with the interaction of two sites, which will be further documented in the discussion of Dos Pilas and its hieroglyphic stairway. Before leaving the problem of Naranjo-Caracol relations, it might be

Venus compound ("starlight glyph")
(CRC St 3, F3)

Caracol Stela 6, back: A young ruler
linked by name to his grandfather.
(© Copyright by University Museum,
University of Pennsylvania, 33rd and
Spruce Streets, Philadelphia, PA
19104. Not to be reproduced without
permission.)

well to mention the stelae of Naranjo that may have been erected at this time, though we have no certain dates for them.

Probably the earliest group of monuments erected at Naranjo in this period was a group of three stelae in a small complex of buildings north of the main architectural complex, connected with it by a short causeway. I have records of only one of these, Stela 38. The style of the hieroglyphs is remarkably like that on Stela 6 of Caracol, especially as to the notation of ends of tuns and the slight indentations made in the faces of Ahaus, and the dress of the figure is clearly early in the Late Classic era. The triplicate staff has angular projections typical of later times, but is held diagonally across the body, and is probably one of the earliest examples of its type. The beginning of the inscriptions is entirely effaced, and the remainder is somewhat ambiguous. It reads: "End of tun. 6 Ahau. 6 katuns. End of tun. 7 Ahau. (?) katuns. End of tun. 5 Ahau. 7 katuns. 3 Ch'en. End 3 tuns. 3 katuns." Two other glyphs follow which may be a title and a name, and then the Emblem Glyph of Naranjo prefixed by a human head with a black mask. The last glyph is a compound of *chuen* which recurs on much later Naranjo monuments. If 5 Ahau and 3 Ch'en can be read as a single date, it would probably be 9.8.0.0.0, a very appropriate date for this monument. The other Ahaus could be 6 Ahau (9.6.17.0.0) and 7 Ahau (9.7.0.0.0). The distance to 5 Ahau would then be 1.3.0.0, and presumably the start of the count would be 9.4.17.0.0 10 Ahau 13 Xul, not long after the fall of the government of Kan Boar at Tikal. If we count 3.3.0.0 forward from 6 Ahau 9.6.17.0.0, we reach 9.10.0.0.0, which, however, is not recorded here.

The next group of three monuments to be erected stands in front of the West Acropolis and includes Stelae 25, 26, and 27. Of these, only Stela 25 retains a partially preserved inscription. This is a very unusual monument. The figure is dressed very simply, with no plumes on its headdress, wearing no earplug, only a simple pendant on its earlobe, a bead in front of the nose, and a double strand of beads for a necklace, and single strands on the wrists. Even more unusual is the text, which, like the texts of Caracol at this time, is incised rather than carved. It begins with a very early date in Cycle 8: 8.5.18.4.0 7 Ahau 3 Kankin, as Morley reads it. Ian Graham's drawing (1978:70) shows it as 8.5.17.4.(?)7(?) 7+(?). I will not dispute Morley's reading (1937–1938:2:26–35), though it seems to have no relation to the body of the text and remains questionable. The rest of the text is a series of katun anniversaries of a date 6 Kan 2 Zip, ending with a lahuntun anniversary 9.9.2.0.4, totaling a distance of 3.10.0.0, clearly stated and placed in relation to Katun 9.9.0.0.0. The lack of any symbols of royalty on this monument suggests that it recounts a time when Naranjo had fallen under the domination of a foreign power, possibly Caracol.

A mutilated lintel, apparently incorporated in a hieroglyphic stairway at Naranjo, or possibly just fallen there, records the end of katun 9.10.0.0.0 and refers to the birth of Kan Cross II of Caracol. It is

title
(NAR St 38, B7b)

name
(NAR St 38, B8)

Naranjo Emblem Glyph
(NAR St 38, B9)

chuen compound
(NAR St 38, B10)

Kan Cross II
(NAR L 1, E4)

carved in a very different script and a different style from earlier inscriptions here, and one wonders if this monarch had returned to his father's birthplace to reestablish his dynasty. The apparent alliance of Naranjo and Caracol at this time may be symptomatic of what was happening at other, less well documented sites, whose paired stelae at this time seem to indicate a wide practice of intermarriages in the royal families, at a time when activities at Tikal appear to have been suspended. As we shall see in the next chapter, with the loss of Naranjo as a tributary city, Tikal turned to the Pasión region. Eventually the rulers of Tikal reestablished Naranjo as an independent border state.

Katun 7 was, according to Morley (1920), represented by Stela 18 at Copan, the earliest at that site to have a human figure on one side. For Katun 8 we have no known monument. The date 9.9.0.0.0 is recorded on Stela 7, the first complete (though broken) monument with a human figure, which originally stood over a cruciform chamber in the large platform of Group 9. The style of the hieroglyphs on this stela is very different from that of the earlier Stela 9. It is a long text, with many of the glyph-blocks containing more than one hieroglyph, but the Initial Series appears to be the only date recorded. The text begins with an unusual *caban* compound followed by three god masks and an ending sign above a double *cauac* (possibly the baktun?) Could this clause refer to a three-part division of the city? In the following clause we recognize some of the hieroglyphs used in ritual passages, or those referring to the past: the 9 manikin mask, God C, the bloodletting expression, serpent heads back-to-back, and the fist glyph. A repetition of God C appears to introduce a new clause recording a birth. Four hieroglyphs are crowded into the next glyph-block, and the name is not clear, but since it is followed by the Emblem of Copan, we can assume that it was the name of a ruler. In the upper right corner of the name block is a curious head with a scroll issuing from its mouth, which may recur on Stela 2 in the Main Group, and on Stela 10, at some distance from it. Neither of these monuments is dated with certainty, but their dates probably fall in Katun 11. An interesting, though somewhat dubious feature of this inscription is an eroded glyph on the right side of the monument, with a *kankin*-like sign, which later recurs on Stela F and on Stela H, referring either to a place of origin or to a family. The glyph immediately before this seems to show the *kankin* element on its side, as it is in the Quirigua emblem, but here shown with a coefficient 4 and a double-eye prefix. The meaning of this allusion is not at all clear, but the possibility of contact with the site of Pusilha is worth keeping in mind.

Although Morley (1920) gives Stela E, which was probably set on a mound facing the Great Plaza of Copan, the date 9.9.5.0.0, this date is questionable, and the discussion of its inscription will be deferred to Chapter 8. The foundation of this monument has never been found. I think it more likely that Stela P (9.9.10.0.0), in the west court, is the earliest monument retained in the Main Group. Its text contains many of the glyphs that were featured on Stela 7: the 9 manikin mask, the God C compound, the bloodletting expression, serpent heads back to back, the first glyph, and god masks wearing animal headdresses. The Initial Series date is the only date recorded, but notations of katuns followed by names may have served to place events in time. The text begins with the common *caban* compound, followed by a human head and two other glyphs, which may consti-tute a name. After a bloodletting notation, there is a record of four katuns and what may be another name. The date of birth of this personage (6 Cimi 14 or 19 Uo) may be recorded on Altar Y, used in the foundation of Stela 4. The four-katun notation is not consistent with his being alive at this time, but since his name here follows a bloodletting rite, it is very probable that he was the father or hus-band of the person first mentioned, who may very well have been a woman, and that the fourth katun implies the span of his life.

On the left side there is a notation of three katuns and a fist glyph, but the name which should follow is completely erased. The "jog" glyph and God C compounds are very prominent in this in-scription, but none of the phrases are well enough known to suggest the subject matter of this text. Such texts outside the southeastern sector occur on lintels and stairways, but seldom on stelae, and it may be that these early Copan stelae, showing the figure holding a

caban compound
(CPN St 7, B7b)

God I + God II
(CPN St 7, A8)

God III + ending sign
over double *cauac*
(CPN St 7, B8)

9 manikin mask + God C
(CPN St 7, A10)

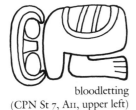

bloodletting
(CPN St 7, A11, upper left)

serpent heads + fist
(CPN St 7, A12)

Copan Emblem
(CPN St 7, B12)

head with scroll
(CPN St 7, A13)

kankin-like sign
(CPN St 7, C11)

4 *kankin*
(CPN St 7, D10)

"jog"
(CPN St P, E12)

flaccid serpent, rather than the usual stiff bar, were posthumous or funerary monuments, representing ancestral figures, not currently ruling lords.

At Pusilha, none of the stelae that may have been erected at this time, Stelae Q, C, F, and G, have clearly legible dates. Stela C is of interest because of its original style, and also because one of the heads in the mouth of the serpent-bar carried by the figure is the head of Tlaloc. The so-called Mexican Year Sign and goggle-eyed heads, though they may have originated at Teotihuacan and were certainly used there intensively in ancient times, probably by the beginning of the Late Classic era had a pan-Mesoamerican distribution and were fully assimilated into the Classic style of the Maya. They are most conspicuous in border sites such as Piedras Negras and Copan, which suggests that these motifs were common among the surrounding cultures. At Piedras Negras and at Yaxchilan, they are often associated with figures of warriors, but the fact that the Maya never seem to have used the atlatl in warfare suggests that other so-called Teotihuacan motifs came to them at second hand and not through direct contact or "influence" from the Mexican city. Two and a half centuries since the first penetration of highlanders into the Peten was ample time for such traits to have been completely absorbed into the artistic vocabulary of lowland art.

That this period had a specific meaning for Pusilha is attested by later inscriptions, which refer to it sometimes by a second Initial Series. Morley's readings of Stelae P and D (9.10.15.0.0) and Stela H (9.11.0.0.0) include the following dates: Stela P, IS 9.7.0.0.0, 9.6.17.8.18, 9.7.4.9.12; Stela D, IS 9.8.0.0.0, 9.5.17.4.18, 9.7.18.5.3, 9.8.1.12.8; Stela H, IS 9.7.12.6.7. These inscriptions have never been studied and the meanings of the dates are unknown. It may be significant that the distance between the earliest dates cited on Stelae D and P is 1.0.4.0. If the date implied on Stela D is a birth date, that on Stela P would be the nearest occurrence of the same day to a katun anniversary. Coggins (1975) notes a similar occurrence of a calendar-name anniversary on Altar V at Tikal at a much later time. However, other instances of this interval are not related to birth dates, and at Piedras Negras, birth dates were celebrated at even hotun intervals, so that the use of calendar names by the Maya remains questionable. It is interesting to speculate whether the retrospective dates at Pusilha have something to do with Copan, since the main sign of the Pusilha Emblem occurs there in 9.9.0.0.0.

At Altar de Sacrificios, a new group of monuments was set up in 9.9.5.0.0, after a period of inaction that lasted nearly a century. Stela 18 was moved to a new location, and an inscription was made on the back. The first twelve glyphs are undecipherable. Below this passage we find an Initial Series recording the hotun date (9 Ahau 8 Uo). The event is the thumb-up hand glyph that I am inclined to interpret as a sign of "receiving" or "attaining" (an honor or status). The infix is often Ahau, but in this case, it is a round element, not unlike an earplug. The next glyph, which may be the name of the ruler, is obscure, and is followed by an animal head. After that is an *u ahaulil* expression, which often follows the thumb-up hand glyph and refers to a previous reign. Unfortunately, we do not know who was ruling at that time, since we have no records immediately preceding. Near the end of the inscription are a Secondary Series and a date 1 Muluc 12 Zotz', followed by a glyph with the coefficient 10. John A. Graham (1972) reads the date as 9.7.15.12.9, but it is possible to give it a later position: 9.10.8.7.9, though this is twenty-three tuns later than the Initial Series. No monument is known for 9.9.10.0.0, but 9.9.15.0.0 and 9.10.0.0.0 are represented by Stelae 8 and 9. The figures on these stelae stand in the Late Classic pose, holding ceremonial bars diagonally in opposite directions, though both figures face to the right.

In the western sector, the earliest known Late Classic monument is Stela 1 from Lacanha, erected in 9.8.0.0.0. The figure wears a quilted or spangled helmet like those of the kneeling figures on Lintel 2 of Piedras Negras and carries a rectangular shield trimmed with feathers. A second Initial Series on this monument records a date in Katun 6. Although the figure bears no arms, the presence of the helmet and shield reminds us of the importance of the military function of chiefs in this troubled period on the frontier. The rectangular shield is virtually unknown in the central area, though occasional examples occur on its periphery. This early relationship between Piedras Negras and Lacanha may prove of some interest, though at the present time we do not have enough material to draw from it any significant conclusions.

Although the earliest date we have from Piedras Negras falls in the sixth katun, the earliest surviving record of the accession of a king at Piedras Negras, on Stela 25, reads 9.8.10.6.16. The only other dated monument of this series is Stela 26, erected one katun later, but there are other monuments in the South Group, too eroded to be placed in time, which may well belong in this or even earlier series.

At this time, stelae were not erected in compact rows, as they later were. Morley arbitrarily fills in the gap between the erection of Stela 29 in 9.5.5.0.0 and Stela 25 in 9.8.15.0.0, with stelae on which there is no vestige of sculpture, and which may have been plain or painted, and by advancing the date of Stela 29 to 9.6.0.0.0; but in view of discontinuities elsewhere at this time, this procedure is questionable. In any case, the motif of Stela 25, showing the ruler seated in a doorway or niche, with the sky-serpent around him and the bird above, is the first of its kind. The inscription is not as clear as one might wish, but it seems to deal with the capture of a prisoner 1.17 before the accession of the ruler, and his sacrifice five days later, which might account for what Morley (1937–1938 : 3 : 49–54) took to be an error of five days in the Secondary Series. Human sacrifice is pictured on two other accession stelae at Piedras Negras.

thumb-up hand
(ALS St 18, GII)

Stela 26, erected a katun later in 9.9.15.0.0, shows the ruler in his military role. This stela records at least two other dates, but its text is badly damaged and all but illegible. It is evident that the frontier location of this city required a strong military orientation. The warriors of Piedras Negras are usually presented in full front view, wearing either a large, turbanlike headdress or a monster head made up of plates, reminiscent of some of the Teotihuacan motifs, with a long chin strap hanging on the chest, ending in a forked tongue. The shields are usually rectangular, and in the early period, instead of a spear, the warrior holds a hooked staff. Such elements suggest interaction of this city with foreign peoples to the west.

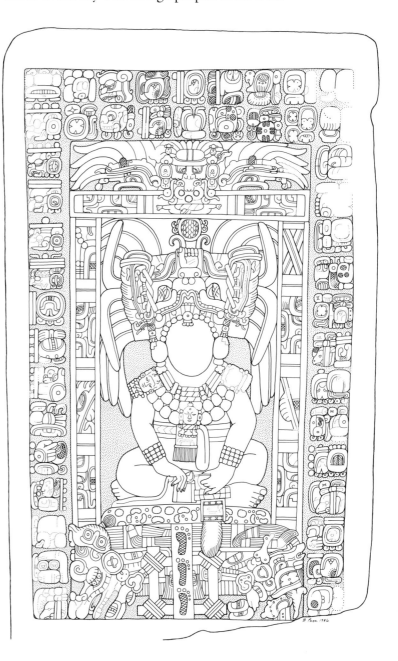

Piedras Negras Stela 25, front: The first known example of the ascension motif of the ruler seated in a niche. (Drawing by Barbara Page.)

The successor to this ruler of Piedras Negras was born on 6 Imix 19 Zotz' (9.9.13.4.1) (see discussion of Stela 36 in chapter 8), twenty-two years after the accession. It is not likely that he was the first-born child of the ruling lord, and he may even have been his grandson, for he was only thirteen years old when he took office.

Yaxchilan was somewhat slower in establishing a strong and stable dynasty. Stela 2 is the only monument that seems to belong to this transitional period, and its brief inscription is not clear. It is a very strange monument, and there is reason to suspect that it was at least partially recarved. Morley (1937–1938:2:404–406) describes the pose of the figure as having feet placed at 180 degrees, but the legs are clearly in side view. Morley and Teobert Maler (1901–1903) seem to agree that the hands of the figure are missing, but the left hand, posed in a "scattering" gesture, is clearly visible, and the right may be partially obscured behind it. The shoulders appear to be in front view, but it is possible that this is because the figure wears an ornament high on its back and a hanging below it simulates an arm. The top portion of a spear overlaps the border at the left. Although the relief is low, the background is deeply cut away, and this in itself suggests alteration. It is difficult to say, however, which was the original design and what parts were recarved or added in stucco. The inscription at the upper left is on the higher plane. It contains only four glyph-blocks, and its sharp edge at the bottom suggests that it may once have extended downward. At the lower left appear some hieroglyphs in very low relief, but not incised, as is usual for such background glyphs. There is reason to think that this inscription (see Chapter 8) implies the accession of a ruler called Bird Jaguar in 9.9.16.10.13, which suggests that at Yaxchilan, as elsewhere, there was an attempt to establish a new dynasty (or revive a previous one) during the tenth katun.

Although we have no dates or texts from the region of San Pedro Martyr at this time, it is perhaps worth noting that Stela 1 at La Florida, though probably a Late Classic monument, exhibits a number of early traits, among them an early position of the feet, a very long, diagonally held serpent-bar, and serpent heads with round eyes and snouts turned back, with an oval on the upper surface. The inscription is too weathered to make out, but the suggestion of a settlement here in the early years of the Late Classic period suggests that the river may have served as an important route of trade at this time.

CHAPTER EIGHT

Growth and Expansion

9.10.0.0.0 – 9.12.10.0.0

A.D. 633 – 682

TIKAL AND THE SITES AROUND IT SEEM TO HAVE BEEN singularly inactive during most of this period. No building of any consequence was going on in the North Acropolis, no rich tombs were found, and we can place no monuments in this period. This does not mean that Tikal was abandoned. Normal activities were doubtless pursued in other sections of the city, but it seems that the king was not in residence, and, as we shall see, there is strong evidence that he was engaged elsewhere in what may have been a military campaign.

Although Morley (1937–1938:1:398–408) assigns a number of stelae at Xultun to this period, his dates are little more than guesses. The limestone in this region is of poor quality, and the stone is now so eroded that most of the inscriptions are illegible. The style of Stelae 4 and 5 seems too late for this time. Only Stela 21, which Morley places later, shows the mixture of early and later traits that is typical of the transition to Late Classic times. The figure holds a ceremonial bar diagonally and with his right hand makes a scattering gesture, a motif that later becomes standard at Tikal on monuments recording ends of katuns. The small frets of the apron and the form of the earplug are early characteristics, and I would guess that this monument was erected between 9.8.0.0.0 and 9.11.0.0.0.

In contrast, the city of Calakmul, dominant in the region of southern Campeche north of Tikal, was flourishing. Although the monuments there are badly weathered, so that very few texts are legible, we can reasonably ascribe fourteen stelae there to the period between 9.10.0.0.0 and 9.12.10.0.0. Its strategic location with access to the Laguna de Términos by way of the Río Candelaria may have contributed substantially to its prosperity. In conquest times, the province of Acalan, a rich trading center, controlled the upper reaches of this river. The prosperity of Calakmul may be a consequence of the development of that important trade route. Unfortunately, there is now little chance of recovering much of the history of this great site. Not only are many of its monuments made of poor stone and badly weathered, but also in recent years there has been extensive looting there, and probably the best of its stelae have been cut up and removed for sale abroad. Karl Ruppert and John H. Dennison made several visits to the site in the 1930s, but they did not attempt to turn the fallen monuments, and only a few are illustrated in their report (1943). Additional photographs and rubbings of inscriptions, now in the Tozzer Library of Harvard University, are not sufficiently clear to permit reading of the texts. Of the texts of three of the fourteen monuments there are no records at all, though they were standing and their dates were partly legible.

The monuments of this period are distributed in five locations at the site, and it seems probable that many had been removed from their original positions and re-erected where they were found. Two are in the early so-called "astronomical" assemblage of buildings, and there may be others there with illegible dates. Four are on the south side of a small structure facing the large pyramid Structure II that overlooks the "astronomical" group from the south, and three others are associated with small outlying Structures IX and XVIII. These may be in their original positions, though the insignificance of the structures is striking. Three stand in a row with two later monuments in front of Structure XV on the edge of a huge palace-type assemblage. The row is arranged in chronological order, beginning with 9.12.0.0.0 and probably ending with 9.13.0.0.0. At no other site are there so many stelae with the same final dates, and this may signify a government less autocratic than that of Piedras Negras, or of Tikal, but lacking legible texts, it is futile to speculate about its nature. Some of the monuments may be paired, one having a male, the other a female figure, but in this period the female figure more often is carved on the back of one that pictures a man. This is clearly so on Stela 9, which is made of slate and therefore better preserved than most. Like many other monuments here, it has two Initial Series: an odd date 9.10.16.16.19 3 Cauac 2 Ceh on the left side, and probably 9.11.10.0.0 on the right. The lahuntun date is repeated on the front and on the back, and on the front is also mentioned the end of the current katun, probably to fix the date more firmly. There is no illustration in Ruppert and Dennison's (1943) report of the figure on the back, but the inscription clearly refers to a woman. The figure on the front resembles other Late Classic figures of ruling lords, though instead of a manikin scepter it holds a scepter that ends in a fret diagonally across its chest, and a shield in the left hand. The wide sun apron with protruding frets and the large tassels on the sandals would elsewhere suggest a later date for this monument, but similar exaggerations are found on a monument from Ichpaatun which was carved at about this time, and the style of the earplugs and the design of the collar are entirely in keeping with the 9.11.10.0.0 date. The name of the woman on the back is preceded by the *kin* title (T1001) which usually designates wives of lords, but the name of the lord on the front is either weathered away or has no identifying title.

Other sites in the north were also erecting stelae at this time. At Naachtun, Stela 2 and possibly Stelae 12 and 18 fall in this period, and at Uxul, Stelae 5, 12, and 13 and Altar 2. The altar depicts a ballgame on the front, and its top is covered with a long inscription that faintly shows three Initial Series, so eroded that about all one can observe is that zoomorphic forms are prominent in the text. A pity, since it is the longest text associated with the ballgame that is known, and were it legible, it might give us some indication of the function of the game.

The prosperity of Calakmul may have been directly or indirectly responsible for the apparent abandonment of Tikal by its rulers. Caracol, too, at this time seems to have stopped erecting monuments. Naranjo, which may have been its tributary town, now passes into the sphere of Tikal. Actually, there are no monuments at Naranjo that we can date with any certainty in this period. Stela 17, which Morley (1937–1938:2:67–69) places here, looks more like an Early Classic monument, and Stela 11 and 34 are more appropriately dated by Berlin (1973) as erected a century later than Morley suggests. Stelae 4, 5, and 20 are the only monuments here that seem to fit comfortably into this period.

Stelae 4 and 5 are of unusual design. Their figures, like that of Stela 25, show none of the attributes of royalty. They wear no long plumes on their headdresses and carry no royal symbols. The figure on Stela 5 holds a round fan (a rare motif that reappears much later on Stela 8). The fish nibbling on a water lily on his headdress and the tall strip of fabric projecting above are details often seen in figure painting on pottery vessels, and seem to imply either less formal occasions or lesser officials. The date on Stela 5 reads best as 9 Lamat 1 Cumku, as originally read by Morley, though later he changed this reading to 9 Lamat 1 Zotz', in my opinion with insufficient reason. This date could be 9.9.14.17.8 or 9.12.7.12.8.

While the north was prospering, the ruler of Tikal had apparently abandoned his city and had established himself at Dos Pilas in the region of Petexbatun, far to the south. What prompted this move we can only conjecture. He may have been expelled by a foreign power or by his own people, or the move could have been strategic, to repel invaders from the highlands and/or to secure access to trade routes along the Usumacinta. Our information about his activities at Dos Pilas is too scanty to yield a definite answer. It comes from a single inscription on a hieroglyphic stairway, large parts of which are destroyed. I am indebted to Ian Graham for a drawing of the text on Stairway 2, from which the following data are taken:

The inscription begins with a Distance Number from 12 Ahau

(9.11.0.0.0) to 9.11.4.5.14 6 Ix 2 Kayab, followed by the "starlight glyph" and the main sign of the Tikal Emblem. The "starlight glyph," mentioned in connection with Caracol and Naranjo, can contain an Emblem Glyph or be followed by it. Here, the contained sign is the scroll T575 used in death expressions, and the Tikal sign is attached. The stairway text continues with T11-*caban,* a *kin* sign, possibly a variant of South, an unknown expression that contains a bird head emerging from a large T575 scroll, a skull with a crossed-bands pendant, and other unknown glyphs. At the end of the passage is a capture glyph and the Tikal Emblem main sign without prefixes, which may or may not imply that the city had been captured, since its precise meaning is still uncertain. In the ensuing inscription, a certain ruler of Tikal is mentioned seven times. His name, like those of later rulers, is distinguished by the prefix of a sky glyph, in his case an oval with a jagged line through it, which looks very much like a cracked egg. One might be tempted to call him Humpty Dumpty, but in respect for his royal lineage, he has been given the name of Lightning Sky. More than half of the second step from the top of the east side is entirely effaced, but the end of the passage refers to Lightning Sky of Tikal. Counting back 2.1 from the lahuntun 9.11.10.0.0, we reach the date 9.11.9.15.19 9 Cauac 17 Yaxkin. The statement that follows begins with a female head and contains two compounds of the sign *imix,* and again ends with the name of Lightning Sky of Tikal. A short phrase follows, and next we count forward 1.9.17 from the same lahuntun as before, reaching 9.11.11.9.17 9 Caban 5 Pop, which marks the capture of Torch Parrot, probably by Lightning Sky, though there are three intervening glyphs of unknown meaning between the two names. Parrots often occur in texts that contain capture glyphs. Since the earliest instance of a parrot worn on the headdress is portrayed on a foreign warrior, one is inclined to think that they may have been invaders from the highlands and that the occasional Torch Parrot may have been their chief.

"starlight glyph"
(DPL HS 2E, IV, D1)

skull with crossed bands
(DPL HS 2E, IV, E1)

capture + Tikal Emblem
(DPL HS 2E, IV, E2b–F2a)

Lightning Sky
(DPL HS 2E, III, F1)

capture
(DPL HS 2E, I, D1)

Torch Parrot
(DPL HS 2E, I, C2)

female head
(DPL HS 2E, II, C1)

captor of Torch Parrot
(DPL HS 2W, IV, E2b–F2a)

T11 katun
(DPL HS 2W, II, E2a)

This is a very puzzling but at the same time a very suggestive passage. It clearly indicates the presence of the king of Tikal in this region, apparently on a military mission, and in view of later events, and the presence of a female head at C1, we may surmise that while he was there, he married a local woman, for in the reign of his successor, the "bundle" emblem of Petexbatun appears at Tikal.

The west steps of the stairway also feature the name of the king of Tikal, who is designated on the first step as the captor of Torch Parrot. Other statements I do not venture to interpret. The first date mentioned, 3 Ix 16 Muan, is impossible in the normal Maya calendar and should probably be read 2 Ix 17 Muan (9.12.5.9.14). A Distance Number of 7 days at B4 would then lead to 9 Imix 4 Pax at B4-A5 (9.12.5.10.1). The starting point of the count seems to have been 9.12.0.8.3 4 Akbal 11 Muan, though it does not appear in the stairway inscription and may have been recorded on some badly eroded panels associated with it. The statement on the second step is also somewhat ambiguous. A Distance Number 1.3 is to be counted from 8 Ahau 13 Zec, seventh tun (9.12.7.0.0), forward (?), but actually back to 11 Caban 10 Zotz' (9.12.6.16.17). Two glyphs that follow, an unknown glyph and a shield glyph, are identical with the glyphs associated with the date 9.13.3.7.18 on Lintel 3 of Temple I at Tikal. Similar events are clearly implied, both in contexts that involve an Emblem of another town. The clause on the Dos Pilas step contains skull glyphs and ends with the name of the Tikal king, possibly indicating his death at the time. The inscription continues, and the last legible date seems to be 9.12.12.11.2 2 Ik 10 Muan. This is followed by a hand glyph, T11 katun, possibly referring to the army, an *imix* compound, a manikin title, and the Tikal Emblem. Lightning Sky is not mentioned here. His successor was already ruling at Tikal. Two panels, called Stelae 12 and 13, however, probably belong with the stairway, and may even form a part of the same inscription. They are only partially preserved and no dates on them have survived, but on Panel 13, near the end of the text, is the name Lightning Sky, captor of Torch Parrot. The text was continued on Panel 12, which is very badly eroded. It ends with an *u ahaulil* "in the reign of" clause, but the name is not clear. The Tikal Emblem follows and the *imix*-comb-*imix* glyph (*bacab*??) that normally ends an inscription. No stelae of this period are known at Dos Pilas. Apparently it was only after the successor of Lightning Sky departed to be king of Tikal that Dos Pilas became an independent city, a *cabecera* in its own right.

At Altar de Sacrificios, most of the inscriptions of this period are scattered in the North Court. John A. Graham (1972) has published an excellent report on the monuments, though his retention of some of the earlier erroneous designations of monuments is somewhat confusing. Thus he describes Stelae 4 and 5 as "wall panels." These panels were set into the retaining walls of the lowest platform on each side of the latest stairway leading to Structure A-I, on the north side of the court. The back of this building is destroyed by the encroaching river, and excavation has shown a long period of innovations and changes within its substructure. It seems very likely that these panels are not in their original position and were dismantled from an earlier building and incorporated in the latest platform when it was built.

The upper part of Stela 4 is missing, but the large Introducing Glyph on Stela 5 is carved in a narrower panel than the text on which it is centered. Thus the top of the stela may have been notched on one side or on both, possibly to support a lintel. The two monuments do not seem to have been designed as a pair. Nevertheless, their inscriptions are closely related. The Initial Series on Stela 4 is 9.10.3.17.0 4 Ahau 8 Muan. The final date seems to be 13 Ahau 18 Kankin (9.10.10.0.0). (Graham's 9 Ahau is surely a misprint.) The inscription on Stela 5, though complete, is even more severely damaged. The Initial Series here is 9.10.11.12.17. If we read the last Secondary Series on Stela 4 as 1.12.17, to be added to the date 13 Ahau 18 Kankin (9.10.10.0.0), we will reach the Initial Series date on Stela 5, 9.10.11.12.17 6 Caban 5 Ch'en (Graham gives 7 Caban). In association with Stelae 4 and 5 are two smaller panels: Sculptured Panels 1 and 2. These are probably vertical panels set into the sloping upper surface of the walls on the sides of the stairway. John Graham reads the final date on both panels as 9 Ahau 8 Ch'en 9.10.11.13.0. His reading of other dates on these panels is less certain, but can provisionally be accepted. A third panel, lower than the other two and apparently illegible, may have been set into the stairway or into the plinth of the temple above. Although none of the panels offers a legible text, it may be worth noting that a female head appears a number of times in these inscriptions. No stela is directly associated with this building, but it is possible that Stela 3, in front of the north end of Structure A-II, belongs with Structure A-I. However, this stela is so badly eroded that even the arrangement of the figure of figures on its face cannot be made out.

Stela 1, on the other hand, though broken and fallen, probably stood originally on a basal platform of Structure A-II. It portrays a woman dressed in jade-net costume, holding a short serpent-bar on her arms. The sculpture is badly damaged, but on the back enough of the inscription is preserved to show an Initial Series of 9.11.10.0.0 11 Ahau 18 Ch'en. Very little else of the inscription is preserved. There are two other jade-skirted figures at Altar de Sacrificios: Stela 7 and Stela 16. Neither now preserves a date, but Morley (1937–1938) draws a period-ending date of 9.14.0.0.0 from Stela 7. The fact that we know of no male figures at this time raises the question whether the jade skirt was worn by women or was a priestly garment. [Editor's note: see Bruhns 1988; Marcus 1987; Proskouriakoff 1961b; Schele 1979; Stone 1988; 1991 for discussion of this problem.] There are, however, a number of scattered and badly eroded fragments here, and any conclusion based on negative evidence is highly suspect.

3 katuns?
(ALS Sc Pan 4, pD3)

vulture
(ALS, Sc Pan 4, pC4)

Sculptured Panel 4 seems to be only a fragment of a much larger hieroglyphic panel, found in the rubble of Structure A-II, not far from Stela 1. We do not know its date, but it contains some interesting glyphs that may be worth mentioning here. In the third and fourth columns of glyphs, near the top of the fourth row there is a birdlike glyph with a coefficient of 3 and a superfix that looks something like the superfix of the katun. This is followed by what seems to be a vulture glyph. I strongly suspect that this phrase may be a military title or refer to the army itself. In the Motul dictionary, one meaning given to the word "katun" is something in the nature of "battalion of an army." The katun glyph, perhaps "battalion," is followed here by the vulture glyph that I have elsewhere suggested may refer to a military chief or governor. There follows a glyph with the coefficient of 11, for which I have no explanation, and then the date 12 Ix 17 Muan. If the Initial Series of this date is 9.11.9.5.14, this day would fall in December, as do at least five other dates in the month of Muan. Moreover, this date is a hotun anniversary of 9.11.4.5.14 6 Ix 2 Kayab, at Dos Pilas, which falls in the middle of January. Late December is the beginning of the dry season, and the 12 Ix date is followed immediately by the "Starlight glyph" with a *caban* main sign, which may indicate the clear sky at this time, a time for military campaigns and for travel in general.

Inscriptions at Pusilha, in the southeastern sector, also tend to contain more than one Initial Series. Stela P, in addition to its date of dedication, 9.10.15.0.0, records 9.7.0.0.0 as well as Secondary Series leading to other dates. At C1 on this monument we discern the Emblem Glyph of Pusilha, with a main sign which is something like the month Kankin and resembles the Emblem of Quirigua turned upright. This Emblem appears again at the end of the inscription of Stela D, which was also erected in 9.10.15.0.0 and whose second Initial Series is 9.8.0.0.0. The phrase containing the Emblem begins with the expression *u caban,* which is normally followed by a name. Here the name resembles that of the person whose birth is recorded on Stela 7 at Copan, erected in 9.9.0.0.0, and whose name may be repeated on Stela E (9.9.5.0.0) and possibly also on Stela 2 (9.10.15.0.0 or 9.11.0.0.0). In no case is this name entirely clear, and its identification is tentative, but the suggestion of a relationship between the first Late Classic dynasties of Pusilha and Copan suggests also the further possibility that the conflict that led to the independence of Quirigua a century later was originated by settlers from Pusilha. This is further suggested by the fact that the last of the five dated stelae at Pusilha was erected in 9.15.0.0.0 and the first Late Classic stela at Quirigua in 9.15.15.0.0.

At Copan, stelae of traditional design, first appearing at 9.9.0.0.0 on Stela 7, continue being erected in the Main Group with little change until 9.11.0.0.0, after which date the style undergoes radical changes. Morley considers Stela E to be the earliest of the monuments in the Main Group and dates it at 9.9.5.0.0. It is the narrowest and smallest of the stelae, and in this respect resembles Stela 7; but, on the other hand, in the design of its headdress and in other significant details it resembles Stela 3 more closely than it does Stela P. Herbert Spinden's (1913) seriation of Copan stelae does not take into consideration the fact that the proportions of the figure as well as the position of its arms are directly related to the overall form of the monument, which may have been determined by other factors than style, and I prefer to leave open the possibility that Stela E partially fills the gap left open by the absence of monuments at 9.10.0.0.0 and 9.10.10.0.0, especially since no other stelae of this period record ho-tun dates. If we place Stela E at 9.10.0.0.0 and Stela 2 at 9.10.10.0.0, the sequence would be complete without violating stylistic probability, though such placing must remain tentative.

Stela 2, in spite of its broader form, is very similar in detail to Stela P, erected in 9.9.10.0.0. Although the central element of the headdress of Stela 2 is a jaguar head, not a mask, as on Stela P, its general form and the arrangement of symbols above are almost identical on the two monuments, as are the serpents pendant from the belt. The inscription on Stela 2 features God C glyphs and the fist glyph and includes a 9 manikin-head expression. On the right side may be recorded the name that appeared on Stela 7, the fist glyph, and 3 katuns. No specific date for the birth of this person is recorded on Stela 7. Since the notation is somewhat ambiguous and may refer to the record of 9.11.0.0.0 just preceding, it does not give us any firm information about this person.

Stela 3 records two Initial Series and depicts two personages. Morley reads the dates as 9.0.0.0.0 and 9.11.0.0.0; Thompson reads them as 9.10.19.5.11 and 9.10.19.5.0. Both agree that the monument was erected about 9.11.0.0.0. At the same time at least five monuments were erected within a 6.5 kilometer radius of Copan, on hilltops, on mountain slopes, and in other prominent locations. Only one of these monuments, Stela 23, was sculptured with a human figure, and this figure, shown in profile, is atypical. The dates suggested for these monuments are: Stela 12, 9.10.14.1.15 (9.12.0.0.0); Stela 3, 9.10.18.12.8 (9.11.0.0.0); Stela 10, 9.10.19.13.0; Stela 19, 9.10.19.15.0; Stela 13, 9.11.0.0.0. Stelae 12 and 23 also record 9.11.0.0.0, and Stela 23 records the beginning of the count, 4 Ahau 8 Cumku. What events are recorded here has not been determined. On Stela 10 we find the same name that was noted on Stela 2 in the Main Group, together with the fist glyph and the katun notation. The katun has no coefficient. It is prefixed by a double *cauac,* and probably refers to a position in the army. I suspect that all these scattered stelae record grants of land and other privileges to persons in the service of the king, perhaps local chiefs who had joined his forces.

Stela 1, erected after 9.11.15.0.0, marks a radical transformation not only in the style and technique of carving on the monuments but also in the costumes worn by the personages depicted and in their physical proportions. Stela 1 is set into the stairway of the ballcourt

name
(CPN St 2, D9aii)

fist glyph + katun
(CPN St 10, E6)

triadic symbol
(PAL TI, mid. pan., D5)

helmet
(PAL TI, mid. pan., C6)

God I
(PAL TI, mid. pan., D7)

at Copan, with an altar in front. Morley disassociates the two monuments (1920:174–177) and apparently misreads the date on the bench of the court (J. E. S. Thompson 1944a:59). The ballcourt in which Stela 1 is set is the last of three superimposed courts. In its alleyway, it has three square markers which were sculptured with quatrefoil panels now entirely weathered away. Shortly before this ballcourt was built, new markers were placed in the earlier court, and they are almost in mint condition. These markers are round, and, like the upper markers, present ballplayers in quatrefoil frames. The central marker shows two ballplayers and a large ball between them marked with a *kan*-cross-winged *cauac*-wing glyph. In the lower panel beneath each ballplayer is the Triadic Symbol, missing, however, its central element. The other two markers show one player each, with the Triadic Symbol below and a smaller standing figure, also wearing a ballplayer's belt. Behind each of the smaller figures is a plant and a hieroglyph, one with the coefficient 9, the other with 7. These are not the usual hieroglyphs with which the numbers 7 and 9 are associated on stelae, and in neither case is the significance of these two numbers known. Between the two figures a ball is suspended on a thick rope. The earlier markers of this court are all but effaced, but enough remains to show that they also were carved with two ballplayers on the central marker and with single players on the end markers. Gustav Stromsvik (1952) reports signs of burning on the surface of these lower markers; so it seems that they were deliberately effaced before new markers were placed over them. The second ballcourt, although similar in plan to the latest court, is not directly under it and has a slightly different orientation. This suggests that large alterations were being made at this time, probably in preparation for the building of the court of the Hieroglyphic Stairway.

Copan Stela I, dated by its altar as having been erected in 9.12.5.0.0, is carved in high relief, but in detail resembles the earlier style. The figure depicted wears a mask with details like those of the glyph for God I of the Palenque Triad. The figure wears a headdress with the Triadic Symbol like the central mask on the panel within the Temple of the Cross at Palenque, associated with God I. The Triadic Symbol also stands for God I in a series of passages in the Temple of the Inscriptions at Palenque. There, three consecutive statements link each member of the Palenque Triad with a specific symbol, followed in each case by a helmetlike glyph. It seems, therefore, that here at Copan, the figure depicted on Stela I is impersonating God I of the Palenque Triad, or whatever entity he stood for. The skeletal form of the serpent-bar held by this figure suggests a deceased ancestor of the royal house.

The Initial Series date, 9.12.3.14.0, on Stela I is quite clear, but two other dates are more difficult to place in time. Their accompanying glyphs G disagree with Morley's reading. The first date 10 Ahau 13 Che'n, Yax, Zac, or Ceh is followed by glyph G9 and within the

Copan Stela I, front: A figure wearing
the mask of 'God I' of the Palenque
Triad. (Drawing by Barbara Page.)

fish-in-hand + manikin cap
(CPN St I, D1)

rodent + 4 + *kankin*
(CPN St I, D2)

bloodletting
(CPN St I, D5)

sacrifice + Copan Emblem Glyph
(CPN St I, D6)

mask with *imix* + manikin head
(CPN St 6, D3 [except top left])

3 katuns + fist
(CPN St 6, D4a)

historic period can have the value 9.9.14.9.0, 9.11.7.0.0, 9.12.19.9.0, or 9.14.12.0.0. The last two dates overrun the dedicatory date and are unlikely. The first two are more probable but fail to explain what seems to be a record of the completion of 8 katuns which follows. A Secondary Series of 10.8 links 10 Ahau with 10 Lamat, Glyph G1, but the month position of this day is unknown and following glyphs are destroyed.

Like earlier inscriptions at Copan, that on Stela I seems to deal with ritual observances. The inscription on the left side begins with the fish-in-hand glyph followed by the cap of the manikin, which seems to serve as a title, but by no recognized name. The next glyph is a compound of *caban,* and that is followed by a compound of a rodent glyph (T758a) with a coefficient 4 and a *kankin* element on its side which later became the central element of the Emblem Glyph of Quirigua. The rodent element I believe may refer to "son" or "offspring." Further on we encounter the 9 manikin-helmet glyph and reference to a bloodletting rite followed by the Emblem Glyph of Copan combined with the sacrifice sign. These glyphs, associated at Yaxchilan with depictions of sacrificial rites, suggest a ritual text, which may or may not have any direct connection with historical events.

Stela 6, erected in 9.12.10.0.0, returns us to a design like that of Stela 1. This monument, however, is not set up in the Main Group, but was found lying on a nearby hillside near Stela 5. The costume of the figure is entirely different from that of former Copan rulers. On the headdress, it displays the sign of Tlaloc and the so-called Mexican Year Sign, worn also at Piedras Negras on the helmets of warriors at about this time. Embroidered on the apron that covers the loincloth is a symbol worn by some Piedras Negras warriors. The broad garters worn just under the knee and the sandals with a high ankle guard are also foreign to Copan. The personage portrayed here may have been a son or younger brother of the ruler pictured on Stela 1, for in the inscription on the left side we find a mask with an *imix* sign on the forehead followed by the manikin head, 3 katuns, and a fist sign, suggesting that the ruler on Stela 1 had died in the interim. The dedicatory date of Stela 6 is expressed by its Initial Series and is followed by the "grain-scattering" glyph and the lahun-tun sign, which probably refers to the augury for the end of the katun which is named. The following clause, containing signs for night and day, is interesting though of unknown meaning. Like most texts at Copan, this inscription contains a number of familiar expressions, mixed with references to ritual observances, which make it difficult to understand their historical meaning. Without attempting to interpret this text, I want to call attention to some individual signs that might help to explain later events. One of these is the upright *kankin* sign at the end of the inscription on the back of the monument, which later occurs, apparently as an Emblem Glyph, on Stelae F and H. On the earlier Stela I, it is shown on its side, in the position it later holds in the Emblem Glyph of Quirigua. This change in position may or may not be significant, but its recurrence at Copan may indicate that Quirigua was originally founded as a dependency of Copan. The problem of its origins will be taken up in Chapter 10.

The name of the current ruler probably appears in the lower half of the third glyph on the right side of Stela 6. It may also be recorded in the third glyph of the left side, though it is eroded beyond recognition. It is here followed by an *imix* mask, and a manikin head, the precise expression which is used with the ruler's name on Altar K. The name on Altar K is a zoomorphic monster head, with a prominent tooth, a long lower jaw, and a comb infix. On the altar, the name and titles are followed immediately by the Emblem Glyph of Copan. Another glyph on Stela 6 that should be mentioned is the name of a future king, Eighteen Jog, which here follows a fish-in-hand glyph. If this is the same Eighteen Jog who was reigning in 9.15.0.0.0, it could be that the ceremony was performed on the occasion of his birth, though usually the fish-in-hand glyph involves the invocation of ancestors.

It is possible that Stela 6 originally stood in the Great Plaza of Copan, and was removed later, though Stela I, which preceded it, was carefully preserved. Altar K, with its Initial Series, which Morley reads as 9.12.16.7.8 3 Lamat 16 Yax, may mark the former location of Stela 6. The remainder of the inscription on Altar K contains some interesting glyphs, whose presence here is not easily explained, though it seems consistent with the exotic costume of the ruler on Stela 6. There is, for example, in addition to the name of the ruler, a jaguar head and a dog glyph with a bird pecking at its eye, a form that appears very early at Yaxchilan. One of the glyphs is reminiscent of the Emblem of Yaxha, and another suggests the central element of the Naranjo Emblem. I don't know what to make of these vague and indefinite hints of wide connections, particularly those that pertain to the Usumacinta region, but it may be worth noting that at this time Copan was beginning to approach its most brilliant period, and may have played an important role in the trade between the lowland Maya and the highland regions. At the end of the inscription on Altar K appears the name of the ruler, the monster with the long lower jaw and the tooth who was pictured on Stela 6. His name is followed by the *imix* mask, the manikin head, and the Emblem of Copan. There is a final statement consisting of three glyphs, the last two each introduced by "4 katuns," the first of unknown meaning, the last the well-known vulture glyph, associated with names of warriors. Perhaps here the katun signs are not used in their calendrical sense, but in the military meaning, to be read as "the great army," or, better yet, they may describe the ruler as (perhaps) a great trader and a great warrior.

At Piedras Negras, a long reign is documented by Stelae 32–37 and 46, in front of Structure R-5 of the South Court, the oldest part of the city. The ruler is designated here by three masks: a turtle head,

"grain scattering"
(CPN St 6, A7a)

upright *kankin*
(CPN St 6, B8)

ruler's name
(CPN St 6, C3b)

ruler's name with comb infix
(CPN Alt K, O2)

imix mask + manikin head
(CPN Alt K, P2)

Eighteen Jog
(CPN St 6, C6a)

turtle head
(PNG St 36, C1)

monkey
(PNG St 36, D1)

head with large eye and curl
(PNG St 36, C2)

a monkey, and a head with a large eye, a curl at the corner of its mouth, and a *kin*-sign earplug. He was born on 9.9.13.4.1 and took the throne on 9.10.6.5.9, when he was only thirteen years old. In his inaugural scene on Stela 33, a woman, probably his mother, stands on the ground below. Presumably he succeeded the king or governor (vulture) whose death in 9.10.6.2.1 is recorded on Lintel 4. The inscriptions on lintels at Piedras Negras are not always easy to interpret. The events recorded on the lintels appear to parallel, though they do not coincide with, those recorded on stelae, and I am not sure whether the term "vulture," which seems to designate the chief of the army, applies to the king himself or to another official. Two stelae in front of Structure K-5, Stelae 39 and 38, may also belong to this reign. Stela 39 (9.12.5.0.0) presents a picture of a warrior, and Stela 38 (9.12.10.0.0) mentions the second katun anniversary of the king's accession, so that it seems there was no change of rulership, or at least of dynasty, at this time. Although the name of the ruler does not appear on these monuments, the texts are badly eroded and this may not be significant. On the other hand, the change of location may signify that these monuments were posthumously erected or represent a regent, for at the time the next ruler was only four years old.

Lintel 4 (possibly a wall panel associated with Structure R-5) has a long inscription, almost completely eroded except for the last six columns, which contain two dates: 9.10.6.2.1 5 Imix 19 Kayab and 9.11.6.1.8 3 Lamat 6 Ceh. These dates, however, are not certain and have been read differently by other scholars. The readings cited here are from Morley (1937–1938:3:91). Since the king acceded only sixty-eight days after the first date, one may infer that this date was the date of the death of the previous ruler, and that the name that follows is that of an interim official, who took charge of funeral services. At the time of the second date, the next king was already in his thirties. The person pictured, however, is probably not the king but the head of his army, with the title of "vulture." He wears a huge feather turban and holds an unusual blunt spear. Before him kneels a slave-carrier, with a bundle of nondescript objects on his back, and behind the carrier are two kneeling warriors. The last date recorded is only thirteen days short of the katun anniversary of the first, and the scene may picture preparations for its celebration.

The date of this anniversary, 9.11.6.2.1 3 Imix 19 Ceh, is the Initial Series of Lintel 2, which was found in the debris of Structure O-13. It pictures the presentation of a boy (the son of the king?) to a group of six kneeling warriors. The heir wears a high pointed hat with a bird on top, and he also wears a mask, which may mean that he is an impersonator. The names of the six warriors are written above them, and three end with the vulture title. All the warriors are handsomely dressed and wear helmets with feathers projecting upward. Their identical costumes signify that they belong to a single group, possibly the personal guard of the king. The dates on this lintel are somewhat difficult to make out, in part from erosion and in part because they do not form a consecutive sequence. As Morley points out, the last Secondary Series, 1.8.12.11, leads back from the final date (9.11.15.0.0) to the date 9.10.6.5.9 8 Muluc 2 Zip, which is recorded on Stela 36 as the date of the ruler's accession. Another numerical series, 3.8, takes us back to 9.10.6.2.1, recorded on Lintel 4. This date is not mentioned here, but its katun anniversary is the Initial Series of Lintel 2. Thus there is no serious difficulty in connecting by Secondary Series the beginning of this inscription with its final dates. There is, however, a long interpolated clause which contains a damaged date that is more difficult to place. I cannot concur with either Morley or Beyer (1939) in reading the first numeral of the Secondary Series as 7 katuns. I think that the 7 is in fact the prefix T12, *ah,* and that the katun here refers to the army. The most likely positions for the intervening date might be 9.10.7.11.15 13 Men 3 Ch'en or 9.10.5.11.5 11 Chicchan 3 Ch'en. Other positions, however, are possible. At the time of the first date the king was twenty-six years old and at the time of the second, thirty-two. The statement could concern his marriage, since it seems to mention a woman. If the statement refers to his mother, earlier positions can be proposed. The coefficient of the katun can also be translated as "1 katun," and the possibilities are too numerous to be discussed here.

In 9.11.15.0.0, the future king was not yet three years old, but there is some reason to think that it is his name that is inscribed in the inverted L-shaped panel on Lintel 2. The first glyph of the panel is a "toothache glyph," lacking, however, the affix cluster that should follow it, were it signifying accession. The "toothache" sign itself is the head of a furry animal, not unlike the first glyph after the birthday glyph on Stela 8. Thus it may designate the heir-apparent. Unfortunately, his name is not clear on any of the records we have. Three other glyphs follow, and finally the Emblem of Piedras Negras. The fact that his name ends with the Emblem Glyph, and not with the vulture, suggests that he is of the royal family and is being presented here as the successor of the king, although he may not be presented in his own person.

After the erection of one more stela, Stela 37, the locus of monuments of this reign moved to Temple K-5, which is adorned with masks of the sun. It is possible that the king had died in the interim, or that he was merely absent on a military campaign, leaving the reign of the city to a regent for his young son. Lintel 7, dedicated in 9.12.5.0.0 and located in Temple K-5, is similar in composition to the celebrated Lintel 3, which shows an audience before the king seated upon a throne. The composition of Lintel 7 is more modest, showing only the king or regent seated on the throne, with a woman on his left and a small figure on his right. The lintel was dedicated at the same time as Stela 39, the first erected at this location, and may

vulture title
(PNG L 2, D'3)

"toothache glyph"
(PNG L 2, K'1)

Piedras Negras Emblem Glyph
(PNG L 2, K'4)

completed
(YAX St 6, C5b)

2 katuns after accession
(YAX St 6, C6)

Bird Jaguar
(YAX St 6, C7a)

bat + *cauac*
(YAX HS 3, VB2a)

eyeless mask
(YAX HS 3, VB3biii)

"fire-fist glyph"
(YAX HS 3, IA4b)

show the future king, now twelve years old, in the care of his mother and a regent. This lintel was found in fragments, and most of its inscription is destroyed. The Initial Series reads 9.9.8.0.?, which is fifty-seven years earlier than the last date and possibly marks the birth of the man portrayed, who would then have been five years older than the king. The readings cited are from Morley (1937–1938: 3:120) and are somewhat questionable. Berlin (1977:99) has proposed the reading 9.12.5.11.5 7 Chicchan 8 Kayab for one of the dates on this lintel, which could be the second katun anniversary of 11 Chicchan 3 Ch'en, a possible reading for one of the dates on Lintel 2. The king's heir was then thirteen years old, but would not accede for nine more years.

At Yaxchilan, most of this period is poorly represented. It has been suggested that Stela 2 may be the divination monument for Katun 10, and that a new dynasty began in 9.9.16.10.13. This conclusion rests on the inscription on Stela 6 and on a statement in the text of the hieroglyphic stairway to Structure 44, which was probably carved more than a century later. Stela 6, like Stela 2, seems to have been carved on an older monument. The figure is in very low relief, and the incomplete design on the butt is on a higher plane. Both stelae present the motif of divination. Morley reads the Initial Series as 9.11.3.10.13 5 Ben 1 Zotz', but I think that the month may be Uayeb, making the Initial Series read 9.11.16.10.13, though I am far from sure of this reading. The next statement seems to say that this date completed 2 katuns after the accession of Bird Jaguar. We know that a lord of that name acceded in 9.16.1.0.0. Therefore, we must conclude that there was another ruler of the same name, who probably began his reign in 9.9.16.10.13, and who may have been the maternal grandfather of the famed Bird Jaguar of later times. His name is mentioned also on the northwest upper step of Structure 44, where it appears in connection with the date 10 Ahau 13 Mol (9.10.14.13.0 ?).

A detailed interpretation of this stairway inscription will not be attempted here, but there are some interesting glyphs on the steps of Structure 44 which may be worth mentioning, though at present their significance is obscure. One of these is the bat glyph combined with a *cauac* sign. It recalls the Emblem of Copan, though this may be sheer coincidence. (At this time, the Main Group of Copan was being rebuilt and stelae were being erected outside the Main Group on surrounding hillsides.) Other interesting glyphs are the eyeless mask (T1013), which suggests reference to death, and repeated occurrences of the "fire-fist glyph," T672, which may in some way refer to ancestors. The steps leading to Structure 44 were probably constructed during the reign of Shield Jaguar, whose origins, in spite of his elaborate genealogy, are obscure. We do not know the dates of his birth or of his accession to power. He was probably not a native son, and may have been a conqueror. Discussion of the early years of his reign will be relegated to the next chapter, although at least five of his dates seem to fall within this period.

Some investigators have called this and the previous period Middle Classic, but at present it would be difficult to define its limits or to describe its characteristics for the area as a whole. It was a period of many changes, but circumstances differed in different parts of the Maya area, and too few inscriptions survive to permit a sound judgment of the relation of various events recorded at different sites. About all one can say is that it was probably a turbulent period of transition, in which various Maya cities were competing for positions of influence and were defining the limits of their domains. The lack of activity at Tikal at this time and the presence of the king at Dos Pilas doubtless can be variously interpreted, but the salient fact is that at the end of this period, the Maya area as a whole was beginning its most opulent period and nearing the peak of its achievements.

CHAPTER NINE

Toward a Peak of Prosperity

9.12.10.0.0 — 9.15.0.0.0

A.D. 682 — 736

THE RESTORATION OF TIKAL AS A MAJOR RELIGIOUS center of the Maya lowlands was a momentous event in Maya history. After what appears to have been the failure of an attempt to reestablish an ancient dynasty of Tikal, as recorded on Stela 26, we observe a series of marriage alliances, both at Tikal (Stelae 23, 25?) and in outlying sites, but there is little evidence of activity in the main center of Tikal at this time. Instead, we find a Tikal ruler (Lightning Sky) mentioned at Dos Pilas in contexts that connote conflict and suggest that the region of Petexbatun may have served as a refuge for the royal family of Tikal during disturbances in this capital city.

The middle of the katun 9.12.0.0.0—9.13.0.0.0 was marked by several events whose rapid succession suggests that they may have been related. The campaign carried on from Dos Pilas was apparently ended on 9.12.5.9.14. At Yaxchilan, Shield Jaguar celebrated a number of victories in 9.12.8.14.1. A little over a year later, on 9.12.9.17.16 5 Cib 14 Zotz', we read on Lintel 3 of Temple I at Tikal of the seating of a new ruler, who has been sometimes called Moon Comb, but is more often referred to as Ruler A. On Stela 16 his name is followed by a "sky-manikin" glyph and the Emblem Glyph of Petexbatun. Since the previous king of Tikal apparently was in residence there, it is not surprising that his successor here uses the emblem of his birthplace. The inscription ends with a record of 3(?) katuns and the *batab* glyph, used earlier with the name of Shield Jaguar. If such *batab* katuns are *ahau* katuns counted from birth, 9.12.0.0.0 was the first *ahau* katun of his life, and he could have been the son of Lightning Sky, whose record appears on a hieroglyphic stairway at Dos Pilas. His first stela may have been Stela 30, dated by its associated Giant Ahau altar as 9.13.0.0.0 and placed within a Twin Pyramid complex. In the general arrangement of the figure it sets a pattern for many of the later stelae at Tikal. It shows the figure in side view, performing the "scattering gesture" suggestive of divination and holding in his left hand a triplicate bar. Its segments have the angular form typical of later times, but like earlier staffs it is composed of only two sections. In this composition it overweighs and obscures other parts of the design. Later, the sections of such bars were reduced, and their design was brought into better proportion with that of the figure. Among the early features retained on this monument are the high wristlets and anklets trimmed with a mat motif and the ends of the apron, which are sharply bent forward to fill the space that in later compositions is filled with an inscription. Such long, sharply bent hangings are also typical among the first Late Classic compositions at Yaxchilan and are frequently shown on certain other compositions transitional to the Late Classic.

On the later Stela 16 (9.14.0.0.0), the ruler wears on his headdress a skull mask, backed by a star symbol, and his kilt is embroidered with symbols of death, possibly indicating mourning. Among forms that link his costume with those of the Usumacinta region are the feather puffs of his headdress, the "death-eye" border of his skirt, and the goggle-eyed mask on the bag that hangs from his right wrist. The death symbols are consistent with the composition presented on the accompanying Altar 5. The altar presents an unusual and enigmatic scene. It pictures two men similarly dressed but with hats of different design, both wearing long streamers with dark spots that suggest bloodletting sacrifice. One holds a sacrificial knife, the other a trident eccentric flint. Between them is a pile of bones and a skull. To me, the skull looks like that of a large animal, but others insist it is a human skull. The motif of this altar is comparable to the motif of Lintel 2 of Temple III, where we see again two men in very similar dress, even to the knots in front of their mouths, in this case each holding an eccentric flint and a staff. Between them, a person dressed from head to foot in a jaguar skin also holds a staff and an eccentric flint. This figure has an enormously extended belly, and it should be recalled that on Altar 5, the glyph following the first date recorded, 1 Muluc 2 Muan (9.12.19.12.9 ?), depicts the lower part of a figure with a comparably round belly. There are three other dates on this altar: 13 Manik 0 Xul (9.13.11.6.7), followed by a phrase beginning with a skull glyph; 11 Cimi 19 Mac (9.13.19.16.6); and 1 Muluc 2 Kankin (9.13.19.16.9). The last date is the nearest 1 Muluc to a katun anniversary of the first, being 1.0.4.0 from the beginning of this inscription. I do not attempt to suggest meanings for the intervening dates, but I believe that the altar may have served as a memorial to the wife of the king, who died prematurely in childbirth. Under the depiction of the memorial rite on the altar is a short inscription beginning with a skull glyph and the *kin*-on-pedestal title before a female head, which seems to designate a queen, and two other glyphs, the last a compound of a jaguar head. The text of Temple III is illegible, but the fragmentary Stela 24 in front of it suggests a

Ruler A (Moon Comb)
(TIK T I, L 3, D4)

"sky-manikin" glyph
(TIK St 16, B4)

Petexbatun Emblem Glyph
(TIK St 16, C1)

3(?) katuns
(TIK St 16, C3)

batab
(TIK St 16, C4)

Maya History

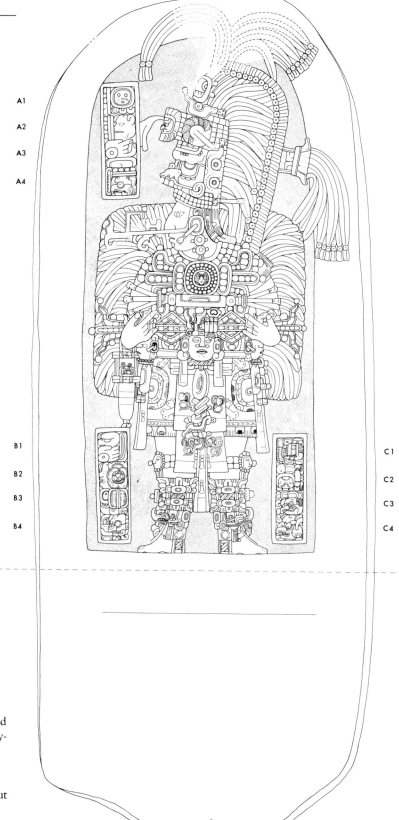

A1

A2

A3

A4

B1

B2

B3

B4

C1

C2

C3

C4

Tikal Stela 16, front: Ruler A dressed in a costume of mourning. (© Copyright by University Museum, University of Pennsylvania, 33rd and Spruce Streets, Philadelphia, PA 19104. Not to be reproduced without permission.)

much later date. Perhaps, however, it is Temple II, on which a woman is depicted, and which stands opposite the funerary temple of the king, that is the temple dedicated to the memory of the woman whose death is recorded on Altar 5. Unfortunately we have no inscription from this temple.

Our best information about Moon Comb comes from Lintel 3 of Temple I, beneath which lies his tomb. On this lintel he is pictured in the underworld, seated on a hassock, with an enormous jaguar extending a protective paw above him. On Lintel 2, the king has risen to his final abode in the sky. The text on Lintel 3 is fairly well preserved, but its meaning is not entirely clear. It is contained in two panels—a square panel pertaining to the king and a narrow, vertical panel referring to two women, probably his wife and daughter—and ends with the date of the king's accession: 5 Cib 14 Zotz' (9.12.9.17.16). Since there is no Initial Series, the Long Count position of the dates is mainly conjecture. The first date in the square panel, 9 Ahau 13 Pop, is probably 9.13.3.0.0; the second, 11 Etz'nab 11 Ch'en, 9.13.3.7.18, and the last, 9.13.3.9.18 12 Etz'nab 11 Zac, as translated by Christopher Jones and Linton Satterthwaite (1982). In Chapter 3, it was noted that the date 9.0.3.9.18, of which the 12 Etz'nab date is the thirteenth katun anniversary, was probably the date when the army of an earlier foreign king, Curlsnout, surrendered to Stormy Sky of Tikal, restoring an ancient dynasty. The anniversary, too, celebrates a new dynasty under Ruler A, Moon Comb, whose mother was a native of Petexbatun. Since these dates fall between Katuns 8 and 6 Ahau, mentioned as fateful katuns in colonial manuscripts, it was suggested to me by Munro Edmonson that the tradition may have originated in Classic times. The first Katun 8 Ahau date in Maya history was 9.0.0.0.0, and the first 6 Ahau was 9.1.0.0.0. The next Katun 8 Ahau was 9.13.0.0.0, followed by 6 Ahau, 9.14.0.0.0. The distance between the two pairs, 13 katuns, was called "the *may*." The final *may* would end on 10.7.0.0.0, beyond the period of known dated stelae.

Coggins (1975) suggests that it was Ruler A who buried Stela 31 under a temple which he built. The mention of an anniversary of the date on that stela in Temple I supports this conclusion. The question remains, however, who mutilated the monument and probably others before the reinstatement of legitimate rule.

The statement after the first Etz'nab date (9.13.3.7.18) contains a shield glyph and a jaguar glyph. The second statement contains a fish-in-hand glyph (indicating descendants?) and a sacrifice glyph followed by the name of the king. In the last two dates we find an abbreviated reference to the name of the next king.

The vertical panel on the right begins with a "1 shell" glyph (first offspring?) referring to the king's wife and her daughter. After that we come to an *ahaulil* (?) glyph with the daughter's name and a passage that may refer to the death of the queen. It is this passage that ends with the date of the king's accession.

round belly
(TIK Alt 5, 3)

skull glyph
(TIK Alt 5, 12)

kin on pedestal + female head
(TIK Alt 5, B)

This ruler is also pictured on the lintel from a palace, Structure 10, which faces the reservoir behind the Central Acropolis. The composition of this figure is consistent with its location, for in front of the ruler is shown a dwarf (?) holding in his hands aquatic plants, and beside him are two cormorants. The inscription is effaced, except for the remains of a date that is clearly 3 Ahau 3 Mol (9.15.10.0.0).

The collection of inscribed bones found above the tomb of Ruler A may prove to be an interesting source of information about his reign, but here I will mention only a few that appear to me to be of particular interest. Miscellaneous Text 28 is essentially a record of deaths, though, unlike those recorded on the Palenque sarcophagus, only deaths that occurred during the reign of the king appear to be recorded. There are six deaths, probably all falling between 9.14.9.0.0 and 9.14.15.6.13. Not all these references, however, are immediately followed by names, and it is not clear how many individuals are mentioned. One of these dates, 9.14.15.1.19, is also mentioned on Dos Pilas Stela 8, where it is said to be the death of a lord of Tikal, who was apparently ruling as a "vulture" (military governor?) at Dos Pilas. The last date mentioned appears to be that of a woman. Two other deaths are recorded on Miscellaneous Text 29, but the dates here are less certain.

A study of the entire collection will doubtless appear in the series of Tikal Reports now in preparation by the research team of the University of Pennsylvania, and it will not be attempted here. There are, however, six carved bones that I wish to mention, for speculations on their motifs have already been published by several scholars, speculations with which I cannot concur and for which I offer here what seems to me to be a better alternative. There are four bones which present an almost identical scene: a canoe manned by one or two paddlers, a central figure of a person of indeterminate sex, and four animals: an iguana, a monkey, a parrot, and a raccoon. A single date, 6 Akbal 16 Zac, appearing with this scene may be 9.11.19.4.3 or 9.14.11.17.3. Scholars confronted with an unnatural scene of this sort are very apt to interpret it in terms of mythical beliefs, and it has been suggested that the scene on these bones represents the journey of the deceased into the underworld. No notice apparently is taken of the fact that the scene is repeated four times and the coincidence (?) that there are four animals in the canoe. Nor is it taken into account that among the Maya the rate of literacy was probably not very high and that symbols incorporated in pictures must have been often substituted for the written word. Since we often find the Maya, especially when they are pictured as warriors, wearing animal heads on their headdresses, presumably identifying the groups to which they belong, I would suggest that the animals in the canoe represent such groups, and that in essence these bones functioned either as contracts with riverine groups to provide transport for envoys of the king, or documents given to his agents empowering them to conscript craft to his service. These documents were made in pairs, so it is possible that they represent only two such agreements, a duplicate of each retained by the king. This seems to be the case with the other set of bones, which includes only one pair.

This pair apparently has to do with a contract to provide the king with fish from the rivers or the sea. In this case, the pictures and the texts on the two bones are identical. Here the persons fishing from a canoe have human bodies but grotesque faces, not persons, but fishermen in general. The inscription is fairly clear, though its exact reading is uncertain. The first glyph is a canoe, the second a mask, seemingly referring to the occupants of the canoe. Next we have an *imix* glyph and a head of unknown meaning followed by "the king of Tikal (?)." However inaccurate the reading may be, the passage clearly identifies the occupants of the canoe as servants of the king and gives them special protection. Since there are no streams or rivers in the immediate vicinity of Tikal, it is natural that the king should make arrangements with riverine groups to provide fare for his table. That such documents appear to come in pairs suggests that they are something in the nature of contracts, the king perhaps retaining one, which may be matched with the other in case of any dispute or attempted fraud.

I have deleted some pages I had written on other pieces of this remarkable collection of inscriptions and pictures on bone, since a serious study of them would require more time than I can give them here, and a cursory examination has not produced any original insights into their character. My general impression has been that they constitute archives and personal mementos of the king, and were not made specifically as offerings for the funeral.

The monuments of Uaxactun and Xultun that may have been erected during this period are so eroded and defaced that neither the sculpture nor the texts offer any additional historical information. The first stela erected at Uaxactun in this period, Stela 1, is tentatively dated by Morley 9.14.0.0.0, so Uaxactun may have been even more retarded than Tikal in resuming erection of monuments.

Naranjo, on the other hand, after having been under a military governorship originating in Tikal, apparently became the *cabecera* of an independent province, ruled by a son of a royal princess of Tikal. Her portrait was erected in three different locations at Naranjo, together with that of her son. Stelae 22 and 24, both apparently set up in 9.13.10.0.0, face each other across a broad plaza. The inscription on Stela 24 begins with the date 9.12.10.5.12 4 Eb 10 Yax, a date thought by some to establish the uniform lunar calendar, although the statement of this event has not been interpreted. It begins with a hand glyph with the lunar postfix T181, resembling Glyph D of the Lunar Series. Although this glyph follows all instances of this date (Stelae 3, 24, 29, and possibly 18), the glyphs that follow it differ,

canoe
(TIK MT 51B, A)

mask
(TIK MT 51B, B)

king of Tikal(?)
(TIK MT 51B, F)

hand + lunar postfix
(NAR St 24, C7)

Lady Uac
(NAR St 24, A6)

Sky
(NAR St 24, A7)

of Tikal
(NAR St 24, A8)

Smoking Squirrel
(NAR St 23, H19)

36 or 38
(NAR St 24, B15)

though all clauses refer to the "Lady Uac (Six) Sky of Tikal." The *kin*-on-pedestal glyph prefixed to her name on the front of Stela 24 suggests that she was a royal personage, perhaps a sister of the king of Tikal. She is shown holding in her arms a vessel filled with ritual objects, recalling the depiction of blood sacrifices and the invocation of ancestors on the lintels of Yaxchilan. The date is 9.13.7.3.8 9 Lamat 1 Zotz', when her son was eleven years old. The date of his birth, 9.12.15.13.7 9 Manik 0 Kayab, is recorded on the east (left) side of the monument. The lady wears around her neck a penitential collar and stands on a captive on whose body is written "West *caban*," perhaps implying that she commanded the allegiance of western lands. In her headdress is the so-called Mexican Year Sign that was worn by warriors of Piedras Negras in 9.11.15.0.0 and first appears at Copan in 9.12.10.0.0.

The text on the sides of Stela 24 contains a number of puzzling statements and unknown glyphs. Immediately after the record of the birth of the future king, who is sometimes called Smoking Squirrel because of the animal sign in his name, there is a glyph with a coefficient of 16 or 18 over the sign of 20, which resembles a lunar sign. Conceivably this could refer to his mother's age, which would then be 36 or 38 years, but this is little more than a guess. Nor do we know the meaning of the next clause preceded by a *hel* glyph that often seems to introduce a new subject or action. The next date is that which is given on the front, with the queen's portrait, but the statement after it is not clear. There follow two statements each introduced by a "jog" glyph and each referring to the queen, whose identity sign seems to be the number 6, *uac*. The first statement begins with a "propellor" glyph and is of unknown meaning. The second begins with a "1 shell" glyph that may signify "first son" or "offspring," and contains also a heart-sacrifice glyph and the sign for West. A third statement begins with the *u ahaulil* glyph, which some scholars call a "father indicator" but which I read as "in the reign of." It concerns a king designated as Ah Chuen, a name followed by a head glyph with the axe-comb expression, which seems to be associated with victory in war (see Kelley 1976 : 135) and refers here to Tikal. A Secondary Series then brings the count to the current lahuntun date 9.13.10.0.0 and concludes with the name of the queen, Ix Uac, and the modified common ending glyph "jog"-comb-*imix*.

Stela 22 seems to portray the naming of the queen's son as the heir to the throne. The composition is somewhat similar to that of Stela 33 of Piedras Negras, erected in 9.10.10.0.0. The woman on Stela 24 may correspond to the woman shown on the Piedras Negras stela. Stela 22 has the same dedication date as Stela 24: 9.13.10.0.0 7 Ahau 3 Cumku, and the woman, very probably the mother of the future king, may have served as the regent when the fourteen-year-old king was still too young to rule. He is shown on Stela 22 seated on a cushion placed on a huge mask with a damaged glyph on its forehead. Its prefix (TVI.602), clearly visible, recalls the number 6 in the name of the woman. On the nose of the mask is seated an emaciated figure of an old man, holding something up in one hand. What his relation is to the boy is not apparent. In his arms, the boy holds a serpent-bar, symbol of noble descent. It may be significant that the serpent head on his left contains the mask of the sun, while that on his right holds only a simple human head. If Coggins (1975: 548–551) is right in associating the right hand with the East and with male progenitors, and the left with women and the West, what may be implied here is that the boy's royal and divine descent is in the female line only.

The text on the sides of Stela 22 deals with events that took place during the childhood of the future king. Whenever his name is mentioned, the Naranjo Emblem Glyph that follows is written not with the usual prefix, but with a sign that has some features in common with God C (T41), though the mouth of the face is covered. One may suspect that this variation in the Emblem may indicate the heir apparent, since it is not used in later references to the king, but I have not been able to substantiate this elsewhere. The Initial Series of Stela 22 records the birth of the future king: 9.12.15.13.7 9 Manik 0 Kayab. The next date, 9.13.1.3.19 5 Cauac 2 Xul, must have been of some importance, for it is probably recorded also on Stela 21, and its katun anniversary, 3 Cauac 2 Pop, is cited also on Stelae 2, 3, and 30. The original date is distinguished only by a Muluc compound and the boy's name. He was then five years old. The next date, 12 Cauac 2 Yaxkin, is only one month later, and the text here makes reference to the "West *caban* (land?)" that was inscribed on the captive of Stela 24. The next two dates, 7 Chicchan 8 Zac 9.13.1.9.5 and 5 Ix 12 Muan 9.13.1.13.14, seem to refer to a person designated by a human head with a *kin* sign on the brow and a hook-scroll on the chin. One might suspect that the *kin* sign may indicate that he (or she) is a priest, but his (or her) function in this context is obscure. It may be that of a teacher of the boy, or that of a priest officiating at mourning ceremonies for his father. The date 5 Oc (8) Cumku 9.13.2.16.10 is most puzzling of all. It is followed immediately by the same compound of the hook-scroll that stood after 12 Cauac 2 Yaxkin, and then by the main sign of the Tikal Emblem Glyph with the prefix T12 (Ah?). Next comes a capture glyph and immediately after it what seems to be a birth glyph and a name. Both the capture and the birth seem to be verbal forms with the half-lunar postfix, but the significance of the juxtaposition of the two verbal expressions escapes me. The lunar postfix, T181, is read by Yurii Knorosov as -*ah*, by Eric Thompson as -*kal*, and by Thomas S. Barthel as the gerundive -*ic*. I have no opinion on this matter.

The head with the *kin* sign and hook-scroll occurs also on the west side of the hieroglyphic stairway of Dos Pilas, at A3b. Several other glyphs that occur at Naranjo in this period also occur on this stairway, linking the young king of Naranjo with the Tikal occupation of this region. This suggests that his mother may have been the

hel
(NAR St 24, C15)

Ah Chuen
(NAR St 24, D12)

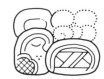

axe + comb
(NAR St 24, E12)

Naranjo Emblem Glyph
(NAR St 22, E8)

head with *kin* + hook-scroll
(NAR St 22, F18)

Ah + Tikal Emblem
(NAR St 22, G2)

name glyphs of future king
(NAR St 21, A6—8)

daughter of Lightning Sky and the sister or cousin of Ruler A of Tikal. The problem of his paternity is more difficult. His father may have been the governor or viceroy pictured on Stelae 4 and 5, whose name we do not know. The Emblem of Tikal occurs on Stela 4, but not at the end of the inscription, and it may refer to the woman he married, a woman who is pictured on Stela 3 and possibly is the same Lady of Tikal as on Stela 24.

On either side of Stela 22 stood Stelae 21 and 23. Stela 21 shows the king as a warrior at the age of eighteen. He holds a shield and a spear, wears a feathered strip as armor, and stands on a captive. There is a trace of a glyph with the number 9 on the thigh of the captive. The date is 9.13.14.4.2 8 Ik o Zip. It is followed by the "jog" and two unknown glyphs. The name of the future king is here introduced by three glyphs, the first of which is an S-scroll in a dotted cartouche, which seems to occur also with his name on Stela 23. The inscription on the back of this monument is virtually illegible, but it clearly ends with 13 Ahau 18 Pax, the end of 15 tuns (9.13.15.0.0). One may recall that on the very early Stela 31 at Tikal the dotted cartouche and two other glyphs stand before the name Great Paw, who was apparently an ancestor of the king. It is also interesting to note that the aberrant prefix of the Emblem Glyph that stood with the name of the king on Stela 22 is here separated from the Emblem, and at the end of the inscription is omitted entirely. Apparently, the boy had achieved his majority. Whether he was already reigning remains a question; we have no clear statement of his accession.

The inscription on Stela 23, though its meaning is by no means clear, nevertheless contains some suggestive clauses. Berlin (1968) interprets the glyphs at F13—F16 as a record of the marriage of the king to a Tikal princess on 9.13.18.4.18, at the age of twenty-two. This, however, introduces a needless complication by implying a second woman from Tikal, whose portrait, moreover, does not appear in the group; nor does this statement follow the date immediately, and the glyph itself, T126.552:23(?), does not resemble in its general composition the usual form of event glyphs. The first clause is introduced by the face glyph with infixed *kin* mentioned several times on Stela 22. The second clause probably begins at F11 or F12. The latter is a compound of T575, with a bird head emerging from the top, a glyph that is found in the text of Hieroglyphic Stairway 2 at Dos Pilas, together with the face glyph mentioned above. If we read Berlin's marriage glyph as "husband" (according to Knorosov), we might surmise that he was from the region of Petexbatun, and that the Tikal lady was a daughter of Lightning Sky mentioned there. The text on Stela 23 can then be construed as describing the ceding of the rulership of Naranjo from the Lady of Tikal to her son. In the *u caban* clause that follows, the new king is not yet named as the Lord of Naranjo. His name is followed by an Emblem Glyph with a face prefix, and then by a vulture glyph, implying a military title, but less than five months later, we find a bone glyph, a skull glyph, and a divination glyph (scattering gesture) and, in the next clause, the normal Naranjo Emblem Glyph follows his name. By 9.14.0.0.0, the "Squirrel King" had attained his royal title without qualification.

Another possibility is that Stela 20 represents the father of the king. David Kelley (1976: 240) has suggested that it is the accession monument of the king himself, reading the double *cauac* glyph of his name as a homonym for *cuc,* which also means "squirrel," but I am skeptical of this rendering, even disregarding the fact that this glyph is suspiciously like the *yax*-double *cauac* glyph at Tikal. The "accession" is marked by the "toothache glyph" but lacks the affix cluster that should follow it. The date is not altogether clear. It could be 6 or 7 Cib, 14 Ch'en or Yax. This gives us four possibilities, but assuming that the date falls somewhere between 9.12.0.0.0 and 9.14.0.0.0, we narrow the choice to three dates: 6 Cib 14 Ch'en (9.12.2.2.16), 7 Cib 14 Yax (9.13.2.8.16), and 6 Cib 14 Yax (9.13.14.11.16). Seven seems to be the better reading of the day number, and this date (9.13.2.8.16) is nearest to the date, 9.13.3.0.0, that is celebrated here and at Tikal is marked with the double *cauac* glyph. I must admit that this argument is far from convincing. Unfortunately, the text on the back is completely eroded and the date is nowhere repeated. It is with considerable hesitation that I suggest that the double *cauac* glyph may signify a close alliance between the provinces of Tikal and Naranjo, perhaps even merging them into a single nation. This entire group of inscriptions, however, deserves more intensive study than I have been able to afford it here. The relationships among the governments of Tikal, Naranjo, and Petexbatun are still obscure, and the degree and manner of political integration of the Classic Maya area remains a pressing question.

By 9.14.10.0.0, four more stelae were erected on the platform of a large temple facing the court. From left to right, the stelae are numbered 28 to 31. The second and the fourth stelae are figures of women. How they are paired with the men is problematical, but the inscriptions of the central pair appear to end with the date 9.14.3.0.0 and those of the outer pair with 9.14.10.0.0. The odd date 9.14.3.0.0 is a katun anniversary of 9.13.3.0.0, the first date recorded on Lintel 3 of Temple I at Tikal. The latter date is followed by "*yax* double *cauac*" both at Tikal and on Stela 29. It was doubtless a date of great importance, but its meaning is still uncertain.

The woman of the inner couple pictured on Stela 29 is the same Lady Uac of Tikal as on Stela 24, for her name is mentioned more than once and ends the inscription. She stands in the same pose, holding a bowl for sacrifice, and the differences in her attire are minor, but the portrait was apparently made by another artist, and she appears both taller and slimmer than on Stela 24. The inscription on the front is mostly destroyed, but on the panel at the right we can discern the sacrifice glyph and a record of 1 katun, and lower, a

marital relationship
(NAR St 23, F13)

Naranjo Emblem Glyph
(NAR St 23, H20)

double *cauac*
(NAR St 20, B1)

accession ("toothache")
(NAR St 20, A4)

masculine name, apparently not that of her son; the Tikal Emblem; a glyph for West; and a _cauac_(?)-_muluc_ compound. The name is somewhat damaged, but it may be that of her husband.

The inscription on the back, like that on Stela 24, begins with the date 9.12.10.5.12, which also appears at Coba on Stela 1. The birth of her son is also mentioned, and a third date, three days after the first, is also recorded here. As we shall see, this date is only one day earlier than a date recorded at Caracol.

As the figures are facing, that of her son on Stela 30 stands behind her, holding a simple staff and an eccentric flint. One is reminded of the figures on Altar 5 and those on Lintel 2 of Temple III at Tikal. The date on the front is 9.14.3.0.0 and the text ends with his name, title, the Emblem of Naranjo, and two additional glyphs of unknown meaning—a face glyph with the number 6 and a bat glyph.

The two outer figures face each other, the man on the woman's right, the woman on his left. Neither figure has the captive base. The panel on which the man stands is broken, but seems to have been composed at least partly of glyphs, the last of which seems to be the main sign of the Tikal Emblem, without prefixes. The inscription on this monument looks deceptively legible, but is actually so pitted and scratched that Morley was unable to read a single date. Since the man is facing to his left, he holds the manikin scepter in his left hand, and in his right what appears to be a small shield seen from the edge. It has been suggested by Joyce Marcus (1976) that the woman who faces him from the other end of the line is not the Tikal lady, but his wife, which is quite possible. Unfortunately we have no good record of the inscription, which might mention her name or her relationship to the ruler. There appears to be a hieroglyph on the back composed with a woman's head and the number 8, but whether this is a reference to the Lady of Tikal or not, it is difficult to make out.

At some time, Stelae 1, 2, and 3 were erected in front of Stela 4, which pictures a man from Tikal, who may have been the father or the husband of the Tikal lady, mother of the Naranjo king. The incised texts on these monuments are partly effaced and are very difficult to read. To Stelae 2 and 3, Morley (1937–1938:2:92–96) assigns the date 9.14.1.3.19 3 Cauac 2 Pop, and I am inclined to accept this reading, though I have not been able to confirm it with confidence. The central figure is the son, who apparently was still reigning at this time, but I suspect that this group may commemorate the death of his mother, though there is no clear statement of this. The son is shown with a rectangular shield and a double-shafted dart in his left hand, and a bag in his right. He stands on a death mask with an inverted _ik_ sign on its forehead. The text on the front of Stela 2 begins with a "jog" glyph, which is followed by _ti_ and a face with what appears to be a weeping eye, suggesting perhaps mourning for his parents, who may be depicted on the other two monuments of the group. The text on the sides is too eroded to reveal more than the mere dates, and even these remain in question. Stela 3 apparently depicts the mother. Although her name is not clear on the front, the text on the sides begins with the date 9.12.10.5.12 4 Eb 10 Yax, which on other monuments is the first date associated with her name. On the right side there is a date 3 (?), (glyph 4?) 2 (Pop?), which may be the 9.14.1.3.19 date. Lady of Tikal appears in the next passage, and at the end, we read 7 Pax, and the Secondary Series 7(?).9.3.15, which leads back to 9.6.12.0.4, the second of the series of Kan dates inscribed on Stela 25, falling in a katun which is mentioned on Stela 38. The last phrase reads "(?) U Katun Ah Double Comb Naranjo Emblem," repeating the name from Stela 38.

Why, at the end of her life, is the Lady of Tikal's name connected with a ruler of Naranjo who lived 150 years (six generations?) earlier? Was the ruler of Tikal Moon Comb also related to this ancient man of Naranjo? What is the meaning of those empty katuns recorded on Stela 25, reaching through those early years when the birth of a king of Caracol is recorded on a lintel, later discarded and reused? We are still far from being able to answer such questions. The intricacies of dynastic changes and successions may no longer be capable of solution. Too much of the record is erased forever, and we are too careless with the remains of the past to save even what little is left. But an occasional glimpse into the changing relationships between sites and provinces brings some life into the static picture we are apt to make of antiquity, and raises the hope that progress in decipherment of the texts will someday make possible a more vivid history of events.

Stela 1 is the worst preserved of the trio. Morley dated this monument 9.13.10.0.0, but Ian Graham's (1978:11) recent drawings do not bear out his reading of other dates on this monument. Like the text on Stela 3, this text steps back far into the past. Here, however, the Emblem Glyph is that of Naranjo, and the text seems to refer to the king of Naranjo.

The last stela erected in this reign is apparently Stela 18, which is set apart from all others in the ancient "astronomical" court. Its sculpture is, unfortunately, entirely gone, and the last three glyphs of the carved inscription on the sides refer not to the king of Naranjo, but to a king of Tikal, and possibly also to the Lady of Tikal. There is, in addition to the carved text on the sides, an incised inscription on the back, which unfortunately is badly eroded, and Morley attempted no reading of it. From Graham's drawing (I. Graham and von Euw 1975: 2:47) it is possible to restore the dates, though not enough of the text to suggest its meaning. It is possible that the first date on the back was once written as an Initial Series, but now it seems that at F2 there is a Secondary Series of 5.12, which leads from a now-eroded 9 Ahau 18 Zotz' (9.12.10.0.0) to (9.12.10.5.12 4 Eb) 10 (Yax). This is the first date associated with the Lady of Tikal on her monuments. Subsequent dates can be reconstructed as follows:

ti + weeping face
(NAR St 2, A2)

$$+ \quad 2. \quad 3.10.12$$

9.14. 13.16. 4	5 Kan 7 Yax
+ 8.18	
9.14. 14. 7. 2	1 Ik 0 Pop
+ 3.12	
9.14. 14.10.14	8 Ik 12 Zotz'
+ 7. 6	
9.14. 15. 0. 0	11 Ahau 18 Zec

The substance of the text does not emerge from this pattern of dates, but since this is the last stela erected in the main group of Naranjo until 9.17.0.0.0, we may assume that it deals with the death of the Lady of Tikal and subsequent funeral rites.

After Naranjo had become an independent city, there is little evidence of activity at Caracol. The only known sculptured stela of this period is Stela 21, probably erected in 9.13.10.0.0. There is a Secondary Series, ?.19.12.4, but the rest of the inscription is destroyed. If there was no katun number, and if the count goes back to an earlier date, this date would be 9.12.8.5.16 8 Cib 14 Yax, a date only one day later than the second date mentioned on Stela 29 at Naranjo. What role Caracol played in the marriage arrangements at Naranjo, it is difficult to say. Conceivably, it could have been the king of Caracol, and not a governor of Naranjo, who married the Tikal lady, or is it merely the allegiance of Caracol to the royalty of Naranjo that is recorded here? There are neither names nor Emblem Glyphs to guide us. The most that we can do at present is to note the close relationships between these three sites in this period, and to suggest that their further study, as well as the study of intersite relationships elsewhere, may prove to be of value.

Long before 9.12.10.0.0, Calakmul was erecting more stelae than any known site in central Peten. Its strategic position between the drainage of the Candelaria, leading to the Laguna de Términos, and the drainage of the Río Hondo flowing into the bay of Chetumal assured its access to important trade routes and may have been one of the reasons why Tikal turned its attention southward to the riverine system at the source of the Usumacinta. The restoration of Tikal to its former position of leadership and its alliance with Naranjo and with cities on the Pasión River did not seem to affect the prosperity of Calakmul. At least twenty-five stelae were erected there between 9.12.10.0.0 and 9.15.0.0.0. Our records of these monuments, however, are very poor. The survey made by Ruppert and Dennison in the 1930s was primarily concerned with mapping the site and its general description, and the description of the monuments in their report is mainly based on Morley's notes made on an earlier visit. Most of the standing monuments were badly weathered, and those lying on the ground were not turned. Since that time, the site has been gutted by looters, and probably some of the unrecorded stelae are now in museums or in private collections.

The stelae of Calakmul were usually set up in groups of four or five, though sometimes there is an additional pair in another location. Monuments in a given group all seem to have the same dedication date, with the possible exception of Stelae 75–79, which may have recorded consecutive hotuns between 9.12.0.0.0 and 9.13.0.0.0. These stelae are described as being carved on all four sides, with figures on the broad sides. Although all but one of them are standing, there are no adequate descriptions of the figures and only partial records of the badly eroded texts. On the left side of Stela 75 there is a record of a birth, but neither the name nor the date is clearly legible. These stelae are ranged in a row in front of Structure XV, facing the great west palace complex. Two stelae dated 9.12.10.0.0 are near the lesser east palace complex in front of the small Structure IX. Both stelae (93 and 94) are fallen. They, too, are described as being carved on all four sides, but there are no published photographs of the sculptured figures.

The second group of five monuments stands in front of a large temple, Structure II, facing the early "astronomical" group that lies between the two palace complexes. This group is arranged in two rows, Stelae 38, 39, and 40 standing in front of Stelae 41 and 42. All these monuments, as well as Stelae 23 and 24, on top of Structure VI of the "astronomical" group, were assigned by Morley to 9.13.10.0.0. Stelae 23, 24, and 38 are said to be carved on the front and sides only—all others on four sides.

Another group of five stelae (70–74) is associated with the date 9.14.0.0.0 and stands in front of a court of the great west palace complex (Structure XV). These stelae are ranged in a row, and all seem to have been carved on four sides, though on some the carving is now all but completely gone. The inscriptions on the two outer monuments of the row begin with an Initial Series 9.12.?.?.?, but that on Stela 70 is better preserved and reads 9.12.8.9.9—not a period ending—and the final dates are unknown. If there was a pair of stelae outside this group at the time, it has not been identified.

For the date 9.14.10.0.0. we have only Stelae 45 and 46 in front of a small platform facing the first terrace of Structure II, and Stela 8, in the "astronomical" group. Ruppert and Dennison (1943) do not illustrate the carving on Stela 8, but a sketch by Eric von Euw shows it to be of peculiar interest. Most stelae that, like Stela 8, are carved on both sides, present on the back a figure of a woman, but in this case both figures are men. The monument is broken and badly damaged. The figure on the front is a stocky individual holding a spear in the right hand and in his left hand a round shield with the figure of a bird below it. It is the figure on the back, however, that invites attention. The head of this person is enclosed in the mouth of a mask drawn with parallel lines, which is somewhat reminiscent of the huge monster masks worn by early warriors at Piedras Negras. More significant is the fact that this warrior carries a rectangular shield trimmed with feathers. This type of shield appears first at Lacanha on a stela dated 9.8.0.0.0. It is characteristic of martial motifs at Piedras Negras, but is extremely rare in central Peten, though it appears sporadically in peripheral sites, for example at Naranjo (Stela 2), at Aguateca (Stela 2), at Dos Pilas (Stela 16), and at Cancuen (Stela 2). It is not an isolated trait, but carries with it a number of characteristic elements of costume. The apron that covers the end of the loincloth, for example, never has, on these monuments, the serpent frets so common in the Peten; instead, it is usually rounded at the end. Just below the knee are broad garters with several hangings. The breast pendants are simple in design and hang by a simple band from the neck. Somewhere in the design usually occurs a goggle-eyed mask. On Stela 2 at Naranjo and on Stela 2 at Cancuen, the rectangular shield is associated with short darts, rather than with the usual long spear of the Maya. The implications of this apparent distribution of an entire complex of traits is not clear at present, but they may be clarified when we know more about sites in the surrounding areas.

The monuments carved in 9.15.0.0.0 at Calakmul are much better preserved than earlier stelae, and the group contains some of the most beautifully carved figures in the Maya area. This group (Stelae 51–55) stands in front of a large pyramid, Structure I, south of the east palace complex. Stela 48, lying at a lower level in front, and Stela 89, on top of the pyramid, also probably belong to this group. All these monuments seem to have been carved only on the front and sides, though all but one had fallen and the backs of some of them were not examined. The central figure, Stela 53, is that of a warrior equipped with spear and shield, carved in the typical ornate manner of the period, but with local peculiarities of costume. The device on the shield is not the usual jaguar-sun but a plain *kan* cross. The headdress is a high turban of typical Calakmul design, with a projecting chin strap, somewhat like those anciently worn by the highland warriors pictured on Stela 31 at Tikal. The long cloak hanging behind the figure and fastened on the shoulders is also essentially a local trait, though it is seen occasionally on monuments of sites on the Usumacinta River, particularly at Piedras Negras. To the right and left of this monument are Stelae 52 and 54, which show a man and woman facing each other. Both hold manikin scepters across the chest, which in the case of the woman is rather unusual, as is the flower she holds in her right hand. The male figure holds a shield and wears the conventional apron trimmed with serpent frets. His tall headdress is, however, of local design. We have no record of the figure on Stela 55, but Stela 51, at the beginning of the row, seems to have been designed by a different artist and is one of the most beautiful monuments at the site. This figure faces outward and, like the central figure, holds a spear and wears a long cloak, though he holds no shield. The head is large in proportion to the body, which is sturdy and broad. Detail is elegantly presented, particularly the curls of hair that fall on his shoulders. In addition to the small glyphic panels on the front of the monument, there is an incised inscription in the background. The only recognizable glyphs, however, are two instances of a bat compound, like that associated with subsidiary figures on the stelae of Piedras Negras.

Stela 89, on the summit of the mound, may have been carved by the same artist. The proportions of the figure are very similar. The ruler portrayed holds a manikin scepter and the conventional jaguar-sun shield. His headdress, however, is unusually simple and resembles the kind of headdress one sometimes sees on seated figures painted on pottery: a tall white band of fabric projecting forward and doubled back at the peak. The dwarf figure on this stela wears an identical cap. In contrast, the pectorals worn by the main figure are heavy and elaborate. As on Stela 51, the inscription on the front is broken up into small panels, and there are traces of incised glyphs on the background. The inscription presents some problems. There is an Initial Series on the left side that reads 9.15.0.0.14 5 Ix 7 Zac. On the right side is a date 7 (Cib?) 10 Zac. Possibly 7 Caban is intended, which is the date inscribed on the front. It could be either 9.12.19.9.17 or 9.15.12.4.17.

Nowhere in this entire region do we find inscriptions well enough preserved to give us a hint of its history. The monuments of Naachtun, a site comparable in size and character to Calakmul, are in an even worse state of preservation. Naachtun is located roughly 40 kilometers to the south, near the higher ground that separates the northern region from central Peten. Like Calakmul, this site has the early "astronomical" arrangement of buildings and large complexes of "palace" type buildings, probably of later date.

Morley (1937–1938:3:342–363) assigns four stelae at this site to the period between 9.12.10.0.0 and 9.15.0.0.0: Stelae 21, 9, 4, and 5. Stela 21 is a full front figure of a woman in high relief, wearing an embroidered dress and a large turban. The huge earplugs and the low straps of the sandals suggest to me an earlier date, though the figure is too unusual to be judged by normal criteria. Stela 4 (9.14.0.0.0???) and Stela 9 (9.15.0.0.0?) are too eroded to be judged by style, but it is perhaps worth noting that the figure on Stela 5 holds a shield with a simple device, wears a very large pectoral, and stands on a prisoner, suggesting a style more like that of Calakmul than that of central Peten.

The only monuments from lesser sites that can be placed with any degree of confidence in this period are Stela 14 of La Muñeca, almost completely eroded, and Stelae 12 and 17 at Oxpemul. There was probably an "astronomical" group at Oxpemul also, though it is now obscured by later constructions. The two stelae, dated 9.15.0.0.0, show none of the elegant elaborations we see at Calakmul at this time, though they share with Calakmul the tendency to use simple devices on the shield of a warrior, to omit serpent frets on the wide aprons, and to have only one face ornament on the belt. In sculpturing technique and in their simplicity, these stelae are more like the stelae of northern Yucatan than those of the Peten. Stela 12 is probably the earliest example we have of the dancing pose, barely suggested by the gesture of the arms and a slight bending of the right knee. Stela 17 pictures a warrior, standing on a crouching captive. There are no fine details, and though the figures wear large headdresses with many plumes, the feathers are arranged in a parallel row, without any attempt at elaborate composition or suggested motion. To the north and east of Oxpemul are sites in the Río Bec style, interspersed with groups of southern affiliation, but most of the monuments in these groups appear to be of later date.

At Coba, in the far north, stelae were probably being erected throughout this period, but their lengthy inscriptions are virtually illegible. The motif on these stelae never varies. They all show figures holding the serpent-bar diagonally, and normally have kneeling captives at the sides. Some of the figures stand on captives, most often on two, crouching back to back. They all wear high, feathered headdresses, and some have jade-decorated skirts. These skirts vary in length, and some of the figures may represent women. The subject matter of the inscriptions is still unknown, nor are there any recognizable names or Emblem Glyphs. Some texts have more than one Initial Series, and there are Long Counts present that have not been explained. The very uniformity and conservatism of these monuments suggest that it is not the history of kings that is the focus of their texts, but that they deal with broader subjects, such as religion, ritual, and cosmology.

As soon as the son of the king had departed for Tikal, Dos Pilas began to erect stelae, using sometimes the Tikal Emblem, and sometimes the Petexbatun variant, which some scholars equate with the Emblem of Tikal. Emblems, however, may refer not to particular sites but to their ruling families, something that is suggested here by the variation in their affixes, which may distinguish matrilineal from patrilineal descent, and which deserve more attention than I have been able to give them here. Stelae 16 and 17 may have been the first stelae erected here after the king's departure. The inscriptions of most of the monuments here are badly damaged, but Stela 8, an all-glyphic monument, though broken and incomplete, gives us some information about two rulers of Dos Pilas at this time. The Initial Series on this monument appears to read 9.12.6.15.11, but the date that follows it, 13 Chuen, G4, 19 Kayab, in the Classic calendar should be 9.12.0.10.11 and is the date of birth of the first "vulture" (military governor?) of Dos Pilas, who would have taken office when he was either nineteen or twenty-five years old, for the date of his "seating" is given as 11 Ahau 18 Uo (9.13.6.2.0). A long passage ends with the designation Shield Manikin Petexbatun, which may be a title above that of a military commander, but below the title of royalty. A short phrase follows, beginning with a backward-count glyph,

Shield Manikin
(DPL St 8, G20)

Petexbatun
(DPL St 8, F21)

imix compound + flying creature
(DPL St 8, G22)

perhaps explaining what his former status was. This phrase contains the *imix* compound with the prefix of a flying snail-like creature, which appears repeatedly on the hieroglyphic stairway at Dos Pilas and is used also on headdresses at Machaquila. Unfortunately, after a Distance Number, 4.9.12 (which may lead to 9.13.10.11.12 5 Eb 10 Zac), the inscription breaks off. Near the end of the next column, however, is another Distance Number, 9.6.8, counted forward to 6 Ahau 13 Muan (9.14.0.0.0). In the brief clause that follows we see again the *imix* glyph with the flying creature above, this time immediately preceding the designation Shield Manikin, and the next Distance Number, 15.1.19, brings us to the date of his death on 11 Cauac 17 Mac (9.14.15.1.19), expressed by the "wing, scroll, *ahau, ik*" expression, and here his name is followed by the standard Emblem of Tikal. The next date, 3 Kan 1 Kankin, is evidently written in the early style of Yaxchilan—9.14.15.2.4(?). It is followed by an interesting clause, which I will not attempt to unravel, except to note that Shield Manikin's name is associated with 3 katuns (possibly giving his age?). Further is a date 9 (Men?) 13 Kayab (9.14.15.5.15), the accession date ("toothache glyph," *ti* vulture) of the next ruler, Cloud Lord, who is mentioned later at Aguateca as well as again at Dos Pilas. The rest of the inscription is missing.

Most of the other texts at Dos Pilas are too badly eroded to be easily read. On Stela 1, the beginning date, 13 Ahau 18 Pax, is probably 9.13.15.0.0. A Secondary Series, 1.9.18, leads back to 9.13.13.8.2 1 Ik 5 Yaxkin. This date is not mentioned on Stela 8. The notation of the event is not clear, but a shield glyph is included in the clause, and possibly the Emblem of Tikal. The portrait shows the lord carrying a scepter and shield. He wears a mask and a warrior's helmet, a flaring sun-god apron with projecting frets, and a very large pectoral ornament, features that are somewhat advanced for the suggested date of this monument. At the feet of the figure is a cormorant with a fish in its beak, and below an earth-band is a prone prisoner. The name of the lord portrayed may have been on the missing upper portion of the monument, but there is little doubt that he is the Shield Manikin lord shown on Stela 8.

At Altar de Sacrificios, there is an apparent break in the sequence of stelae between 9.11.10.0.0 and 9.14.0.0.0. Some eroded monuments may partially fill this gap, such as Stelae 3 and 16. Stela 17 is a Giant Ahau stone, for which J. A. Graham (1972) suggests the date 9.15.0.0.0, relying on the hypothesis that Giant Ahaus are always names of katuns. In view of the similarity of this monument to Stela 2 and the fact that lahuntuns as well as katuns were recorded, I am inclined to place these two monuments closer in time, e.g.; at 9.14.10.0.0 and 9.15.0.0.0, or 10.1.0.0.0 and 10.1.10.0.0. We are left, then, with only Stela 7, which Morley (1937–1938:2:335–337) dated 9.14.0.0.0, to represent this period. Again it seems to be a portrait of a woman holding a serpent-bar. The inscription, unfortunately, is illegible. It is barely possible that this is a portrait of the same woman

death
(DPL St 8, I10)

accession ("toothache")
(DPL St 8, H18b)

ti vulture
(DPL St 8, I18)

as that on Stela 1, though the interval of time, fifty years, seems rather excessive. It is strange, too, that all three Late Classic portraits at this site are in female dress.

Another Giant Ahau date occurs on a curious monument, Stela 13, at Machaquila, located far to the east of Petexbatun on a tributary of the Pasión (I. Graham 1967). The date 6 Ahau is probably 9.14.0.0.0, though if we allow for the possibility of lahuntuns, it could be 10.0.10.0.0. In the first instance it would be the first stela erected at Machaquila. Its curious shape, however, with a projection at the top, carved with a mask, is somewhat like the form of stelae at Cancuen, which are eighty years later. The fact that this monument stands in the same group with an all-glyphic Stela 11 recording the date 9.15.10.0.0 is a strong argument for the earlier placement of the Giant Ahau.

So far as we know, Piedras Negras was not directly affected by events on the upper Usumacinta. During almost the entire period, it was ruled by a single sovereign, who acceded when he was twenty-two years old and ruled for about forty-two years, almost as long as his predecessor. The dynastic sequence has been discussed elsewhere (Proskouriakoff 1960). In spite of his long rule, we know very little about him. Even his name is not clear on his monuments. Better records of the inscriptions may give us more information, but erosion has made identification of signs extremely difficult.

After the accession monument, the next to be erected was Altar 1, marking Katun 9.13.0.0.0, undoubtedly a date of great importance. Thompson's revision of Morley's reading of the dates on this altar (J. E. S. Thompson 1944b) can be provisionally accepted, though some of the dates may remain doubtful. The date 9.12.19.13.4 is the first hotun anniversary of 9.12.14.13.4, which is only three days after accession, and whose katun anniversary is recorded on Stela 8. The date 9.12.19.15.9 is possibly a hotun anniversary of 9.12.14.15.9, which may be recorded on Naranjo Stela 28, though this is less certain. Other dates on this altar deal with period endings and cover large stretches of time. It is possible that they deal with astrological computations, and it may be for this reason that the next stela erected, Stela 2, shows the ruler as a diviner, scattering grains. Normally, this gesture is reserved for ends of katuns and lahuntuns, but since there is no stela for 9.13.0.0.0, the representation may refer to this date. Another possibility is that it represents the augury on the birth of a son, for on the side of this monument is the portrait of a woman and on the top, a curious small figure shown propped up in some sort of container.

On the next monument, Stela 4, the ruler is shown in full regalia, wearing a sun-mask apron, a helmet such as was worn by warriors on Lintel 2, but with a great array of plumes and symbols attached, and with two captives kneeling at his feet. His portraits on the next two stelae, 1 and 3, are virtually destroyed, but the portraits of a woman on the back are excellently preserved with their inscriptions.

Both inscriptions begin with the day of her birth, 9.12.2.0.16 5 Cib 14 Yaxkin, naming her as Lady Katun. Two more glyphs complete her name, the last an *ich-ben* expression with a sign that resembles *akbal*. The glyphs that follow two dates about twelve years later may refer to her marriage or engagement to the king. On the next stela, Stela 3, she is shown sitting on a throne, apparently illustrating an event on the twenty-fifth anniversary of her husband's accession, when she was awarded an honor designated by a hand glyph with its thumb up, holding an *ahau* sign. She was then thirty-seven years old and may have become the head of her family, lineage, or matrilineal clan. About three years earlier, she had become the mother of a girl, who is shown sitting with her on the throne. An earlier event apparently refers to her marriage, and is marked by a moon compound preceding her name and a *manik*-hand compound followed by a glyph presumably designating her husband. This glyph is somewhat different from the two glyphs that follow the statement of the anniversary of his accession, but they have enough details in common to suggest that the reference is to the same individual. The freedom of composition of glyphic elements, noted by Eric Thompson (1962:99) makes it difficult sometimes to identify equivalent statements, and this is particularly true of names and titles, since these in themselves may vary.

Stela 5, which follows Stela 3, is an elaborate composition showing the ruler seated on a jaguar-throne, beneath a canopy in the form of a sky-serpent, with a masked bird above. Three small figures appear behind the throne: a figure of death, a figure of a monkey, and a figure of an old, toothless man with a sharp Roman nose. These figures are patently symbolic, although we do not yet know their significance. Possibly they refer to functions of the king, to kinship groups, or to heavenly bodies. The king holds a manikin-headed staff before a figure standing in front of him. The king at this time was over fifty years old, and getting on in life. Perhaps the composition indicates that he was naming a successor or relegating some of his duties to a younger man. The last is more likely, since, if the glyphs above the young man are his name, he did not succeed to the throne, though a generation later, we find a name very similar to his on an accession stela. It is unfortunate that the weathering of the sides of this monument has made the inscription illegible and that the motif on the back is completely eroded.

On Stelae 7 and 8, we again find the ruler shown in the guise of a conqueror. The relief now is high and rounded, the curve of the belt of the figure further accentuating the three-dimensional quality of the carving. Both monuments recapitulate the life of the ruler, citing his birth, his marriage, and his accession. Berlin (1968) first suggested that the four consecutive dates 9.12.14.10.14 through 9.12.14.10.17 inscribed on Stelae 1, 3, 7, and 8 probably refer to marriage festivities. The key hieroglyph in reference to this marriage he considered to be the crossed-bands compound, which he transcribed

Lady Katun
(PNG St 1, C3)

ahau
(PNG St 1, D1)

Lady + *ich-ben*
(PNG St 1, E1)

hand + *ahau*
(PNG St 3, E3a)

moon compound
(PNG St 3, D2b)

name of husband
(PNG St 3, C4)

crossed-bands compound
(PNG St 8, A4)

rodent + T110
(PNG St 8, A5)

woman's name
(PNG Sh Pl 1, C2)

as T47.552 : 23, though I think the prefix is T126. This hieroglyph occurs on the front of Stela 8 with the latest of the four dates and is preceded by two other statements, which occur with the first date on Stelae 1 and 3. Actually the first date associated with the events of this period is probably five days earlier. It is marked by a compound of *imix* with infixed *ahau* and the verbal affix 181, referring to the woman. With the first of the four consecutive days we have on Stela 1 a single glyph: a compound of the moon sign, T23 : 683b? : 130. On Stela 3, the statement is expanded by adding the name of the woman, a compound of the *manik*-hand glyph T86 (671)17? : 178 (as Thompson transcribes it), followed by two highly decorated bird heads, which evidently refer to the ruling lord. On Stela 8, following the record of the next day, more glyphs are added. The moon compound as before is followed by the woman's name. The glyph after the *manik* compound is damaged. Then comes the crossed-bands glyph (*icham?*), a rodent glyph, and a jaguar with an infix in place of the lower jaw. The rodent and the jaguar apparently constitute another designation of the ruling lord. The rodent has the suffix T110, which can also appear as an infix. It frequently stands with an alternative designation of a person, and occurs with the birth date of the ruler on Stela 8. On the south support of Altar 2, the rodent glyph recurs with the birthday of the next ruler, and a variant element in his name. At Yaxchilan, it follows three names on the early Lintel 18. At Tikal it appears in a compound following a unique glyph, which Coggins (1975) suggests may signify birth or pregnancy, and stands in front of what appears to be a woman's name. There is a possibility, therefore, that the rodent signifies relationship and might read "offspring," "son," or "heir." The alternative name may be a name given at birth, and distinct from the official name acquired with rulership, or it may refer not to the subject but to the parent.

The latest date pertaining to this reign is inscribed on one of the four shells found in Burial 5 (W. R. Coe 1959). It reads 9.13.17.14.17 2 Caban 15 Kankin and is 136 days before the accession of the next ruler, whose life will be covered in Chapter 10. The interval is ample, but not too long for the completion of mortuary ceremonies and the installation of the new monarch, and although there is no recognizable statement of death, it may very well be that the inscription was made for the burial and that the deceased was the ruler whose stelae stand before Temple J-4, at the other side of the main court of the acropolis. The text, however, deals not with the king, but with the woman on Stelae 1 and 3, very probably his wife. It records her birth, the event signified by the *imix-ahau* glyph pertaining to her, here followed by *u caban* and the ruler's name with 4 *ich-ben* katun. Next, with the last of the nuptial days comes the moon compound that was noted on Stelae 1, 3, and 8, but the woman's name here is different. It has an *ix* prefix attached to a quincunx with the superfix T12 that seems to go with descriptive names. Perhaps the woman is here described as "the widow," since the quincunx seems to be associated in some way with death or with funerary rites. The expression with the last date is not clear, but it seems significant that in this clause the *u caban* expression refers not to the king, as before, but to the woman. The king may be mentioned again before the end of the inscription, not by his official designation, but by the jaguar compound used in his alternate name, and the inscription then ends with 4 *ich-ben* katun, *ich-ben kin,* with wing suffix. The *kin* glyph occurs also in the name of the ruler pictured on Stela 25, and with the name of the child on Stela 3. In the mother's name, the corresponding glyph is *akbal.* The significance of such glyphs is unknown.

Another text recording a katun anniversary of the accession of this king occurs on a beautifully carved jade bead dredged from the sacrificial cenote of Chichen Itza (Proskouriakoff 1944). Many of the pieces of jade from the cenote probably came from looted graves (Proskouriakoff 1974). It seems unlikely that this jade could have come from Burial 5, suggested to be the tomb of this ruler, since W. R. Coe (1959:124) states that Burial 5 was disturbed by the collapse of the vault before the construction of the floor above it. If Coe is correct, this may put the identity of the occupant of this burial somewhat in doubt.

During this entire period, Yaxchilan was ruled by Shield Jaguar, whose influence reached far beyond the frontiers of his provinces. Although he seems to have claimed descent from early settlers of Yaxchilan, he probably was not himself a native of that city. We have no record of his birth or of his accession to power. He begins his career at Yaxchilan with a series of "captures," but we cannot be altogether sure whether he captured the city from its rightful lord, or rescued it from a foreign foe and restored its legitimate dynasty; whether he ruled it by virtue of conquest, or by virtue of marriage to a woman of the royal family. It was in his rule that Yaxchilan acquired a second Emblem Glyph, the "spot" Emblem T36:168:511, apparently the Emblem of his native land. Although this Emblem is not known elsewhere before his time, we might surmise that Shield Jaguar's native territory lay on the opposite bank of the river and that the two sites, now joined under a single rule, gained sole control of riverine traffic. The earlier dates concerned with his conquests are sometimes written with the month coefficient one less than we expect, a type of notation also found at Etzna at about the time of his arrival, as well as in Postclassic times in northern Yucatan, which is another reason for locating his original home somewhere to the north.

In front of Structure 41, on a high hill commanding a view of a large sweep of the river, were found three of Shield Jaguar's earliest stelae: Stelae 18, 19, and 20. They are reported to have been carved on both broad faces, but only the front faces are well preserved. Maler (1901–1903:2:126) describes the carving on the backs of these monuments as badly eroded and refers to the designs as the "deity" motif, here considered as depicting divination. I question Maler's

Shield Jaguar
(YAX L 25, F2)

Yaxchilan "spot" Emblem Glyph
(YAX St 18, D5)

capture
(YAX St 19, A3)

name of captive
(YAX St 19, A4)

identification of the divination motif on these stelae, but not having seen the monuments, have no alternative but tentatively to accept it, which would suggest that Shield Jaguar's homeland shared this tradition with Yaxchilan and was probably adjacent to its territory. The carving on the faces of these monuments, however, is very different both from that of earlier Yaxchilan monuments and from that of stelae erected here later. Stelae 18, 19, and 20 are all tall monuments, and all present Shield Jaguar with a spear and a bag in his hands, standing before a kneeling figure which is well dressed and does not appear to be bound. Stela 19 records a day 11 Ahau 3 Pop (9.12.8.14.0?) and refers to a capture of a certain prisoner whose name appears as a death mask with an *ahau* sign on its forehead. The central lintel of Structure 44, apparently carved much later and in a different style, very probably portrays the same capture, referring it to the next day, 12 Imix. Most of this inscription is destroyed, but the *ahau* death mask is clear, and although neither the month position nor the capture glyph survives, there is an *imix* compound of the type that often appears to refer to captives. On the step below that lintel is an Initial Series, 9.12.8.14.1 12 Imix 4 Pop, the day following 11 Ahau 3 Pop, and there seems to be little doubt that all three inscriptions refer to the same event.

The date on Stela 18 undoubtedly refers to the same capture as does the last date recorded on the step in the southeast doorway of Structure 44. The month position is clear as 14 Mol, but in neither case is the day sign clear, nor is its coefficient on Stela 18. Morley's original suggestion for the Long Count of this date on Stela 18 was 9.10.19.14.6 3 Cimi 14 Mol, and for the date on the step, 9.5.13.6.1 2 Imix 14 Mol (Morley 1937–1938:2:429–432). J. E. S. Thompson (1952) corrected the latter to 2 Chuen 14 Mol 9.14.16.17.11 (actually, 9.14.17.15.11). Morley's date is certainly too early. Thompson's, I suspect, is too late. One Calendar Round earlier, 9.12.5.2.11, seems more acceptable if we read the date on Stela 18 as 3 Eb 14 Mol 9.12.5.2.12, written in the style current in Etzna at this time and used in Postclassic times in northern Yucatan.

The date of Stela 20 is even more difficult to reconcile with the Structure 44 inscription. It appears to read 6 Ix 16 Kankin and records a capture. The next glyphs are damaged, but the third glyph down is a *kan* cross expression that also appears with the date 5 Ix 17 Kankin on Lintel 46 (9.14.1.17.14, according to J. E. S. Thompson 1946), where it immediately follows the capture glyph. It is especially unfortunate that the Initial Series on this lintel is completely gone. It may be that the Maya themselves mistranslated this date and that it should read 6 Ix 17 Kankin (9.13.9.14.14?). There seems to be no simple and uniform solution to the problem, and we may be dealing here with two different events.

Stela 15, on the upper terrace, is a smaller monument and is squared at the top. Its composition is different from that of the other monuments, for Shield Jaguar is shown grasping his captive by the hair. The date appears to be the same 12 Imix 4 Pop that is recorded on Lintel 46, though here the prisoner is named T12 Ahau, without attachment to a mask. The carving of this monument shows no significant differences in style from other stelae associated with Structure 41, though I suspect it may have been erected later. There is a *ben-ich* notation with Shield Jaguar's name, which might date this stela, but its number is not clear on Maler's photograph (Maler 1901–1903:2:Pl. 79). Another small monument featuring Shield Jaguar, Stela 13, is also squared at the top. It is said to be carved on both sides, though only one is preserved. This stela stood on one side of Stela 11, which features his successor, and it is undoubtedly a posthumous monument. His name is associated here with 5 *ben-ich* katun, his dress is simple and he carries in his hand a plain staff. Another probably posthumous monument that associates his name with the death-scroll mask T1013 as well as with the 5 *ben-ich* katun expression is Stela 10. On the back of this monument is an unusual divination motif that shows the figure in front view, below the standard sky motif, showing ancestors enclosed in frames above the sky-serpent. Morley suggests the date 9.16.15.0.0 for this monument, and he could be right, but only if we assume that the front was copied from an earlier portrait. The composition, like that of some later stelae, shows Shield Jaguar with two other standing figures, a young woman in front of him and a young man behind. There is also a crouching figure with his hand on his shoulder in a gesture of submission behind the figure of the young woman. The dress and accoutrement of these figures as well as their rigid poses suggest that the scene represented is earlier.

death-scroll mask + T1013
(YAX St 10, pH1)

Stelae 22 and 23, found fallen in front of Structure 44, though incomplete, are narrow, and may also have been small monuments. Only the lower parts of the sculptures were preserved, and neither monument shows a date. Both appear to be later than the early monuments of Shield Jaguar, and on Stela 23, his name is followed by a notation of 5 katuns. Both faces of Stela 23 show a single human figure standing in profile, but not enough sculpture remains on either monument to permit a confident evaluation of its style. By the middle of the fifteenth katun, the style of carving at Yaxchilan had already changed radically. The scenes of capture in Structure 44, though they may refer to earlier events, in no way resemble presentation of similar events on the stelae in front of Structure 41. On the lintels of Structure 44, the figures are shown in action, and the strong, carefully modulated relief, as well as the balance of space and figure, distinguishes them as masterpieces of Maya design. Unfortunately, all three lintels are broken and badly mutilated.

Much better preserved are the lintels of Structure 23, probably the work of the same artist. They were excavated by Alfred P. Maudslay, and two (Lintels 24 and 25) are now in the British Museum. Structure 23 is one of three buildings built by three successive kings, presenting on their lintels very similar motifs. They stand in a row on a low terrace running along the foot of the hills fronting the river. Structure 22 on the same terrace has already been mentioned in Chapter 5. In each of the three buildings, one lintel features a lord, and the remaining two depict ritual scenes featuring a woman. The central Lintel 25 of Structure 23 is an "invocation" scene, in which a woman, holding a bowl of sacrificial objects, kneels before an image of an ancestor, shown in the jaws of a two-headed serpent rising from the smoke of a burning sacrifice. The date, 5 Imix 4 Mac, is the same as that on a step of Structure 44, where its position is 9.12.9.8.1. On the front edge of Lintel 25, a Secondary Series leads to 3 Imix 14 Ch'en 9.14.11.15.1 (?). Both dates are followed by the fish-in-hand expression. The phrasing is not identical, but what seems to be implied is a commemorative rite directed to an ancestor who died in battle forty-two years earlier. The fourth katun notation with Shield Jaguar's name on the face of the lintel apparently refers to the later date and to the scene portrayed, when he was over sixty years old. It is interesting to note the spotted turban, the Tlaloc-like masks, and the so-called Mexican Year Signs worn on the warrior's head and appearing also in the mouth of the lesser tail-head of the serpent.

T1012:102
(YAX L 25, S2)

Neither the identity of the woman nor that of the dead hero pictured on this lintel is altogether clear. Her name may be inscribed on the front of the lintel, beginning with the *kin*-on-pedestal prefix and followed by a God C (T1016) compound. Her relationship to the dead hero may be indicated in the next two expressions ending with the sign T1012:102, which occurs also in the curve of the cloud-scroll under his portrait, and which could be his name.

It is not clear whether this woman is the one who is pictured on Lintels 24 and 26 or another. The tattooed designs on the cheeks of these two distinguish them from the portrait on Lintel 25. On the edge of Lintel 26, the woman is designated only by her *kin*-on-pedestal title, and of the front edge of Lintel 24 we have no record. However, on the face of that lintel, where the woman is shown performing a blood sacrifice, as stated in the caption at the left, her name is also linked twice to the T1012:102 expression, so that she is very probably of the same family, if not the same person. The date on the face of Lintel 24 is 5 Eb 15 Mac (9.13.17.15.12?) and the katun notation with Shield Jaguar's name is again 4 katuns, and again we see the Tlaloc mask and the Mexican Year Sign, this time worn on the woman's headdress.

Lintel 26 was broken in half, and only its upper portion is well preserved. Five hieroglyphs are indicated by Ian Graham (Graham and von Euw 1977:57–58) on the lower portion, but are not drawn and cannot be seen on the photograph. On this lintel, the male figure, presumably Shield Jaguar, wears quilted or feathered armor, as in his battle scenes in Structure 44, but he carries only a knife in his hand and wears a penitential collar of rope. A woman holds his shield and his jaguar helmet. The day sign of the accompanying date is not clear. Its coefficient is 12, and its month position is the seating of Pop. This could be 12 Eb 0 Pop 9.14.12.6.12. The Initial Series on the front edge of this lintel is damaged, but it reads best as 1 Ahau 13 Yaxkin 9.14.11.13.0, a date less than a year earlier than the value suggested for the date on the face of this lintel, and forty-one days earlier than the date on the front edge of Lintel 25.

Considering the uncertainty of these dates, and our present state of knowledge of Maya writing, it would be unwise to attempt a detailed interpretation of the events commemorated on Structures 44 and 23. What stands out clearly, however, is the enormous importance ascribed to the dates 9.12.8.14.1 and 9.12.9.8.1. It is surely no coincidence that soon after this date, on 9.12.9.17.16, a ruler was inaugurated at Tikal after the absence of his predecessor in the region of Petexbatun. Were the kings of Tikal and Yaxchilan adversaries in a conflict to control trade on the Usumacinta, or were they allies against a common foe?

About this time, more monuments began to appear in the vicinity of Quirigua. It must be admitted, however, that their dates are little more than guesses. Morley places Stela T and Stela U at 9.13.0.0.0 and 9.14.0.0.0. The coefficient of the katun of the Initial Series of Stela T is clearly 13, but the argument for the date of Stela U is weak. Since there is a day 9 Ahau in the text, I would prefer to read it as 9.12.10.0.0 (9 Ahau 18 Zotz'), admitting that the margin of error is great. Both these monuments stood on a high, leveled hill overlooking the site of Quirigua and the Motagua River. This suggests a defensive purpose, but since the main group of Quirigua may not have been built at this time, the question arises what territory was being surveyed and what defended—that of Copan, that of Quirigua itself, or that of Pusilha. In view of Copan's expansion at this time, and its subsequent prosperity, one might surmise that it was the rulers of Copan who established a lookout at this strategic spot, to gain control or to protect traffic along the Motagua. Perhaps the Copan rulers also set up the small group with Stela S on the lower level at the settlement. Located on the left bank of the Motagua, this site may once have been subject to Quirigua, or some other larger site. Its independence, as we shall see, was to come later.

Pusilha continued to erect monuments until 9.15.0.0.0, but I have been able to gain little from its inscriptions. Stelae M and E are dated by Morley (1937–1938:4:54–60) 9.14.0.0.0 and 9.15.0.0.0. These readings are by no means certain, but are as good as the eroded state of the monuments allows. The asymmetric pose of the figure on Stela E argues a later date, but lacking corroborative detail, a stylistic judgment is of little value. The Initial Series is irregular, with a long interpolation between Glyph A and the month notation. The statement that follows is destroyed. It ends with an Emblem Glyph difficult to make out, but probably not the Emblem here proposed for Pusilha. The next sign seems to be a "jog" followed by a "1 shell" (first offspring?) clause referring to a woman. Parts of the clause are destroyed. The rest is legible, but of unknown meaning.

I believe Stela C to be the earliest monument erected in the north end of the main court at Copan after its completion. The date suggested by Morley, 9.17.12.0.0, seems much too late. The stela stands in the middle of the court, its two figures facing east and west. Its very high relief makes its figures look almost like statues, and the detail is flamboyant and extravagant, but there is just a vestige of the earlier style in the position of the hands, which almost hide the ceremonial bars the figures hold on horizontal forearms.

The reading of the dates on this monument is difficult, and there seems to be no entirely satisfactory solution. Each side of the stela begins with an Initial Series Introducing Glyph followed by the notation of thirteen calabtuns and an Ahau Calendar Round date. The first Calendar Round is 6 Ahau 18 Kayab. A Secondary Series of 11.14.5.1.0 connects it with the date 6 Ahau 13 Muan, shortly followed by the phrase "seating," perhaps of the *haab*. Assuming that this 6 Ahau 13 Muan is the one that fell on 9.14.0.0.0, the Distance Number indicates that the first date fell before the traditional beginning date of the Long Count on 4 Ahau 8 Cumku. The Distance Number reaches back 2.0.5.1.0 before this date, regarded as the completion of thirteen baktuns in a previous cycle. If written in the manner used by the Maya at Palenque to designate such negative dates, it would read 10.19.14.17.0, counting from the end of the previous pictun. If, following the indication provided by the opening of the text of the Copan stela, we count it instead from the end of thirteen calabtuns, it would read 12.19.17.19.14.17.0—a rather awkward number. Adding the Secondary Series to this number, we have 13.10.9.14.0.0.0 as the expression of the contemporary Calendar Round 6 Ahau 13 Muan. Thirteen pictuns would seem to have done as well as the larger calabtun.

Actually, all the Calendar Round dates on this monument can be accommodated in the fifteenth katun of Baktun 9. If we change Morley's (1920) reading of 5 Ahau 18 Uo to 5 Ahau 8 Uo, and put all the dates thus obtained in chronological order, an interesting pattern of regular intervals between dates emerges:

9.14. 0. 0. 0	6 Ahau 13 Muan
+ 7. 4. 0	
9.14. 7. 4. 0	6 Ahau 18 Kayab
+ 2. 1. 0	
9.14. 9. 5. 0	5 Ahau 8 Cumku
+ 7. 4. 0	
9.14.16. 9. 0	5 Ahau 8 Uo(?)
+ 2. 1. 0	
9.14.18.10. 0	4 Ahau 18 Uo
+ (13. 0)	
(9.14.19. 5. 0	4 Ahau 18 Muan) (suggested by Morley [1920])

Whether these actually are the positions for these dates is in question, but however the pattern may be changed by adding or subtracting Calendar Rounds, the regularity will remain. This is not a historical pattern, and I suggest that this stela was erected in 9.14.0.0.0 and records a prophecy for the coming katun. The last date, whether it was inscribed here or not, is a lahuntun anniversary of the third, and it is recorded on Stelae A and H. It may have been chosen for whatever ceremony is recorded on these stelae, a self-fulfilling prophecy, so to speak. As for the figures, I would conjecture that the bearded figure is the prophet and the other the king. Unfortunately no names, if they were recorded, are legible. Such "double portraits" seem to appear after the death of a king, the priest having officiated at the burial ceremonies. An alternative interpretation may be that he is an ancestor validating the new ruler's royal status.

Stela F was erected in 9.14.10.0.0 and Stela 4 in 9.14.15.0.0. These monuments are even more independent of the constraints of the conventional stela form, and their figures stand out strongly in three-quarters relief, with natural rendering of body forms, surrounded with intricate detail. This is probably why Spinden (1913) considered them the most advanced in the evolution of the art of Copan and Morley placed them in a Calendar-Round later than their dates indicate; but art does not necessarily progress uniformly in one direction. An exceptionally talented artist can revolutionize a style, and I prefer to accept the clear evidence of the dates. The preference for such statuesque forms was short-lived, and after 9.15.0.0.0 there was a return to more blocklike forms, though the flamboyant detail continued for some time. Perhaps stone of suitable quality was no longer attainable.

The inscriptions on these monuments are brief and, like all inscriptions of Copan, are not easy to interpret, for, with some exceptions, they contain few intermediate dates and use many head glyphs and elaborate forms not found elsewhere in texts. The text on Stela F begins with an Initial Series Introducing Glyph and the date 5 Ahau 3 Mac, lahuntun of 15 katuns (9.14.10.0.0). It ends with T12 (usually read as *ah*) *ben-ich* over a *kankin*-like element, which in this form is usually the main element of an Emblem, indicating that this personage comes from another town or province. The upright *kankin* is not known as the main sign of an Emblem Glyph elsewhere, but there is a possibility that it may have been the Emblem of Pusilha. On the other hand, if placed on its side, it resembles the Emblem of Quirigua, and one may wonder if that Emblem derives from it. The woman portrayed on Stela H at Copan (9.15.0.0.0) also appears to have the upright *kankin* as her Emblem. The argument for some family connection between rulers of Quirigua and Copan based on the similarity of Emblems is admittedly weak, but it is reinforced by the fact that the first stela erected in the main group of Quirigua in 9.16.0.0.0, described in Chapter 10, bears a marked resemblance to the stelae of Copan, and that there is no stela at Copan with the

ah ben-ich + *kankin* variant
(CPN St F, B10)

Two-legged Sky
(QRG St A, B17)

Eighteen Jog
(CPN St A, C10a)

same date. It may also be of interest that the often repeated date 9.14.13.4.17 at Quirigua, when the king later known as Two-legged Sky first assumes or is given the governorship of that town, falls shortly before the erection of Stela 4 at Copan in 9.14.15.0.0, which initiates the rule of Eighteen Jog. The name Two-legged Sky was given the king of Quirigua by D. H. Kelley in a paper (1962) which gives his interpretation of this and of another incident recorded there. Since this name is very similar to that of Stormy Sky, differing only in the replacement of the manikin helmet by the *cauac* sign, I would have preferred to call this Quirigua ruler Rainy Sky, but I will retain here Kelley's designation, Two-legged Sky.

Almost due south of Palenque, against the foothills of the Chiapas highlands, the site of Tonina exhibits considerable activity during this period. The stelae here are more like statues than like the slabs of the Peten, and their inscriptions are cramped on the back and often difficult to make out. There are various other sculptures, and it is clear that this, like Tortuguero, was a border site. It is probably the quality of the local stone that is responsible for Tonina's statu-esque style.

CHAPTER TEN

On the Crest of the Wave

9.15.0.0.0 − 9.17.10.0.0

A.D. 731 − 780

AFTER THE ESTABLISHMENT OF PEACEFUL RELATIONS along the Usumacinta some forty years earlier, the prosperity of the larger Maya cities steadily increased, reaching a peak by 9.15.0.0.0. Tikal, in its protected place in the center of northern Peten, and possessed of a longer tradition than the border cities, seems to have become a religious capital and a place of pilgrimage for surrounding regions. Otherwise it would be difficult to explain its enormous constructions, and at the same time the conservative nature of its monuments. By 9.15.0.0.0, the North Acropolis was crowded with small temples, and the greater temples, with their towering roof-combs, were raised on pyramids of enormous size. Stelae, with their accompanying altars, were placed at the base of the stairways leading to the temples, and at the end of each katun, a stela was erected in an arrangement called a "twin pyramid" group, with a varying number of plain stelae and altars, ranged in front of the east pyramid. The plain monuments may have been added later, and may have been stuccoed and painted, though they now have no vestige of design or writing on them.

So far, seven such groups with stelae have been reported, and there may be others. In two, all monuments are without carving. There seems to be no stela recording the date 9.15.0.0.0., but since this was a period of mourning between the death of one ruler and the accession of the next, this is not surprising. Twin Pyramid Group O is usually assigned this date. Moon Comb (Ruler A) may have died or was about to die at that time. Ruler B, Dark Sky, was seated on 3 Lamat 6 Pax (9.15.3.6.8). The first stela erected in his reign seems to have been Stela 21. It is a badly damaged monument, and the first half of the inscription is virtually effaced. A date of seating is noted at the end of the inscription without mention of a name, "seating as *batab;* divination" (hand scattering grain). This may mean that the

Ruler B
(TIK St 5, B4)

matrilineage name
(TIK St 5, A6)

Petexbatun Emblem Glyph
(TIK St 5, D12)

woman
(TIK St 5, C7)

portrait is not that of the king himself, but of a priest representing him in the ceremony. A Secondary Series, 1.11.12, leads back from a missing hotun notation to 3 Lamat 6 Pax (9.15.3.6.8). If 9.15.5.0.0 is the final date of this stela, it is the earliest stela which shows the figure standing in bare feet, suggesting that he stands in a room or enclosure. His pose is identical to that of stelae erected in twin pyramid assemblages, and I wonder if it had not been originally designed to represent the missing Katun 15. On the other hand, Stela 20, which represents Katun 16 and stands in twin pyramid Group P, is not a divination figure, and seems strangely out of place in this complex. Unfortunately, if there was a name on this monument, it no longer survives. The latest date on the roof-comb of Temple VI is 9.16.15.0.0. One might even wonder if in the final renovations of this temple the two monuments had not changed places.

The next monument erected was Stela 5, which stands on the North Acropolis in front of Structure 33, together with four plain stelae in line and one in front. The inscription on the front is all but destroyed, as are the first glyphs on the left side, though these can be reconstructed as the seating date 3 Lamat 6 Pax, pertaining to Ruler B of Tikal. At A6 we find the last of three names listed on Stela 26 which I have suggested may be three matrilineages of Tikal (see Chapter 7). Here, however, it has the prefix *yax*. A number of the following glyphs are familiar and suggestive of meanings that are, however, still questionable. On the other side of the stela, a Secondary Series leads from the seating date to 4 Ahau 3 Yaxkin (9.15.13.0.0), naming Dark Sky as *batab* of Petexbatun (?), the Emblem here written as a face glyph.

The rest of the inscription has been interpreted by some scholars as referring to the mother and the father of the king (e.g., Jones 1977). I do not fully understand the two phrases, but I cannot agree with this interpretation. The final passage clearly states that the preceding event occurred "in the reign of Moon Comb," the former ruler, who was *batab* of Petexbatun. The event is signified by a hand holding an upside-down *ahau* and refers to a woman who comes from a site perhaps somewhere to the north. Her identity is not clear to me, but she may have been the daughter of the former king, mentioned on Lintel 3 of Temple I, and the natural inheritor of his title, since there is no mention of a son. The new ruler may have become king by virtue of his marriage to the daughter of the former monarch. Unfortunately no one has yet made a comprehensive study of Emblems and what they signify. Dark Sky, like his predecessor, uses the Emblem of Petexbatun, but after the king's death, his Emblem is a human head with a dark spot on the cheek and a jaguar tail under the chin, suggesting an abnormality in his claim to the throne.

Clemency Coggins (1975) has suggested that Temple VI is the location of the tomb of Dark Sky (Ruler B), but it seems to me to be more likely that this ruler was buried below Temple IV. A considerable lapse of time between the death of one king and the accession of another is not unusual, and I suspect that the latest renovations on Temple VI were made by the surviving daughter of the previous king.

The lintels of Temple IV repeat the motifs of those of Temple I, with minor variations. Lintel 2 is the underworld scene. As before, the ruler is shown seated and holding a manikin scepter. This time, the jaguar behind him appears in human form, but wearing jaguar spots on his body, a jaguar ear on a fillet that turns over his nose, an artificial beard under his chin, and the number 7 on his cheek. Unfortunately, a panel of glyphs in this scene is all but completely destroyed. A vertical panel at the left begins with the date 3 Ahau 3 Mol (9.15.10.0.0), followed by a Secondary Series, 2.11.12, leading to 6 Eb 0 Pop. The nature of the event on this date is unknown, but it is followed by the name Dark Sky, a title, and his own peculiar emblem: a face with a spot on its cheek. The next day, 7 Ben 1 Pop, is followed by a "starlight glyph," which seems to be associated often with journeys, but it is not clear to me whether the reference is to travels of the king himself, or of dignitaries from other towns coming to Tikal to pay their respects to the new king. This is a very difficult inscription to interpret, and I will not attempt it here. It concludes with the date 9.15.15.14.0.

On both lintels of Temple IV, the inscription begins with the date 9.15.10.0.0 and continues, noting a pair of consecutive days. On Lintel 3 these days are 11 Ik 15 Ch'en and 12 Akbal 16 Ch'en (9.15.12.2.2; 9.15.12.2.3). On Lintel 2, they are 6 Eb 0 Pop and 7 Ben 1 Pop (9.15.12.11.12 and 9.15.12.11.13). After the first date of Lintel 3, and after the second date of Lintel 2, is the "starlight glyph" discussed in Chapter 8 in connection with the presence of an earlier ruler in the region of Petexbatun. The distance between the two "star" notations is 191 days.

Lis Brack-Bernsen (1977) calculated that by the Thompson correlation, a partial eclipse of the sun occurred on the day 10 Imix preceding the first of these dates, and that the name Dark Sky derives from this event. John S. Justeson (1975) identified the turtle glyph that follows the "starlight glyph" at B4 on Lintel 3 as the Emblem of Yaxha.

I do not pretend to understand the meaning of these very unusual inscriptions, but a panel of twenty four glyphs on Lintel 2 is almost completely destroyed and it very probably would have given us at least the date of death of Ruler B, which we do not know. Also destroyed is most of the inscription on a lintel from Structure 10, which begins with the date 9.15.10.0.0. This lintel is in a palace structure at the back of the acropolis, and before the figure is shown a dwarf with two cormorants. Christopher Jones (in Jones and Satterthwaite 1982) describes it as a portrait of a man, but I suspect it may depict a woman, although the shield, manikin, and bag are normally items of male accoutrement.

The inscription on the roof-comb of Temple VI, which stands at a distance from the Main Acropolis, and facing it, begins with the

event
(TIK St 5, D7)

Emblem Glyph of woman
(TIK St 5, D8)

Emblem Glyph of Ruler B
(TIK T IV, L 2, A6)

"starlight glyph" + Yaxha Emblem
(TIK T IV, L 3, B4)

date 5.0.0.0.0, well over a thousand years before the earliest stela erected at Tikal. Not only is the correct Calendar Round position recorded for this date, but also the Lunar Series, and after some eroded and unknown glyphs, the passage ends with the Emblem of Tikal. One might think that the foundation of Tikal was recorded here, if the date were not so out of line with the earliest remains found at the site. Perhaps they were writing about the origins of the royal family and exaggerating its antiquity, a practice not unknown in our own history. After the emblem there are four more glyphs, the last of which is 8 Vulture, as on Stela 5 at A8.

A long Secondary Series lead from the initial date to 6.14.16.9.16 11 Cib 4 Zac, still somewhat early for Tikal, but possibly when the first permanent settlements appeared. Three hundred years later (7.10.0.0.0 3 Ahau 13 Pax) was when the first stelae with inscriptions begin to appear on the Pacific Coast. Strangely enough, Cycle 8 does not seem to be mentioned at all. A Secondary Series, 1.14.0.0.0, skips us directly from 7.10.0.0.0 to 9.4.0.0.0, the date that begins the royal history at Palenque in the Temple of the Inscriptions; the date of the first stelae at Yaxchilan, at Calakmul, and at Caracol; the date when Classic Maya culture is for the first time spread beyond the confines of the Peten.

A large part of the text that follows is destroyed, but 9.4.13.0.0 was probably recorded, for a short Distance Number from this date leads to three closely spaced events: 5 Cib 9 Ceh (9.4.13.4.16?), 4 Ix 7 Kankin (9.4.13.6.14?), and 4 Manik 0 Mol (9.4.13.7.7). The month glyphs, unfortunately, are damaged, as well as the glyphs that may have identified the events. These dates in the main part of the inscription on the roof-comb pertain to the history of early Tikal, and may document the violent events leading to a hiatus in the sequence of known dates at Tikal. It is possible, however, that Stelae 10 and 12, of unknown date, partially fill this hiatus.

Contemporary dates are inscribed in separate panels. The only two that are partly legible are 4 Caban 15 Pop (9.16.14.17.17 ?) and 7 Ahau 18 Pop (9.16.15.0.0 ?). Although I can find no suggestion of death in the glyphs that follow, the Caban date, if this reading is correct, is not far from the accession date of the next ruler. The date of his seating, 9.16.17.16.4 11 Kan 12 Kayab, is given on Stela 22, erected on 9.17.0.0.0 in Twin Pyramid Group Q. He has been given the designation of Ruler C. However, it is still uncertain whether the expression "seating as *batab*" is equivalent to accession or refers to the office of the diviner. Stela 22 introduces new features of design, which become standard on later Tikal monuments. Among these are the "cloud-rider" figure in the sky and the jaguar-tail costume. I suspect that the purpose of the ceremony may be to announce the choice of the next ruler, who is to reign after the death of the king, but it would be difficult to test this, since the inscriptions are not well enough preserved.

The proliferation of monuments that took place in the previous

name glyphs of Ruler C
(TIK St 22, A3–B3)

period was concentrated in the larger sites, which probably ruled over provinces of considerable size. After 9.15.0.0.0, conflicts seem to break out sporadically, and gradually we find more and more smaller sites erecting monuments, suggesting the formation of smaller principalities. Whether these were entirely independent or subject to the major centers is yet to be determined, for the significance of Emblems and titles remains problematical.

Uaxactun seems to have resumed the erection of stelae after a long period of inactivity. Morley (1937–1938:1:208–211) dates Stela 1 at 9.14.0.0.0, but this is little more than a guess. The next monument, Stela 2, he places at 9.16.0.0.0, the only certain date of this period. Stelae 8 and 11 he places "in the last quarter of Baktun 9." The erosion of these monuments is severe, and the texts are virtually illegible in the published photographs.

The monuments of Xultun, a site of considerable size, are, if anything, in even worse condition, and most of Morley's readings (1937–1938:1:395–410) are unreliable. The dates that he assigns to Stelae 8, 4, and 5, for example—9.8.10.0.0, 9.11.0.0.0, and 9.12.0.0.0 (with questions marks)—I find unacceptable by stylistic standards. The monuments he assigns to the period under discussion, Stelae 13, 14 and 16, are much too fragmentary or eroded to yield any stylistic criteria. We cannot even say whether this site, like Uaxactun and Tikal, exhibits any considerable gap in the erection of its monuments.

Nor does La Honradez yield any legible texts. The published photographs are inadequate, and I have been unable to confirm Morley's readings of the dates (1937–1938:1:431–459). All one can say is that there are several sculptured monuments there that probably date from this period. Like Xultun, the site is large, and only a small portion of it has been explored. Both sites are located in the northeastern corner of the Peten, and both apparently suffer from the poor quality of stone available there. No very large constructions are reported, but the ruins spread over a considerable distance, and further exploration and fuller reporting of the monuments may prove to be of crucial interest, for they are located at the headwaters of the Río Hondo, which flows into the Bay of Chetumal and was undoubtedly a major route of trade in ancient times. Chochkitam in this general region also has at least one stela of this period, but yields no legible text. To the east, Stela U at Nakum is dated by Morley (1937–1938:2:12–13) at 9.17.0.0.0. It is too badly weathered to yield a text, but appears to be the earliest monument there and testifies to the expansion of monumental activity at this time to many more sites than were erecting monuments before.

From Naranjo, we have no surely dated monuments of this period. Judging by the damaged inscription on Stela 18, it seems possible that after the death of the dowager queen from Tikal, the city had decided to reclaim Naranjo and held it during the reign of Dark Sky. However, Stela 20 and Stela 6 could have been erected in this

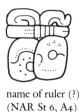

name of ruler (?)
(NAR St 6, A4)

sky title + *chuen* variant
(NAR St 6, A5)

interval, and since Stela 20 seems to have been moved and is standing with later monuments, others of its group may be buried under the debris of the acropolis or in its fill.

Stela 20, in style, resembles the monuments of the previous fifty-tun period. The inscription on the back is virtually destroyed, and on the front there is only one Calendar-Round date, which is ambiguous. Morley (1937–1938:2:145–147) read it as 7 Cib 14 Yax or Ch'en. A reading of 6 Cib is also possible, though less likely. Because of its proximity to later monuments, Morley considered no dates earlier than 9.15.15.3.16 7 Cib 14 Yax. My style dating has placed it between 9.12.0.0.0 and 9.16.0.0.0, and the date could be 9.13.2.8.16, in the reign of the son of the Tikal lady. The event is marked by a "toothache glyph," but without the usual affix cluster. Kelley has suggested that it is the accession stela for the son, and that the animal name for this son is here rendered *cuc*, a homonym for "squirrel," but I am not convinced of this, and prefer to leave the date of this monument uncertain.

The date of Stela 6, which also has a "toothache" expression, is best read as 9.16.4.10.18 9 Etz'nab 11 Muan. A Secondary Series 1.5?.?.2 (1.5.7.2 ?) brings us to 9.17.10.0.0, the date of Stelae 13, 19, 33, and 36. This series is part of the inscription on the back, which is very badly weathered. The "toothache" expression here seems to be complete and is followed by a name(?) somewhat like that recorded on Stela 20, but with a sky title attached to a *chuen*-like sign, which might identify the ruler. No Emblem Glyph, however, seems to be present. Tentatively, we might suggest that this is the accession monument of the series that begins with 9.17.10.0.0, and is discussed in Chapter 11.

Our record of events in the region of Petexbatun during the preceding period is somewhat sketchy, but Ian Graham (1967) published excellent drawings of a group of monuments at Aguateca with dates beginning in 9.15.0.0.0. Fragments of Stela 5 of this group show a clear record of Katun 9.13.0.0.0, and at that time it was assumed to be the dedicatory date of the monument, but the addition of other fragments, showing the upper half of the figure, and the fact that this katun is preceded and followed by other dates make it unlikely that this is the latest date. The first date recorded preserves only a part of a bar and the month Zotz', and the best reading for an Ahau date would be (8 Ahau) 8 Zotz' (9.16.5.0.0). The mention of the much earlier date may be due to the fact that 9.13.0.0.0 was the date of the first stelae erected at Tikal by Moon Comb, who was a native of Petexbatun.

The first monument to be erected in this location is probably, as usual, the central monument, Stela 3, recording Katun 9.15.0.0.0 4 Ahau 13 Yax, and this is followed by an unusual combination of a thumb-up hand with an infix of grains that suggests divination. The name of the person to whom this expression refers occurs also on Stelae 1 and 2. It is here followed by his titles and an Emblem Glyph.

From Dos Pilas Stela 8, we know that this person succeeded to the title of "vulture" another known as Shield Manikin, who died in 9.14.15.1.19, a date which also appears on one of the bones in the grave under Temple I at Tikal, suggesting that he may have been an officer of the king's army, if not actually a relative. Cloud Lord, as I have called the new "vulture," succeeded Shield Manikin in 9.14.15.5.15, less than 4 uinals after his death, which confirms my impression that "vulture" was a military and not royal title. He was later known as Captor of Kin Jaguar, and bore the manikin title. Kin Jaguar is mentioned in Temple IV at Tikal at a later date. This may be a posthumous allusion, but it may imply that Kin Jaguar was not a name, but a title that could refer to more than one individual.

The pose of the lord shown in Stela 3 is rigid in comparison with those on other stelae of this group. The ornamental features, such as the pectoral, the head attached to the belt, and the wide apron below, are exaggerated in size, but lack the elegance we see on later monuments. The headdress, although elaborated with plumes, appears to be based on a warrior's helmet, such as was worn at Piedras Negras and Palenque. The figure holds a manikin scepter and a round shield held with its face away from the observer, so that its device is not visible.

Stela 2, erected in 9.15.5.0.0 to the right of Stela 3, shows the ruler in a radically different guise. He is dressed in the style of the lower Usumacinta, probably originating in the ancient city of Teotihuacan or in its far-flung colonies. The headdress is a huge round turban, such as on Lintel 4 of Piedras Negras, and includes the so-called Mexican Year Sign, which is shown there as early as 9.11.15.0.0 on Lintel 2. The rectangular shield first appears at Tikal during the reign of the foreigner Curlsnout, and the broad garters worn just below the knee are typical of Piedras Negras in this period. The goggle-eyed mask of the apron and the shells decorating the collar are other features that recall the Teotihuacan style of dress, while the abbreviated form of the mask worn in front of the face is similar to masks attached to the headdress of Shield Jaguar of Yaxchilan in his role of captor of prisoners. The claws worn on the feet and hanging from the shoulder also give an alien touch to this extraordinary portrait, while the spear, the shield, and the crouching prisoner beneath his feet emphasize its warlike character. The identical motif, with only minor variations, occurs on Stela 16 at Dos Pilas, undoubtedly depicting the same personage, since it records the same events and features the same name in the text.

Texts on these monuments are similar to those on the lintels of Temple IV at Tikal in that they begin with a record of two consecutive days, the first of which at Aguateca and Dos Pilas is marked by the "starlight" compound. These dates, however, are more than seven years earlier than similar dates at Tikal: 9.15.4.6.4 8 Kan 17 Muan and 9.15.4.6.5 9 Chicchan 18 Muan. On the stela at Dos Pilas, the "starlight glyph" contains the main sign of the Emblem of Seibal,

thumb-up hand with grains
(AGT St 3, A3b)

name of ruler
(AGT St 3, B3)

Captor of
(AGT St 2, F5)

Kin Jaguar
(AGT St 2, F6)

Maya History

"starlight glyph" + Seibal Emblem
(DPL St 2, C1)

axe + *imix*
(DPL St 2, D2)

event
(AGT St 2, E2)

manikin head + T184.74
(AGT St 1, A13)

Captor of Ich-Ben Turtleshell
(AGT St 1, B13)

T12:II:370 + Petexbatun
Emblem Glyph
(AGT St 1, A14)

with the prefix *ti;* at Aguateca, it contains a scroll and the Seibal Emblem follows. The next clause begins with an *imix* compound with an axe prefix, which is often found in clauses which suggest conflict between towns and may indicate execution of prisoners (*imix* compound) ordered (*pati ?*) by the king (manikin head). This clause also includes an *u cab* (?) expression, the "heart" or "sacrifice" glyph, and shields. On the Aguateca stela, the passage is abbreviated and contains only the "axe and *imix*" compound and the expression "T586; manikin head" (by order of the king?). The Dos Pilas text is incomplete, but the text on Aguateca Stela 2 continues, relating an event that took place six days later. The passage includes two statements, similar (except for the names involved) to statements on Stela 3 at Piedras Negras that link the name of a woman with that of a man, shortly before the date that Berlin has proposed for her marriage. I am not prepared to assign a definite interpretation to these statements, for they involve the broader problem of the role of women in the conduct of political affairs, which seems to have been of crucial importance. The question of marriage alliances throughout the Maya area and the clauses associated needs more detailed attention and will not be discussed here. There is an indication, however, that it was by virtue of a marriage of a chief of Seibal to a royal princess from Petexbatun that Seibal began to erect stelae for the first time. This suggests that the coherence of the Maya area as a nation was achieved by a series of such marriage alliances, a point that has not been covered adequately here, but one that invites further investigation.

Another puzzling feature of these texts is the repeated reference to a Kin Jaguar. In one statement, the Cloud Lord of Aguateca seems to be named the Captor of Kin Jaguar, but Kin Jaguar is also mentioned on the funerary lintel of Ruler B, Dark Sky of Tikal, though this reference may be posthumous.

Aguateca Stela 1 (9.15.10.0.0) may record the death of the Captor of Kin Jaguar in 9.15.9.16.11, and a new ruler took office in 9.15.9.17.17, one month and six days later. He is known as Captor of Ich-Ben Turtleshell; T12:II:570(109): 102 as Thompson transcribes it. I see no element corresponding to 109. The "bone" element, 570, may conceivably be read as *baac* (bone), and the prefix as *ah*. *Ah baac* can mean "son," and what may be implied here is that the Captor of Turtleshell was of the second generation of Aguateca rulers. The next ruler has the designation Ah III Baac. Captor of Turtleshell's name is preceded by the manikin head with the postfix T184.74, and is associated with the Petexbatun Emblem.

The expression "Captor of Ich-Ben Turtleshell" suggests that the second ruler had captured (or won a battle with?) a chief from Piedras Negras, for the turtleshell is the Emblem of that town, and this is in a measure confirmed by the mortuary motif of Stela 10 at Piedras Negras, probably erected in 9.15.10.0.0.

Stela 4 is in fragments, and its text is badly eroded. Its central portion was never turned, and only a rough sketch is presented in Graham's report (1967). Except that it presents a warrior holding a spear and a shield, we know very little about it. Normally, it would have been the third stela erected here, but Stelae 2 and 1 record the two hotuns that follow the erection of the central Stela 3. Since Stelae 1 and 2 name different individuals, it is possible that Stela 4 was paired with Stela 2. The date of Stela 5 is, unfortunately, also uncertain. Since the publication of Graham's report on Aguateca, more fragments have been fitted to this monument, and it now shows the upper half of a figure, dressed in the manner of the figure on Stela 1, with a short cape composed of three flaps, decorated on the shoulders with the "mat symbol." The pose of the figure is very much like that on Stela 1, but the headdress is more elaborately designed and the detail more intricate and delicately rendered. These qualities of the carving suggest that the stela is later than Stela 1 and that the date 9.13.0.0.0, which is followed here by the "divination" glyph, is too early. The first glyph of the inscription is still missing, but the second is partially preserved and records the month Zotz', with a broad bar before it. If this is the date of dedication, it could be the date 9.16.5.0.0 8 Ahau 8 Zotz'. The reading is to some degree corroborated by a Secondary Series of 15 tuns, 0, 1 or 2 uinals, and an unknown number of days. If we read this number as 15.0.3, it brings us back to the inauguration date of the second ruler: 9.15.9.17.17. The name preceding this series contains the turtleshell and the bone glyph, though the glyph immediately preceding is not the captor glyph, but a sky compound with the suffix T184.74 that elsewhere is attached to the manikin title of the ruler. However, several signs are missing here, and we do not know exactly how the name was written. Three glyph-blocks are missing after the Secondary Series, and then there is a "toothache glyph," followed by a "count (forward?)" glyph. Since the next glyphs we see record Katun 13, there must be a lower panel with a Secondary Series now missing. After the divination glyph for Katun 13, there is a glyph often seen at Yaxchilan: T516b, which usually occurs on lintels depicting the king with another, smaller individual, often a woman with a bundle. The inscription ends with an unfamiliar name: a sky title, the manikin head, captor of (unknown glyph) 4 *ben-ich* katun, and a destroyed Emblem. It is possible that this reference is to something that happened many years earlier.

T516b
(AGT St 5, D3)

Stela 6, which stands in front of an adjacent building, appears to duplicate the motif on Stela 4, showing the ruler as a warrior with a barbed spear. The inscription on this monument is difficult to make out, though some of the numbers can be read, and Graham's reading of them can be provisionally accepted. The text begins with a birth on 9.15.16.12.1 12 Imix 14 Cumku and a Distance Number of more than 1 katun. The dates that follow are somewhat dubious, but there is no question of the record of 9.17.0.0.0, which is probably the date of dedication, though the inscription continues with at least one

Paw Jaguar
(SBL HS I, IXpBI)

Parrot-feather Jaguar
(SBL HS I, IVE2)

hand scattering
(SBL HS I, IIFIa)

manik hand
(SBL HS I, IIIC2a)

other date. If this stela pictures the successor of the Captor of Turtleshell, he must have acceded to power between 9.16.0.0.0 and 9.17.0.0.0.

We turn now to the site of Seibal, whose foundation or conquest by Aguateca was recorded at that site in 9.15.4.6.4. There are no records of this event in Seibal, but the text of its hieroglyphic stairway, the earliest text we have from the site, covers the period 9.15.13.13.0 to 9.16.0.0.0, starting almost ten years later, in the fourth tun of the rule of the second Aguateca king, Captor of Turtleshell. The text, unfortunately, is incomplete, and the order of reading uncertain, since some fragments of the stairway are missing and others may have been moved from their original position. Like the earlier stairway at Dos Pilas, which recorded a name and Emblem of a personage from Tikal, this stairway names the current ruler of Aguateca at least three times, and twice more refers to a manikin title, which may belong to the same king or to a king of Tikal. Two Seibal rulers are mentioned, the first designated as Paw Jaguar, the second as Parrot-feather Jaguar, who is first named with the date 9.15.16.7.17.

Hand-scattering glyphs (divination?) are associated here with the ruler of Aguateca in connection with the date 9.15.14.17.18 and probably also with the record of 9.15.15.0.0. The Paw Jaguar of Seibal, on the other hand, is associated with the normal compound of the *manik* hand sign, which follows his name and is in turn followed by the manikin title once with the interpolation of a mask resembling the God I mask of Palenque. Since the *manik* hand elsewhere stands between two names, the manikin glyph here probably refers either to the Aguateca ruler or to the ruler of Tikal.

It is interesting to note that in the case of Parrot-feather Jaguar, the *manik* hand changes its affixes and stands *before* his name with a glyph that resembles a capture glyph and *kan* cross. However, the interrupted passage seems to end with the Emblem of Aguateca, just before a Secondary Series of 3.10.3, which links the date of the event, 6 Caban 10 Kankin (9.15.16.7.17) to the end of Katun 16.

The question naturally arises whether these Seibal Jaguars were relatives of the Jaguars of Yaxchilan, who were rewarded by the Aguateca-Tikal alliance for their aid by being installed at Seibal as semi-independent lords, or whether the Jaguar names were titles that were used in lieu of the manikin glyphs implying a lower-than-kingly status, just as the vulture, a military title, seems to have been used elsewhere. One would hesitate to suggest something in the nature of an incipient feudalism that was arising at this time, and was responsible for the erection of stelae at many minor sites that formerly did not erect monuments. However, with the sphere of Tikal influence apparently extending much farther south than formerly, it is not incredible that the power that could not be maintained for long at such a distance could be in some measure preserved by granting a considerable degree of independence, and high titles of rulership, to certain lords in exchange for continued fealty.

And in this respect it is interesting to note that at the very end of the stairway inscription, the count of the dates leaps back to 8.18.19.8.7 2 Manik o Mol, cites the end of Katun 19, and apparently returns to the date associated with Parrot-feather Jaguar: 9.15.16.7.17. The date 8.19.0.0.0 is near the date when Stormy Sky must have restored the ancient regime at Tikal. One wonders what act of service to the ancient king of Tikal performed by their ancestors was the basis of these later Jaguars' claim to the rulership of their province. We are reminded that early Jaguar names at Yaxchilan also go far back into the past. Stela 6, dated 9.17.0.0.0, is actually not a stela but a panel, part of an assemblage of a stairway that will be described in Chapter 11.

At this time Seibal, though an important town, was probably not entirely independent of the rulership at Aguateca and Dos Pilas, which, in turn, may have been either subject to Tikal, or allied with it by family ties. The question whether Jaguar names imply a military title, an honorary title, or a family connection is germane to the understanding of the social organization of the ancient Maya. It deserves more serious attention than has been afforded it.

At Altar de Sacrificios, we have only Stela 15 in this interval of time. J. A. Graham (1972) reads its dates as 9.16.18.15.1 and 9.17.0.0.0, but no part of the noncalendrical text survives. Other, lesser sites begin to erect monuments toward the end of this period also.

To the east of the Petexbatun area, the site of Machaquila, located on a tributary of the Pasión, whose first stela may have been erected as early as 9.14.0.0.0, erected an all-glyphic stela in 9.15.10.0.0, Stela 11. The meaning of its texts is not entirely clear to me. It contains two statements. The first concerns a mask introduced by an *etz'nab* compound, possibly the name of an earlier ruler. The second, beginning with a "jog" glyph, contains a shell glyph, which may denote an offspring or son referring to a woman. This passage ends with a name consisting of the same mask as the first, with a flaming-sun prefix followed by the Emblem Glyph of Machaquila. These may be the names of two consecutive kings of Machaquila, or the first reference may be to a more ancient ancestor.

Stela 12 in this group is badly weathered, but apparently depicts a figure holding a serpent-bar with a single head, with a manikin in its jaws. The date is damaged, but probably correctly read by I. Graham as 1 Ahau 3 Zip, lahuntun (9.16.10.0.0). Graham suggests the date 4 Ahau 13 Yax (9.15.0.0.0) for the date of Stela 10 in this group, but the "dancing" pose of the figure, as well as its stylistic similarities to Stela 17, make me inclined to give it a somewhat later date, and both monuments will be discussed in Chapter 11.

North of the Petexbatun area, and west of Lake Peten, the site of Itzimte began to erect stelae in 9.15.0.0.0. Sixteen stelae are reported, but only five of these appear to have been sculptured. Morley (1937–1938:3:377–399) places all the carved stelae in the interval 9.15.0.0.0–9.16.0.0.0, but they are a motley lot, so different from one

etz'nab + mask
(MQL St 11, B4b)

flaming sun + mask
(MQL St 11, B6a)

Machaquila Emblem Glyph
(MQL St 11, B6b)

another that it seems hardly possible that they were carved within twenty years. Stela 5 (9.15.0.0.0) is a conventionally designed monument, with the figure holding a scepter and shield. Stela 1, to which Morley has assigned the date 9.15.5.0.0, is, on the other hand, of such peculiar design that it is difficult to place it. It is a profile figure, holding a high triplicate staff ending in a serpent head and flint point. The shield, worn on the left arm, has been cut into and is not symmetrical, suggesting that there was some attempt to recarve the figure or to mutilate it. The very elaborate earplug and the contrasting single string of beads worn around the neck is only one of the many incongruities in this design. The monument does not pair well with any of the other monuments with which it is associated. There is no record of the face of Stela 2, which was apparently completely eroded. Morley's reading of the Initial Series on the side as 9.15.10.0.0 may be correct. The date 9.16.0.0.0 for Stela 3 is also acceptable. This is a dancing figure, a motif that began to be popular at this time, especially in lesser sites. The figure is wearing sandals, as has been noted on Stelae 10 and 17 at Machaquila. Stela 4, which Morley believed to have been erected in 9.15.15.0.0, is, in my opinion, much later. Its figure has the same stocky proportions as that on Stela 3, but unlike the forms of Stela 3, the forms here are angular and the relief is flat. A telling detail is the flat, rectangular earplug. I would put this monument not earlier than 9.17.10.0.0, and perhaps even later. There are some incised glyphs on the background, but they cannot be clearly made out.

Of the thirteen stelae reported from La Florida, only two have legible texts, and these are very brief. La Florida is located on the Río San Pedro, a possible route to the gulf for the cities of central Peten, and one that was later used by colonial *entradas* en route to Tayasal. Stela 9 records the date 4 Ahau 13 Yax (9.15.0.0.0) and appropriately shows the figure in the grain-scattering pose of divination. The figure wears a long robe and over it a sort of sheath or apron that hangs from the shoulders to below the knees. The sex of the figure, however, is ambiguous. A human head prefix at A6 and a bundle at the feet of the figure suggests that it is a woman, but women are not usually shown in the pose of divination, and at Naranjo, sheaths of this kind are worn by warriors. The figure on Stela 11 at Naranjo, moreover, also wears a long robe under a sheath, and carries a staff and shield. The brief inscription gives no indication that the Naranjo figure is a woman, and the artificial beard under the chin suggests a male figure. Thus we are left with some uncertainty as to the sex of the La Florida figure, for men apparently also wore long robes on certain occasions. The designs of the sheath worn by the La Florida figure is of some interest, for its border and the mat designs within it recall the design of the short capes worn at Aguateca at about this time. Stela 7, conventionally designed, shows a male masked figure holding a manikin scepter and records 7 Ahau 18 Pop (9.16.15.0.0). Other designs and texts at La Florida are in very

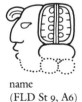

name
(FLD St 9, A6)

poor condition. Stela 1, showing a figure holding a long serpent-bar diagonally could be quite early, though the very high cuff on the left wrist tends to belie this judgment. Stela 10 is of some interest because it is an all-glyphic monument with the inscription arranged in a mat pattern, somewhat in the manner of Copan Stela J and the back of Quirigua Stela H.

Farther down the Río San Pedro, near its confluence with the Usumacinta, is the site of Moral. Here, a single stela was found, probably dating from 9.16.5.0.0. This stela was difficult to photograph because its corners are rounded, and the record of the inscription is not very good. It is carved on both faces, the front with a figure holding a manikin scepter and two prisoners at his feet, the back with a scene of capture. The Initial Series on the back reads 9.16.5.0.0 8 Ahau 8 Zotz', the fifth tun, "divination." Following glyphs are not clear, but there seems to be a Secondary Series that leads back to a date which E. Wyllys Andrews IV reads as 6 Ahau (9.14.0.0.0), but which I think is 8 Ahau 8 Uo (9.13.0.0.0). The date of the capture is recorded on the left side of the monument, but it is not clear. Andrews (1943:59) reads it as 12 Ahau 13 Ceh (9.16.0.7.0), but the month looks more like Ch'en or Yax (9.16.8.6.0 or 9.15.8.2.0). On the right side of the monument is recorded the end of Katun 16: 2 Ahau 13 Zec. There are at least two other dates on this monument. One is 12 Manik, its month position obscured by a break in the monument. The other is 12 or 13 (?) 19 (Mac?), on the right side of the monument, which Andrews seems to have missed.

Calakmul at this time was still erecting stelae, though not in such great numbers as before. Stelae 25, 26, and 27 stand back of Mound 6, west of the "astronomical" group, and facing the main acropolis. They were all probably carved on all four sides, but Stela 25 was not turned by the Ruppert and Dennison (1943) expedition, and Stela 26 was broken into pieces and not reassembled at that time. Both faces of Stela 27 are reported to be in bad condition. Fortunately the dates 9.15.5.0.0 on the central Stela 26 and 9.15.10.0.0 on the two others survived. Stelae 59 and 60, facing this group across the court, apparently also record 9.15.10.0.0, though they appear to have been in very bad shape and give us no further information.

Stelae 61 and 62 stand on a landing leading to a small structure built on the edge of the first terrace of the acropolis, which they face. Only the butt of Stela 61 was noted, but it is probably of the same date as Stela 62, which is reasonably well preserved, and which appears to record the katun end 9.16.0.0.0. The inscriptions on the sides, however, are badly eroded. The front shows an elaborately garbed figure standing stiffly on a narrow band of angular *caban* signs. He wears a mask in front of his eyes, and a chin strap that projects far to the front, and his costume is overburdened with large and elaborate ornaments. He holds a scepter and a bag in his left hand, which is the direction he is facing, and on his right arm supports an unusually small three-part staff with angular projections, from behind which project water lilies on which fish are nibbling. The design is elaborate, but is executed in flatter relief and with less grace than the stelae of the preceding period, which were apparently made of better stone.

Stelae 57 and 58 both record Katun 9.17.0.0.0. They stand in front of Structure XIII, on the lower terrace of the acropolis. Presumably they are badly eroded, for Dennison does not illustrate them. No stelae marking the lahuntuns of Katuns 16 and 17 are known.

It is evident that both the quality and the quantity of monuments were falling off at this time at Calakmul. On the other hand, though sites to the south of Calakmul had been erecting monuments for some time, the geographical range of stelae seems to have been expanding to the north at this time. Few of the monuments can be dated, of course, with any certainty, but the incidence of monuments in small northern sites appears to be increasing. Oxpemul is the northernmost site that has an early "astronomical" arrangement of buildings, somewhat modified and probably later than the early group at Uaxactun. As at Calakmul, the stelae associated with this group are all Late Classic and probably later than the first constructions. Nineteen carved stelae are reported from this site, but most of them are in poor condition and there are no good records of the texts. Eleven of these monuments are dated by Morley (1937–1938:4:370) within this period.

Stelae 12 and 17 (9.15.0.0.0) were mentioned in Chapter 9. Their provincial style is very evident. Stelae 9 and 10, two of the five monuments aligned in front of the "astronomical" group, are quite different. Morley dates Stela 10 in 10.0.0.0.0 and Stela 9 in 9.16.0.0.0. Both are masked figures, and entirely different in style from the earlier monuments. The figure on Stela 9 stands on a coiled serpent and holds in his right hand a huge battle-axe. The detail is simple and large scale, and only two small feathers adorn the headdress. I should have guessed a later date for this monument than Morley proposes, but perhaps it is the unusual motif that accounts for the lack of royal accoutrement and fine detail. Stela 10 is in many ways similar, but unfortunately the others are too badly eroded to show whether this assemblage was all part of one operation. Stelae 11 and 13, dated 9.15.10.0.0 by Morley, are not illustrated in Ruppert and Dennison's report (1943).

At Yaxchilan, next to Shield Jaguar's Structure 23, which features ritual scenes, such as autosacrifice and invocation of an ancestral figure, is a small building, Structure 24, set at right angles to it and facing east. Its three lintels, 27, 59, and 28, are carved only with texts on their front edges, and they record deaths, presumably of the immediate family members of Shield Jaguar. The first death recorded is that of a queen on 6 Chicchan 8 Yax (9.13.13.12.5). If the 6-katun *batab* notation that follows refers to her age, she would have been over a hundred years old when she died. Possibly, however, this reference is the duration of her lineage, for the *batab* glyph is followed by

6-katun *batab*
(YAX L 27, D1)

four other head glyphs of women, the first of which is shown over a shield. A Secondary Series—1.17.5.9—leads to 6 Ix 12 Yaxkin (9.15.10.17.14), the death of Shield Jaguar. Another series, 6.16.0, leads to 3 Ix 17 Zip (9.15.17.15.14). The name here is not altogether clear, however, though its final glyph, a birdlike mask, is seen with other names. Counting 1.17.9 forward we come to another death on 10 Akbal 16 Uo (9.15.19.15.3), the death of a woman whose name ends with the God C glyph, and who is apparently the woman shown in the sky with Shield Jaguar on Stela 11. One other death is recorded 4.9.14 later on 6 Caban 10 Zac (9.16.4.6.17), again the death of a woman, probably the woman of the bloodletting scene on Lintel 24. At this time, Bird Jaguar had already been ruling for more than three years. Another lintel (56), which Ian Graham (1979:121) ascribes to Structure 11 on the river's edge, may also refer to this woman. Its impossible Initial Series, 9.15.6.19.1 7 Imix 19 Zip, was corrected by Charles P. Bowditch (1903:20−28) and Morley (1937−1938:2:497−500) to 9.15.6.13.1 but, of course, remains in question. The event recorded, which begins with a compound of the fire-glyph, appears to be of a ritual nature.

The famed warrior Shield Jaguar, king of Yaxchilan, was now over eighty years old, and his name is associated with records of 5 *ben-ich* katun. The discrepancies that seem to exist between the records on his stelae and those on the steps and lintels of Structure 44, which were made after 9.15.0.0.0, I have not been able to reconcile completely. Even if we accept J. E. S. Thompson's (1946) date for the capture of Chuen as 9.14.17.15.11, we must conclude that Shield Jaguar's later years were spent in diplomacy rather than in conquest. After his death we find his name mentioned at Sacul in central Peten, at Palenque, and at Tikal. Between his death on 9.15.10.17.14 6 Ix 12 Yaxkin, recorded on Stela 12 and Lintel 27 at Yaxchilan, and the accession of Bird Jaguar on 9.16.1.0.0 11 Ahau 8 Zec, there is an interval of close to ten years. In an earlier article I suggested that there may have been some question about Bird Jaguar's right of succession (Proskouriakoff 1964:180), but since I have been unable to find any record of Shield Jaguar's accession, I now believe that the lady whose name contains the God C glyph, and whose portrait appears in the sky with that of Shield Jaguar on Stela 11, was the true hereditary monarch, and that Bird Jaguar could accede to kingship only after her death on 9.15.19.15.3.

Bird Jaguar was born when Shield Jaguar must have been at least sixty years old, and their relation to each other is problematical. He may have been the son-in-law of the God C lady and the maternal grandson of an earlier Bird Jaguar, for whom he was named. It is a curious coincidence that the divination (819-day period) date of his birth on 9.13.17.12.10 8 Oc (13 Yax), recorded on Lintel 30 (Structure 10), was 1 Ben 1 Ch'en (9.13.16.10.13), which is the second katun anniversary of the date of Stela 6, in turn said to be the second katun anniversary of the accession of the earlier Bird Jaguar, the predeces-

Lady Shield
(YAX L 27, C2)

name of woman who died on
6 Caban 10 Zac
(YAX L 28, X2)

fire glyph compound
(YAX L 56, H1)

Lady Skull
(YAX St 11, A'3)

Lady "God C"
(YAX St 11, A'4)

Bird Jaguar
(YAX L 30, G2)

sor of somewhat doubtful authenticity of Shield Jaguar. Of the thirty-one stelae reported from Yaxchilan, only three furnish us with any significant information about the reign of the great Bird Jaguar, though at least two others can be attributed to him. Stelae 11 and 12, which stood in front of Structure 40, next to Structure 41 on the highest hill of the town, record Shield Jaguar's death and the events that preceded the accession of Bird Jaguar.

The front of Stela 11 pictures two persons apparently of comparable rank, the figure on the right somewhat more dominant. They are holding similar staffs of distinctive and intricate designs, trimmed at the top with feathers and sinuous elements projecting above. At the foot of the lesser figure is inscribed the date 12 Cib 19 Yaxkin (9.15.9.17.16). With one exception, El Cayo Lintel 1, this motif is peculiar to Yaxchilan, where there are five examples of it, and in every case the date associated with it falls on the last day of Yaxkin or on the first day of Mol. Although the end of Yaxkin is recorded elsewhere, there is no evidence that at other sites any special attention was focused on this time of the year. Diego de Landa, however, describes a ritual in the month of Mol "in honor of all the gods" celebrated in Yucatan, for which preparations were made in the month of Yaxkin (Tozzer 1941:158–159). Although the Long Count position of most such dates at Yaxchilan is not given, all but one are surely in the lifetime of Bird Jaguar and therefore can be given precise dates. The one exception is the date on Stela 16, to which Morley gives an earlier date, but which I believe can be no earlier than Bird Jaguar's reign. It may interest some scholars that all these dates can fall within six days of the summer solstice:

> Stela 11: 12 Cib 19 Yaxkin 9.15.9.17.16—June 26, A.D. 741
> Structure 13, Lintel 33: 5 Cimi 19 Yaxkin 9.15.16.1.6?—June 25, A.D. 747*
> Stela 16: 13 Chuen 19 Yaxkin 9.16.17.6.11?—June 19, A.D. 768
> Structure 2, Lintel 9: 1 Eb 0 Mol 9.16.17.6.12—June 20, A.D. 768
> Structure 13, Lintel 50: No date
> El Cayo, Lintel 1: No date

> *In a former article (1964) I read this date as 9.16.16.1.6, which is incorrect.

I am reluctant to stress the possible association with the solstice, but a seasonal rite certainly seems to be indicated. The rains begin in June, and their postponement could spell a major disaster for the community. On the other hand, excessive rains may cause a dangerous runoff from the hills that could require recourse to supernatural intervention. The double portrait, suggesting an exchange of staffs, however, is shown only on Stela 11 and on Lintel 9, and probably both fall near the end of a reign.

Perhaps more significant is the fact that the date on Stela 11,

12 Cib 19 Yaxkin, is the third katun anniversary of the accession of a ruler at Tikal in 9.12.9.17.16, and on 5 Cib 14 Zotz', after a period of disturbances, and that this anniversary is associated with the name of Shield Jaguar, a contemporary of the Tikal king, who was no longer living. Possibly the descendant who bears his name is here impersonating him.

A row of glyphs across the top of the scene record the date 9 Ahau 18 Xul (9.15.15.0.0). The statement is damaged and difficult to read, and although there appears to be a record of a *ben-ich* katun, neither its number nor the name referred to is clear. A central vertical row of glyphs in two panels begins with the *u caban* glyph and refers to Bird Jaguar. Below the scene is a large panel, with the record of Bird Jaguar's accession on 9.16.1.0.0 11 Ahau 8 Zec. The text ends with references to Lady "God C" and to Shield Jaguar, whom Bird Jaguar succeeded.

On the back of the stela is depicted an earlier scene, in which Bird Jaguar wears a mask and holds a manikin scepter before three kneeling captives. The mask appears to signify that he is not acting in his own right, since he is not yet king, but in the name of the couple shown in the sky above him. The date is 9.15.19.1.1. Not long before, he had been in Piedras Negras (see below, p. 124), and the prisoners may be hostages taken when he was there, and portrayed on Piedras Negras Lintel 3 after he had returned. On 10 Akbal 16 Uo (9.15.19.15.3), as recorded on Lintel 28, Structure 24, the woman who is shown in the sky with Shield Jaguar died, and soon after that Bird Jaguar succeeded to the throne of Yaxchilan.

The accession of Bird Jaguar on 9.16.1.0.0 11 Ahau 8 Zec is recorded on Stelae 11 and 12, and on Lintels 1 and 30–31. The four statements, however, are by no means identical. On Stela 11, the accession is indicated by the "toothache" expression and the normal affix cluster, but between the two is inserted a vulture glyph, perhaps referring to the king's former military career. On Lintels 30 and 31, the "toothache" element is followed by an eroded form, which may be a personified affix cluster, but is not clear. On Stela 12, the clause begins with a seating glyph and the affix cluster, but the name does not follow immediately and consists of two separate characters with a bat substituted for the bird element (Flying Jaguar?). The intervening glyphs include a "claw-crossed bands" expression and a title consisting of a sky glyph and scroll-eyed mask. Possibly this expression refers to the restoration of the original dynasty rather than to the person of the king himself. Identical forms appear with the name of Bird Jaguar on Lintel 21 and on Lintel 33, where the king claims descent from the early settlers of Yaxchilan. The scroll-eyed mask at Tikal was used to refer to the ancient ruler Great Paw and probably indicates the founder of a dynasty. It may be relevant that both names on Lintel 21, the first a skull compound associated with the date 9.0.19.2.4, the second with the name of Bird Jaguar on the date 9.16.1.0.9, are introduced by the same compound of a bat glyph, with

"toothache glyph"
(YAX St 11, C4)

the coefficient 4, for this may account for the substitution of the bat for the bird in the statement of the seating of Bird Jaguar on Stela 12. The variety of bat glyphs and their uses is poorly understood and requires a special study. The back of Stela 13, the third monument in front of Structure 40, apparently depicts Shield Jaguar, but the front is eroded, and the arrangement suggests that it may be part of the Bird Jaguar series.

Another monument erected in Bird Jaguar's reign is Stela 1, which stands in the middle of the plaza on the shore of the river. Its Initial Series reads 9.11.10.0.?, but, as Morley (1937–1938: 2: 560–566) has shown, 9.16.10.0.0 is probably intended, since the Calendar Round dates that follow are 1 Ahau 3 Zip (9.16.10.0.0) and its 819-day period, (1 Oc) 18 Pop (9.16.8.16.10). Only the back of this monument and a very badly eroded inscription on the front are preserved. The back depicts a divination motif, and the figure shares a number of traits with the earlier Stela 6, which was a recarving of a still earlier monument. It is interesting to note that Stela 1, carved in apparent imitation of Stela 6, erroneously incorporates the katun number of that monument. It seems that the carvers of this inscription were thoroughly confused by their instructions.

Although neither Stela 3 nor Stela 4 can be given a final date with any certainty, the style of both suggests that they belong in the period of Bird Jaguar's reign. Both present the king standing between two female figures, and both show the static composition and the delicate detail characteristic of the time. Both monuments were

vulture
(YAX St 11, D4)

affix cluster
(YAX St 11, E1)

seating
(YAX St 12, C2)

affix cluster
(YAX St 12, D2)

Bat
(YAX St 12 D4)

Jaguar
(YAX St 12 C5)

sky + scroll-eyed mask
(YAX St 12, D3)

early name: skull compound
(YAX L 21, B8)

4 + bat glyph
(YAX L 21, C6b)

found broken, and no legible date is recorded on the surviving part of Stela 3. On Stela 4 there is a damaged date: ? Akbal or Ben, 16 (?). Although the glyphs immediately preceding are gone, the presence of Glyph Z of the Lunar Series, which always appears at Yaxchilan with 819-day period notations, suggests that the date may be such a date, especially since the scene is one of divination. If this is so, and if the date pertains to a period ending, it could only be 1 Akbal 16 Kankin 9.17.4.15.3, the divination base for 9.17.5.0.0. However, Bird Jaguar would then have been sixty-six years old, and since his name is nowhere associated with more than 3 *ben-ich* katun, we cannot be certain that he was still living. On the other hand, Stela 3, on which his name is mentioned, may be of even later date, though here, too, the statement is not altogether clear. It appears to record the first katun anniversary of his rule, which would be 9.17.1.0.0, but instead of the usual statement of accession we have a compound of the vulture glyph, which might refer not to his kingship, but to his military command after the death of his predecessor, and since no date accompanies the statement, this may have been at any time after 9.16.10.0.0. Morley (1937–1938:2:569–573) suggested 9.16.10.0.0 for both monuments, which is very unlikely, but if the suggestion of 9.17.5.0.0 for the erection of Stela 4 is correct, 9.17.0.0.0 could be tentatively ascribed as the dedication date of Stela 3. Stela 9 is a very small monument found in front of the small pyramidal Structure 36. Its brief inscription mentions Bird Jaguar, probably the great Bird Jaguar, though its pose and the costume of its figure are so unusual that it is difficult to judge its date. Morley (1937–1938:2:426) reads the month position of its one Calendar Round date as 0 Mac, but a better reading might be 'completion of Mac" or 0 Kankin. In rare instances the tun sign can also be read as 5, so that 5 Mac is another possible reading.

Many sculptures of this period are in the form of lintels. A great deal of building must have been going on at Yaxchilan in this period of stability and relative peace. Lintels 15, 16 and 17 of Structure 21 duplicate the themes on the earlier Lintels 24, 25, and 26, which were carved in the reign of Shield Jaguar. On the central Lintel 16, Bird Jaguar, in battle dress, is shown with a seated bound figure holding a fan, his left hand raised to his mouth. The date is 6 Caban 5 Pop (9.16.0.13.17 ?) and records a capture. Lintel 15 shows an invocation scene comparable to that of the earlier Lintel 25: a woman kneeling before the image of an ancestor shown in the mouth of a serpent rising from the smoke of a burning sacrifice. The woman is identified as one who appears in other contexts with Bird Jaguar. She has the *kin*-on-pedestal (queen?) title, the name 6 Cauac, and is associated with the Emblem Glyph of Ik. The third lintel, Lintel 17, depicts the bloodletting rite performed in the presence of Bird Jaguar by another woman, whose name includes the day sign Ix. Although we do not yet know the signs which would reveal the relationship of these women to Bird Jaguar, the parallel motifs in Structures 21 and

Lady 6 Cauac
(YAX L 15, C2)

Lady of Ik Emblem site
(YAX L 15, C3)

Lady Ix
(YAX L 17, H)

lady of the conquered land?
(YAX L 24, G2a)

23 permit us to conclude that Lady 6 Cauac bears to Bird Jaguar the same relationship as does Lady "God C" to Shield Jaguar. Although this relationship is unknown, we might tentatively consider it as that of wife and husband.

The lady with the tattooed face shown with Shield Jaguar on Lintels 24 and 26 is more difficult to identify, since the inscription on the edge of Lintel 24 is missing. On the face of the lintel there may be a reference to her as "the lady of the conquered land," the glyph consisting of a hatchet over a *caban* sign. A similar reference occurs in the inscription on the edge of Lintel 26, where she is given also the *kin*-on-pedestal title, naming her as the "queen of the land(?)." Of course, the arbitrary translation of "queen" may be incorrect; possibly the *kin* title implies only that she belongs to the royal family. The name of the woman on Lintel 17 stands in a peculiar context which includes the sign, though not the Emblem, of Tikal, and a jaguar glyph. What the relationships of these two women are to their respective kings is problematical. I suspect, in each case, that they are of an older generation.

The problem of kinship and succession in ruling families is not yet solved, and Lintels 38, 39 and 40 of Structure 16, near the northwestern end of the riverside esplanade, are not helpful in this respect. The inscriptions on all three of these lintels begin with the fish-in-hand glyph, which appears to be related to mourning ceremonies and the invocation of ancestors. On all three lintels the sculptured motif presents a human figure in recumbent pose holding a serpent with heads at either end, from whose jaws emerge the busts of manikins. The figure on the central lintel is probably Bird Jaguar, but the position of the date 4 Imix 4 Mol is indeterminate, since it is not necessarily the date of the rite, but could refer to the ancestor addressed. In the right panel the name of Bird Jaguar is preceded by the eyeless mask which usually refers to persons deceased. With the figure of the woman on Lintel 38 we have two names: that of Lady "God C," who probably was Shield Jaguar's wife, and that of the woman 6 Cauac "from Ik?" who probably was the wife of Bird Jaguar. This appears to imply that Shield Jaguar's wife was the mother of Bird Jaguar's wife, but of course this is not a necessary conclusion. Unfortunately the names on the third lintel are not at all clear. The date appears to be 13 Ahau 18 Zip, but is also somewhat uncertain.

Perhaps the most interesting arrangement of buildings in Yaxchilan comprises three temples erected during Bird Jaguar's reign at some distance from one another on prominent foothills, overlooking the esplanade along the river: Structures 33, 42, and 1. Each of these temples has three carved lintels spanning the front doorways, and Structure 1 has, in addition, a lintel, 8, over an end doorway. On each of the ten lintels, Bird Jaguar appears with another person. Five of these persons are men, and five are women, but there are probably only three individual men shown. The figures on Lintels 6 and 8 in Structure 1 have identical names. Of the name on Lintel 42, only the last hieroglyph is intact, and the figure's identity is somewhat uncertain.

Although the three Yaxchilan temples are not arranged as compactly as the three temples, of the Cross, the Foliated Cross, and the Sun, at Palenque, they exhibit an intricate pattern of dates and motifs that relates them to one another. I have suggested elsewhere (Proskouriakoff 1964:189ff.) that Bird Jaguar was arranging marriages of members of the royal family. Here I would like to suggest that these arrangements involved either three matrilineal clans (see Proskouriakoff 1978), or, as suggested for Tikal by Philip C. Thompson (1982), two matrilineages and one patrilineage. The problem of royal succession and kinship relationships is probably not capable of categorical solution on the basis of our present knowledge, but there is a strong body of evidence that matrilineal descent played an important role in the system. The alternating names of the Shield and Bird Jaguars of Yaxchilan favor Thompson's suggestion of two matrilineages. If we assume that the succession was from father to son, then we might be tempted to interpret the Jaguar element of the name as denoting the patrilineage, and the prefixes as alternating matri-names. However, if the succession went to the father's sister's son, then the constant element could represent the matrilineage. Either case, however, involves unsubstantiated assumptions, and the problem remains for the present unresolved.

In the central Structure 33, the dates summarize the interval covered by the group as a unit. Lintel 1 records 11 Ahau 8 Zec 9.16.1.0.0, the date of the great Bird Jaguar's accession, though it is not so stated here. The king wears a high, elaborate headdress and holds a manikin scepter. Behind him stands a smaller figure of a woman, elaborately dressed and holding a bundle in her arms. Her name suggests that she is either a daughter or a granddaughter of the deceased Shield Jaguar. The fact that she stands behind the figure of Bird Jaguar may indicate that she is his daughter.

The central Lintel 2 records the hotun anniversary of the first date: 4 Ahau 3 Zotz' (9.16.6.0.0). Wearing the same garments as before, Bird Jaguar stands facing a smaller figure of a man identically attired. Bird Jaguar holds in his hands two cruciform wands with birds attached at the top, and a third wand of the same design is held by the smaller figure. These wands recall the crosses of Palenque temples. The name of the smaller figure includes the glyph T145.188, which appears in the name of Bird Jaguar's successor, whom I have called Shield Jaguar's Descendant. This glyph is rare and appears to be distinctive of his name, and although in this case the name of Shield Jaguar is omitted, I believe the reference is to the same individual. Following his name is the "spot" Emblem Glyph, which is one of the two emblems that occur with the name of Bird Jaguar. Possibly, the young man is being appointed the ruler of the dependency of Yaxchilan.

On Lintel 3 is recorded the hotun end 9.16.5.0.0 8 Ahau 8 Zotz'.

part of name of Shield Jaguar's Descendant (YAX L 2, J1)

Here Bird Jaguar wears an enormous scroll headdress, and his belt is the classic rigid belt adorned with three human heads, rather than the fitted belt he wears on the other two lintels. The figure facing him is similarly dressed, but wears on his head the more conventional mask headdress. Each figure holds a manikin scepter in the right hand. A notation of 3 katuns in the name of the lesser figure suggests that he is of the same generation as the Bird Jaguar himself, but I am uncertain of his identity. His name ends with the same hieroglyph as that of the man on the central lintel of Structure 42, and both of these figures wear a mustache, but the last glyph is normally not the identifying name, and on Lintel 42, only a part of the previous glyph is preserved, and it is suspiciously like the name of the captive of Bird Jaguar's "battle companion," shown on Lintels 5 and 8.

Lintel 42 is the central lintel of Structure 42, and depicts Bird Jaguar in essentially the same costume he wears on Lintels 1 and 2, though his headdress is not quite as elaborate. He holds a manikin scepter before the figure of a young man whose name is largely destroyed. The young man is equipped with a hatchet and shield. The date is 9.16.1.2.0 12 Ahau 8 Yaxkin. The same date appears on Lintel 5 of Structure 1, where Bird Jaguar is shown facing a woman holding a bundle. This lintel was clearly designed by a different artist. In some details, the costume of Bird Jaguar is different from that shown on Lintel 42, but in essentials, such as the high headdress and the fitted belt, it is the same. He is holding in his hands two wands, like those he holds on Lintel 2, but with double crossbars. If this is a motif connoting marriage arrangements, the question arises which of the two men is the bridegroom. I would suggest that it is the young man of Lintel 42, and that the bride is related in some way to the future king shown on Lintel 2.

The next date recorded is 8 Cimi 14 Mac (9.16.1.8.6) on Lintel 6 of Structure 1, and on Lintel 43 of Structure 42. On this day the king wears a jaguar headdress and a batlike mask on his belt. He holds a staff which supports a device of basketwork on which a manikin is seated. If this motif is concerned with marriage arrangements, however, it is only in a preliminary way. The lady Bird Jaguar visits on that day is Lady Ix, who was depicted in Structure 21 performing a blood sacrifice. On Lintel 43 she is shown holding a bowl with instruments of sacrifice. The young man shown on Lintel 6, the central lintel of Structure 1, holds a similar empty bowl, and both he and Bird Jaguar hold pointed instruments ending in claws, which no doubt also pertain to autosacrifice. The young man is here designated as the captor of a certain prisoner, although, if our reading of the dates is correct, this capture does not take place for over two years, on 7 Imix 14 Zec (9.16.4.1.1). It is recorded on Lintel 8, on which he and Bird Jaguar both take prisoners. On this lintel, Bird Jaguar wears a headdress with the goggle eyes of Tlaloc, and on the

captor of
(YAX L 8, B)

name of captive
(YAX L 8, C)

same day, wearing his battle costume, he is shown with a woman on Lintel 41. She is called Lady Ik and also appears with Bird Jaguar on Lintel 17 of Structure 21, in a scene of ancestral invocation. A significant feature of these encounters is that both women are shown standing to the right of Bird Jaguar, and the young man is shown on the left; normally, this arrangement is reversed.

It is unfortunate that Lintel 41 is only a fragment. I had formerly assumed that Lady Ik was Bird Jaguar's wife, but it is possible that she was his sister or daughter, and the bride of his battle companion. The inscription, however, gives us no hint, and appears to pertain to the victory, since it is followed by a "starlight glyph."

Only two days after Bird Jaguar's interview with Lady Ix and with the battle companion, he is shown with a woman in Structure 1, as depicted on Lintel 7. The date was 10 Lamat 16 Mac (9.16.1.8.8). The woman holds a bundle, and one might think that she is the bride of the battle companion, except for the fact that Bird Jaguar has changed his garments, and is now wearing the huge scroll headdress that he wore on Lintel 3, and is dressed in a similar fashion, with change only in details. Whether this woman was to be the wife of the battle companion or of the older man on Lintel 3 I cannot venture to guess.

Though no two texts seem to be exactly alike, one sign is prominent in all or most of them: T516. A variant in the form of a turtle head with dark spots in front of its eye, which Thompson lists under T743, I am confident is a variation with an analogous meaning. The sign occurs in different compounds but always has the suffix T130, which seems to be an integral part of it. On Lintels 1, 3, and 42, it is preceded by a hand glyph holding an *ahau* sign (T59 : 533 : 670), and this is preceded by a "jog" glyph. On Lintel 2, the "jog" glyph leads directly to the turtle variant of T516 prefixed also by *ti*. On Lintel 42 the formal T516 variant has the prefix T229, a common substitute for T12. Elsewhere it can take a verbal form with the addition of the lunar postfix. Such verbalization of nouns is not uncommon in Yucatec, as, for example, in the words *acan* and *acantah,* though I do not propose this as a specific reading.

The erection, at an earlier time, of pairs of stelae depicting a man and a woman seemed to connote an effort to consolidate provinces under a single dynastic rule. Here, the intention seems to be to integrate with an earlier dynastic system the intrusive line of Shield Jaguar and his descendants.

Three unusual carvings are associated with Structure 33. All may be earlier than the reign of Bird Jaguar, but none can be dated with certainty. One of these is the more-than-life-size statue found inside the building. It is a full-round representation of a seated dignitary with an inscription on the back, of which only a fraction remains legible. One can make out a Secondary Series, 7?.2.14, and a "forward count" glyph, but no dates remain. It is tempting, in view of the rarity of full-round sculpture here, to link the missing dates with the date 9.10.17.2.14 13 Ix 17 Muan on Monuments 6 and 8 of Tortuguero, where that date is followed by a "starlight glyph" and a reference to the death of a certain Jaguar. The statue may have been carved later, but could have been an ancestral portrait. A rare glyph, which appears to make reference to the ballgame, occurs both on the Tortuguero slab and on a buried terrace under the Yaxchilan temple.

Recently, the Mexican archaeologist Roberto García Moll excavated the lower part of a stalactite column that stood in front of Structure 33. It is incised (?) with a divination motif (Simpson 1972) and shows two male figures standing in profile, one slightly taller and more robust than the other, with a seated figure, probably of a woman, between them. The lesser of the two figures is performing a divination rite, and the woman, with a basket before her, cups her hands as if to receive the drops falling from the hands of the diviner. Interspersed among the drops are the signs *yax* (green) and *kan* (yellow), perhaps describing beads of jade and amber. There are columns of glyphs, possibly designating the actors in this scene, but if any dates were recorded, they would be on the missing upper portion of the column.

Thirteen carved panels were uncovered on steps beneath the temple. The first shows a seated figure, with a large ball and steps at the right margin. The next two seem to depict women holding serpents, as on mortuary motifs. The remainder depict ballplayers in action, large balls marked with a hieroglyph, and stepped panels representing the courts and containing inscriptions. These are badly eroded and for the most part illegible. Step VI may refer to Shield Jaguar, but its date is illegible. Steps VII and VIII are better preserved, seem to form a pair, and are of some interest.

On Step VII the stepped panel is on the left side. The inscription begins with a date 13 Manik 5 Pax, which is followed by a hieroglyph with the axe-comb prefix, elsewhere associated with war or conflict and perhaps here with contest. A Secondary Series, 5.19.0.17, leads to a day 9 Kan. The next glyph is either a "jog" compound or 12 Xul, but the correct month should be 12 Zec. There is another date, 1 Ahau 13 Xul, preceded by a long Secondary Series (3?.8.10.14.11), which, however, does not seem to lead to this date. I am at a loss to place either of these dates in time.

In the panel at the right, there is recorded an Initial Series, 9.15.13.6.9 3 Muluc 17 Mac, preceded by eight hieroglyphs with the coefficient 13, which appear to be names of periods. Whether we construe these periods as running concurrently or in sequence, if we take them to be written in the vigesimal system, the number would run into billions of years. This passage ends with the name of Bird Jaguar. In the inscription following the date we find a hieroglyph consisting of a stepped form and a circle, virtually a mirror image of the stepped form and ball on the opposite side of the panel, apparently a glyph for the game or for the court itself. In the center of the

axe-comb prefix
(YAX HS 2, VII, A2)

panel is a ballplayer in elaborate costume, and on the enormous ball is an upside-down figure with knees bent, suggesting a prone captive drawn on a whirling ball. Behind the ballplayer at the right are two fat little dwarfs, with star (or half-Venus) signs attached to their shoulders and tails behind. One is tempted to wonder if they are symbolic of comets, and if the long Distance Number is a prediction of a comet's return.

The next panel is of similar design, but reversed, the steps being at the right. The costume of the ballplayer is even more elaborate, with a creature (somewhat like a bat?) attached to his chest. The first date recorded is a day 9 Lamat 16 (Ch'en, Yax, or Ceh) and further we read: 7 Caban (?) completion of (Mol?) (o Ch'en?). The ball is similar to that on Step VII, and the glyph with the tumbling figure appears to record a name which ends with a ballcourt glyph, mentioned above, with a *ben-ich* prefix. This is an interesting text, but one that we are not yet prepared to unravel.

The chronology of Yaxchilan is complicated by the fact that most of our information comes from sculptured lintels with Calendar Round dates only and that arrangement of lintels in a single building often covers a span of more than a single reign. Shield Jaguar's name often occurs on lintels carved long after his death. Adjacent to Structure 10, with its all-glyphic Lintels 29, 30 and 31, which record the birth of Bird Jaguar and his accession, and apparently built on an extension of its platform, is Structure 13, with its central Lintel 32 portraying Shield Jaguar. Its other two lintels, 33 and 50, feature the staff motif mentioned earlier, their style suggesting that they were carved in Bird Jaguar's reign or even later. Lintel 32 is carved in a different style that seems much earlier. It could have been reset in this late building or copied from some earlier source. Its inscription refers to the fifth katun of Shield Jaguar and to his Lady "God C" or to a descendant of hers, possibly the girl pictured on Lintel 1 of Structure 33. The fact that her headdress consists of a mask with the Triadic Symbol of rulership suggests, however, that she is the older woman, who continued to rule for some years after the death of Shield Jaguar. She is shown holding a bundle in her arms, while Shield Jaguar holds a manikin scepter before her.

An identical motif, carved in a later style, occurs on Lintel 53 of Structure 55, and again the fifth katun of Shield Jaguar is mentioned. This structure is in the extreme southeastern section of the ceremonial center, and is probably much later than the buildings of the central group. Nevertheless, the dates as well as the motif on Lintels 32 and 53 appear to be identical, recording 7 Ben 16 Mac. Formerly (Proskouriakoff 1963; 1964) I read this date as 6 Ben, but Graham's drawing shows that to be incorrect. In view of the 5 *ben-ich* katun associated with the Shield Jaguar's name, the most reasonable Long Count position for this date is 9.15.18.7.13, though Shield Jaguar had died some seven years earlier. In view of the fact that we do not yet know the glyphs that signify family relationships, and in view of the

stepped form + circle
(YAX HS 2, VII, Q2)

name
(PSD L 1, B4)

moon sign
(PSD L 1, B5)

locations of both these buildings that suggest their late date, and relying also in part on the skull glyph with a feminine prefix that appears in both these inscriptions as well as in the name of the young girl portrayed on Lintel 1, I am inclined to suspect that Lintels 32 and 53 both document the ancestry of that young girl, referring to two of her grandparents. Lintel 52 of Structure 55 is dated 9.16.15.0.0, probably the contemporary date of the building, and this lintel depicts Bird Jaguar with his successor, Shield Jaguar's Descendant, both holding manikin scepters. Nine years earlier he is depicted on Lintel 2 of Structure 33, where he and Bird Jaguar hold the three bird-and-cross wands, which may stand for three royal lineages. On Lintel 52, we might assume that he has reached an age when he is eligible for rulership. The third lintel of Structure 55, Lintel 51, is badly eroded, but appears to represent a woman seated on a large mask and holding a serpent on her arms. This may be a posthumous representation of the "God C" woman, whose grandchildren (?) are pictured on the other two lintels here.

At least three lintels that come from the vicinity of Yaxchilan are now in foreign museums. A lintel in the Leyden Rijksmuseum voor Volkenkunde presents a portrait of Bird Jaguar in the act of divining before a lesser personage wearing a long cloak. This person's name ends with a moon-sign glyph that ends the name of Bird Jaguar's battle companion on Lintel 8. The date of the divination rite is 7 Ahau 18 Pop (9.16.15.0.0).

Another lintel, now in the Berlin Museum für Völkerkunde, shows Bird Jaguar with spear and shield before a bound captive. The costume of the king is here similar to that which he wears on the lintels in Temple 33, with a closely fitted belt and narrow apron. Behind the crouching captive is another standing figure in a high hat and a skirt made of an animal pelt. The date is not clear, but is probably 9 Etz'nab 11 Yaxkin (9.15.8.3.18?), roughly two years after Bird Jaguar's intervention in the succession of Piedras Negras kings (discussed below). The date is followed by a capture glyph, as one might expect. Ian Graham has shown that this lintel and the Leyden lintel probably come from La Pasadita, a small site near Yaxchilan (Simpson 1976).

The third lintel, now in the Museum of Modern Art in New York, belongs in the reign of Bird Jaguar's successor and is described in Chapter 11.

While Yaxchilan was enjoying a period of unprecedented prosperity, trouble was brewing at Piedras Negras. The last monument erected in the previous reign was Stela 8 (9.14.15.0.0). In 9.15.0.0.0, Stela 11 was erected on the terrace of Temple J-3, next to the stairway leading to the acropolis. It records the accession of a new ruler, whose names and dates, however, are more easily read on Altar 2, which is on the plaza below, centered on the great stairway. He was born on 9.13.9.14.15 7 Men 18 Kankin and was enthroned on 9.14.18.3.13 7 Ben 16 Kankin, when he was twenty-eight years old. On the sides of Stela 11 are depicted two men and a boy, doubtless the would-be successor to the king and his guardians or tutors. The next monument, Stela 9 (9.15.5.0.0) was probably centered on the stairway of Temple J-3, and shows the king as a warrior in battle dress, as does "Lintel" 5, a panel in the entrance of the temple. The long inscription on this panel is unfortunately all but destroyed. The next monument, Stela 10, apparently stood near Stela 11, and is of most unusual design, for it depicts a tomb, in the manner of that which is depicted on Lintel 3 of Temple 1 at Tikal. It shows a person seated on a hassock, with a huge jaguar standing behind him, stretching a front paw over his head. Although I once suggested that the jaguar may symbolize a military alliance, others have shown convincingly that this is a mortuary motif, which is here clearly indicated by the sky-bands in the base panel. Very little of the inscription remains, and I am unable to identify the deceased with any confidence, but in view of the simple garb of the figure and the fact that the death of rulers is not normally reported here, I am inclined to think that it is the heir to the throne, who has met with an untimely death. We have seen that at about this time Stela 1 at Aguateca describes a ruler of that town as Captor of Ich-Ben Turtleshell, and it is possible that the heir to the throne of Piedras Negras had been captured or killed by the monarch of Aguateca in some sort of confrontation between the two cities. On Stela 40, placed near the southwest end of the stairway to Temple J-3 of Piedras Negras in 9.15.15.0.0, the throne is shown empty. Behind it is the bust of a woman, holding what Morley called an "aspergillum," a scroll with feathers, held by women on accession monuments when a king is too young to rule, probably here the wife or mother of the deceased heir. Above her, kneeling on a canopy, is a prophet or diviner, scattering grains from his right hand. This figure has long been called "The Sower" under the misconception that he was planting corn, though everyone knows that corn is never sown (see Simpson 1972 for a detailed study of the "scattering gesture"). From the sky above descends a rope with attached knots and scrolls, which passes behind the woman's bust. References to "the rope" are made in several prophecies in the Books of Chilam Balam. In some cases it is associated with hanging, but the relevant passages, as translated by Ralph L. Roys (1933:82, 155) suggest merely communication or command: "The rope shall descend; the cord shall descend from Heaven. The word shall descend from Heaven." And again: "The rope shall descend. The cord shall descend. There comes from heaven the word of the true path." In the context of Stela 40, the rope seems to imply command from heaven concerning the royal succession. The weathering away of the inscription on the edges of Altar 2 leaves us uncertain as to what happened next.

After the erection of this altar, activities were shifted to the East Group. Here, two stelae were erected in front of Structure O-12, eight in front of Structure O-13, and fragments of one or two were

names of ruler
(PNG Alt 2, Support 2, A3–C1)

Piedras Negras Stela 40, upper half
of front: A scattering rite, carried out
in divination of succession? (Drawing
by Barbara Page.)

found in the plaza between the two buildings. Three altars were found in this group, so it probably remained the center of activity at least until 9.19.0.0.0. Most of the stelae were broken, scattered, and badly eroded. The destruction was probably ancient and deliberate, and must have occurred shortly after 9.19.0.0.0, perhaps when the site was invaded by a foreign group.

Morley assigns the date 9.16.5.0.0 to Stela 22, on the terrace of Structure O-12. It is very unusual to erect a stela in a new locale before the end of the reign, but Stela 22 gave no indication of having been an accession stela, and the circumstances were certainly unusual. The situation was explained many years later on "Lintels" (actually wall panels) 1 and 3 of Structure O-13. Lintel 1 is only a fragment, but on Lintel 3 a number of interesting facts are revealed. This lintel is without exception the most remarkable piece of sculpture produced by the Maya. The modulation of the relief ranges from delicate detail to the almost three-quarters round of the protagonists of the scene, with some elements actually undercut. The scene takes place in a throne room. The main figure, seated on the throne, leans to the left to address a council of seven individuals, seated on a step below the chamber. The head of the main figure is in the center of the composition, but the throne is displaced to the right, and the focus of the seated group, four facing right and three left, balances the displacement of the throne. Standing on the floor of the chamber at the extreme right is a compact group of four persons: a man, a woman, and two children, a boy and a girl. At the left are three men, apparently conversing with each other. Between this group and the back of the throne is an incised inscription, and on the right of the throne a briefer text in inset low relief. A raised curtain frames the scene at the top, and above it and on the sides is the main inscription. This inscription begins with the first katun anniversary of the accession of the king of Piedras Negras, 9.15.18.3.13. On this day a Jaguar from Yaxchilan is mentioned; perhaps he arrives by canoe? This much is reasonably clear; the rest is somewhat dubious, and the reconstruction offered here might be questioned. Two days later occurs an event designated by a compound of T516, a glyph that often occurs on Yaxchilan lintels when the ruler is shown with another person, and this is followed by a parrot glyph with a very unusual prefix resembling T226 or 227. A very similar expression occurs on Yaxchilan's Stela 11 in the scene where Bird Jaguar, masked, appears before three kneeling captives less than a year later (9.15.19.1.1). Who were these men? Were they captives to be sacrificed at the accession ceremonies of Bird Jaguar, who was not yet king, or were they aspirants to the throne of Piedras Negras, taken as hostages until the Jaguar could return to settle the dispute about the Piedras Negras dynastic succession?

At Yaxchilan, Bird Jaguar accedes to the throne in 9.16.1.0.0, arranges his family affairs, and apparently returns to Piedras Negras, where he is shown occupying the throne on Lintel 3. A "toothache

canoe verb
(PNG L 3, I2)

glyph" in the incised inscription next to the throne suggests that he was inaugurated on 9.16.6.9.16 5 Cib 19 Mac and that the council took place one month and three days later on 9.16.6.10.19 2 Cauac 2 Muan. His name is given here as Bat Jaguar, in the same way as it appears on Stela 12 at Yaxchilan, but the significance of this variation is unknown. Is this only another way of saying Flying Jaguar, or does it imply a relative or representative of his?

The former king of Piedras Negras was still living, but perhaps too ill to rule, and the council shown on Lintel 3 appears to have been called to name his successor. The three men on the left may have been aspirants to the office, possibly taken as hostages by Bird Jaguar, and depicted on Stela 11 at Yaxchilan. Be that as it may, the successor chosen seems to be the boy in the group at the right. The figures of this group are very badly damaged, and it is not altogether certain whether there were two children or one, but the outline of the broken portions seems to indicate a small figure in front of the standing man. Four glyphs under the feet of the man probably identify him, and perhaps also the boy. Among them are two animal glyphs that appear to indicate relationship, followed by the Emblem Glyph of Piedras Negras, suggesting that the man is a native of the city. Under the feet of the woman is the name of the former king of Tikal (Ruler A) and a compound of Glyph C. She evidently is a noblewoman from Tikal, possibly a relative of the king.

I assume it is their son who is chosen to be the next king of Piedras Negras and is shown on Stela 14, an accession stela erected in 9.16.10.0.0. The main inscription does not mention the second visit of the Yaxchilan king, but it may record the death of the legitimate king on 9.16.6.11.17, though the glyphs here are somewhat eroded. A date three days later may refer to the boy, his successor, and finally a long Secondary Series leads to a date that J.E.S. Thompson (1944b) reads as 9.17.11.6.1 12 Imix 19 Zip.

The boy-king was inaugurated on 9.16.6.17.1, as recorded on

animal; relationship?
(PNG L 3, S′1)

manik-hand name
(PNG L 3, T′1)

rodent; relationship?
(PNG L 3, S′2)

Piedras Negras Emblem Glyph
(PNG L 3, T′4)

Ruler A
(PNG L 3, V′1)

God C compound
(PNG L 3, W′2)

Stela 14, which is the last monument with an ascension motif, depicting the ruler elevated in a niche, that we know. However, subsequent monuments erected here are in very bad condition, and Stela 16, erected in 9.16.15.0.0, seems to record another accession (9.16.12.10.8). Although a rough sketch of the front of this monument made by Mary Butler (1931:171) suggests a standing figure, it is so weathered away that we cannot be sure, especially since the arrangement of the figures on the sides, two men and a boy, is virtually identical to that on Stela 11. It seems that the boy-king did not rule long, and that the old dynasty was reinstated.

The destruction of the monuments in this location makes the sequence difficult to follow. If Stela 13, broken into four pieces, but unusually well preserved on its face, was indeed erected on 9.17.0.0.0, it is stylistically ahead of its time, and is perhaps the work of the genius that later produced Lintel 3, the throne in Structure J-6, and Stelae 15 and 12. The theme, as on Stela 40, is again divination, this time, however, on the occasion of the end of the katun. Perhaps the previous link with the family of Tikal had initiated the custom of katun prophecies. The style, however, is innovative. It introduces a new naturalism in expression and a more mobile composition than was ever achieved at Tikal. The dress of the figure is relatively simple, but the great sweep of the plumes of his headdress and the sway of his body as he stretches forward his hand focus attention on the gesture. He holds no insignia but the bag, on which is inscribed "13 Ahau," the name of the katun. Stelae 17 and 18 probably also belong to this reign, and bring the count of hotuns to 9.17.10.0.0. In the next hotun another king is inaugurated, whose reign sees the culmination of sculptural virtuosity begun on Stela 13.

Returning to the inscription on Lintel 3, it is interesting to note that on the occasion of the anniversary of his accession, the name of the king of Piedras Negras is expressed in three glyphs. After that, only the last glyph of his name is used. We do not yet understand the structure of Maya names and designations of persons, or the significance of titles and honorifics that accompany personal names. I venture, however, to interpret tentatively an inscription at the site of Chinikiha that may refer to this king. Chinikiha is a little-known site at some distance from Piedras Negras to the northwest, on a tributary of the Usumacinta River. Although Maler (1901–1903: 1:10) describes it as a large site, the only monument known is the top of a throne or altar or sarcophagus, a slab carved with an inscription on the edge and inscribed with glyphs on the top. There is no photograph of the inscribed glyphs, and Maler's drawing does not allow of an easy reading of the dates. The carved inscription, however, contains the first glyph of the name of the Piedras Negras ruler, combined with an unknown prefix. The dates are incomplete, and the day of a Secondary Series is missing, but if we assume that the dates are within the lifetime of the king, we can reconstruct them as follows:

name of Piedras Negras ruler
(CNK Mon 1, 12)

7 Ahau 3 Kankin	(9.14.18. 3. 0)
+	1. 0
1 Ahau 3 Muan	(9.14.18. 4. 0)
+	1. 5.14. (16)
2 Cib (9 Zec)	(9.16. 4. 0. 16)

Stela 22 of Piedras Negras, which Morley (1937–1938: 3: 217–220) assigns to 9.16.5.0.0, offers us no help in this matter, but it is interesting to note that the first two dates enclose the date of the king's accession (9.14.18.3.13), and the last falls in the interval between the two visits of the Yaxchilan Jaguar to Piedras Negras. Only five days later (9.16.4.1.1), Bird Jaguar and his companion take captives (Yaxchilan, Lintel 8). Could his raids have reached as far as Chinikiha?

On the top of the throne (?) is an incised inscription, but it is known only from Maler's sketch. It has two seating expressions, but the dates are not clear.

A number of lintels and panels from the central region of the Usumacinta are now in museums and private collections. Since we do not know their exact locations and associations, they do not tell us very much about history, but occasionally testify to the presence of independent towns in the vicinity of better-known sites.

Dumbarton Oaks Relief Panel 1 (M. D. Coe and Benson 1966) records the birth of a ruler in 9.10.16.8.14, when the Series 2 king of Piedras Negras was about twenty-three years old. He was probably of the next generation, and could have been the king's son or nephew. Forty-one years later (9.12.17.13.1), three tuns after the accession of the next king of Piedras Negras (Series 3), his name is indirectly associated with the Piedras Negras Emblem—possibly a reference to his relationship with the king, who was fifteen years his junior. In 9.13.15.2.9, at the age of fifty-eight, he acceded to the throne of an unknown site, and lived until 9.15.1.6.3, dying at the age of eighty-four. Three years earlier (9.14.18.5.7) another accession seems to be recorded. Possibly, being over eighty then, he had stepped down from the throne in favor of his successor, or perhaps he was deposed by the new king of Piedras Negras, who had come to the throne of that city only thirty-four days earlier. The glyphs relating to the final date, 9.15.2.7.1, are illegible.

Another panel in the Dumbarton Oaks Bliss collection comes from a lintel of Kuna, in the vicinity of Lacanha. It appears to depict a mortuary motif, showing a bearded figure seated on a mask and holding a ceremonial bar that terminates not in serpent heads, but in manikin masks. The Initial Series, 9.15.15.0.0, is followed by a statement containing a quincunx glyph and a fist glyph, the first associated with burials, the second with deceased persons. The glyph that follows is a compound of comb and half-moon, then a jaguar head with a knot prefix, and possibly an Emblem. The quincunx, fist, and comb-moon glyphs are repeated elsewhere in the text. A Secondary Series leads back to 9.15.11.17.3 4 Akbal 16 Xul. An incised

name of ruler
(DO Sc Pan 1, C1)

panel records a birth on a day that Michael D. Coe reads 13 Men 18 Yaxkin, but that I suspect is 13 Chicchan 18 Yaxkin (9.15.12.0.5). The text is by no means clear, but it is interesting to note here the repeated use of the comb-moon glyph, which at Yaxchilan ends the name of a man who is depicted with Bird Jaguar on Lintels 3 and 42.

The site of Bonampak, in the Lacandon region, began to erect stelae about 9.17.0.0.0, but since most of its monuments were erected later, its discussion is relegated to Chapter 11. The date 9.17.0.0.0 was 13 Ahau, and the thirteenth katun after 9.4.0.0.0, when the Maya area expanded westward along the Usumacinta River. In 9.17.0.0.0 a number of sites on the eastern and southern frontiers of the central area begin their histories. Since the dedication dates of their monuments tend to be later, however, they will be dealt with in Chapter 11.

Copan, by 9.15.0.0.0, was at the peak of its creativity. Its Great Plaza had been laid out, the ballcourt had been rebuilt, earlier monuments relocated, and Stelae J, C, F, and 4 had been erected. Morley (1920) places Stelae C and 4 later, apparently on the basis of Spinden's stylistic judgment, but the texts of these monuments indicate earlier dates. Stelae A, H, and B were added in 9.15.0.0.0. Stelae A and H probably depict the king and his wife, though we have not yet identified glyphs that pertain to family relationships. On the back of Stela H, which depicts a woman, is the Triadic Symbol over a sun mask, which is the principal motif in the Temple of the Cross at Palenque. The symbol is often worn as a headdress by women at Yaxchilan, and at Palenque it appears with a change in matrilineage. The inscription on Stela H is brief. It begins with the date 4 Ahau 18 Muan (9.14.19.5.0), which occurs also on Stela A. Morley has noted that this date is 13.0 after the last prophetic date recorded on Stela C, and another addition of thirteen uinals would reach 4 Ahau 13 Yax (9.15.0.0.0), the katun date for all three monuments. Most of the glyphs that follow the 4 Ahau 18 Muan date on Stela H are badly damaged, but one can recognize the name of Eighteen Jog in the fifth glyph from the end. The last glyph is a *kankin*-like sign with a vague prefix and a double superfix, no doubt the *ben-ich* superfix of an Emblem. What makes this alien Emblem important is its resemblance to the Emblem Glyph of Quirigua, the central sign of which is also a *kankin*-like sign, but laid on its side. Earlier, this sign occurs at Copan, upright and with the *ben-ich* superfix on Stela F, without that superfix on Stela 6, and laid on its side on Stela I, a masked figure with the Triadic Symbol that begins a new dynasty (see Chapter 8).

In contrast to the text of Stela H, that of Stela A is long and complex. It begins with an Initial Series 9.14.19.8.0, 12 Ahau 18 Cumku, and then steps back three uinals to 4 Ahau 18 Muan, the date recorded on Stela H. The passage after the Initial Series and that after the 4 Ahau date both contain parrot or possibly turtle heads which are difficult to distinguish here. I can make nothing of the passage

quincunx glyph
(LAC L 1, D2)

fist glyph
(LAC L 1, C3)

Emblem Glyph?
(LAC L 1, D4)

Eighteen Jog
(CPN St H, B3b)

kankin variant
(CPN St H, B4b)

scroll and sun
(CPN St A, C9b)

Yax Dog?
(CPN St A, D9a)

Copan Emblem Glyph
(CPN St A, F4)

Tikal Emblem Glyph + unknown
Emblem Glyph
(CPN St A, E5–F5)

Palenque Emblem Glyph
(CPN St A, E6)

East + West
(CPN St A, E8–F8)

South + North
(CPN St A, E9–F9)

that follows the latter date, and can only remark that the skull and quincunx glyphs that it contains hardly seem appropriate to nuptial ceremonies, or to accession rites. Near the end of the inscription on the back, however, there is a "jog" glyph introducing a phrase that refers to Eighteen Jog, King of Copan. The first glyph after the 'jog" is a scroll-and-sun glyph, which I believe may stand for the high priest, whose name (Yax Dog?) shortly follows. This, conceivably, could refer to the coronation of the king. Next follows 4 Ahau 13 Yax, the end of Katun 15, but the 13 Ahau immediately after it is not identified since the last glyphs on the back are eroded.

On the opposite side from that of the Initial Series, the text begins with the sign for North, and after two unknown glyphs, by four sky glyphs, each with a coefficient of 4 and a prefix. These, in turn, are followed by four Emblem Glyphs: that of Copan, that of Tikal, an unknown one, which Marcus (1973) has suggested represents Calakmul, and finally the Emblem Glyph of Palenque. It is interesting to note that the sky glyph in the second place, corresponding to Tikal, is in the form of a *moan*-bird, and that the prefix of the last, corresponding to Palenque, is a deer foot. The main element of the glyph that follows the list of Emblem Glyphs appears to be that of a woman, though it is difficult to be sure. It is followed by a sky glyph that at Copan is often used as a title, and then by a *caban* variant with the same prefix. Since below the female (?) head there is a "death-eye" glyph (T575), I wonder if this expression is stating that the Emblems represent the matrilineages(?) of the nobility of the land. The text continues with the glyphs for East, West, South, and North, but the order of these world directions does not seem to correspond in any way to the order of the places mentioned. I have no suggestions to offer concerning the final glyphs of this inscription. Barthel (1968) has suggested that at this time the entire lowland region was organized into four divisions, or at least so conceived. He may be right, but I can find no confirmation of this elsewhere, and I rather think that Eighteen Jog was simply boasting here about his broad family connections or travels. The third glyph from the end of the text is the lahuntun glyph, for which I can offer no explanation. The last two are eroded.

At the end of the next hotun, on 9.15.5.0.0, Stela D was set up in the north end of the Great Plaza of Copan. The inscription on this monument is presented in full-figure glyphs, and the final glyphs are illegible. Normally, Copan monuments were erected at lahuntun intervals, so that the hotun date must celebrate a particular event, perhaps the completion and dedication of the Great Plaza. Judging by the bearded figure on the front, it represents a priest, wearing the mask of the Mexican god Xipe, associated with human sacrifice. The possibility that it is the funerary monument of the king, Eighteen Jog, or of his wife, cannot be altogether eliminated, though his name is associated with a later date at Quirigua. On the step back of Stela D is an inscription with two dates that Morley reads 9.14.16.11.8 1 Lamat 1 Zotz' and 9.15.17.0.0 1 Ahau 8 Xul. I would prefer to amend the second date to 9.15.4.15.0 2 Ahau 8 Xul, just three uinals before the date on Stela D.

There seems to be no stela at Copan that can be assigned either to 9.15.10.0.0 or to 9.16.0.0.0. For a possible explanation of this hiatus, we must turn to Quirigua, where the first stela was erected in Katun 9.16.0.0.0. However, there is a text on the upper surface of Altar Q at Copan, erected after 9.17.0.0.0, which probably refers to events that occurred soon after the death of Eighteen Jog, the ruler of Copan. It concerns certain "parrots" that seem to turn up in troubled times. We have encountered them in the Petexbatun region when the king of Tikal was resident there (see Chapter 8), and they are mentioned in the last inscription of Yaxchilan (Chapter 11). I have suggested that they may represent highland peoples who occasionally raided the lowland towns, but it is also possible that they were local armies attacking or rebelling against established powers. At Copan, parrots may be mentioned on Stela A, though their glyphs here are atypical and could represent the heads of turtles. On Altar Q, after the date 5 Caban 15 Yaxkin (9.15.6.16.17), we find a hand with its thumb up holding a manikin head followed by a compound of crossed torches and a *ben-ich* sign over a parrot head. After the next date, only three days later, the clause again contains the crossed torches and a different compound of the parrot glyph. A Secondary Series then leads to 9.15.7.6.13 and a long passage that I have not ventured to interpret, after which the text jumps to Katun 17.

Another reference to a "parrot" occurs on a small cylindrical monument, inappropriately called Stela 11. It pictures a bearded man holding a ceremonial bar without serpent heads, perhaps because he claims no celestial ancestors. He wears no headdress, but scrolls are attached to his head, a particularly large one projecting forward, like those one sees attached to the manikin helmets, usually signifying rulership. A single date, 8 Ahau, begins the text, and I suspect it may be the 8 Ahau (18 Yaxkin 9.15.6.17.0) of Altar Q. Eighteen Jog is named in the middle of the inscription and is followed by a glorified skull glyph, probably implying that he is recently deceased. There follows another glyph, a sign for West (?), a parrot glyph and the Emblem Glyph of Copan, apparently signifying that the parrots were now in control of the government of Copan. One may well wonder if the huge macaw heads above the figure on Stela B have

hand + manikin head
(CPN Alt Q, A2)

torches
(CPN Alt Q, B2)

ben-ich parrot
(CPN Alt Q, A3)

parrot
(CPN Alt Q, B5)

skull glyph
(CPN St II, A5)

parrot
(CPN St II, B6)

Copan Emblem Glyph
(CPN St II, A7)

Two-legged Sky
(QRG St A, B17)

any relevance to what appears to be the seizure of the government of Copan by the parrots. It is the one puzzling feature of these events, suggesting the involvement of the clergy and the possibility of an internal revolution rather than an invasion from the outside. It may very well be, however, that the parrots were the defenders rather than the aggressors in a conflict that resulted in the death of the king.

It is clear that to understand the events of this period we must determine the identity of the parrots, which is not easy to do in the present state of our knowledge. David H. Kelley (1962), in his version of the events at Quirigua during this period, ascribed the death of Eighteen Jog to the king of Quirigua and dated it on 9.15.6.14.6 6 Cimi 4 Zec but in a later work (1976), he seems to abandon this idea, and suggests that Two-legged Sky, king of Quirigua, was the son of Eighteen Jog of Copan. This agrees better with my appraisal of the situation, though, since his name is never associated with the complete Emblem of Copan, it is possible that he was either the son of the queen by an earlier marriage, or was the son of the man on Stela F, and a younger brother of the queen. Family relationships and the rules of succession have not yet been established for the Maya, but I have reason to think that matrilineal descent was very important in royal families, and that the so-called Triadic Symbol, the headdress of the mask in the Temple of the Cross at Palenque, often worn by women at Yaxchilan, and at Copan depicted on the back of Stela H and earlier worn by the man on Stela I, refers to royal lineages, or to their founders.

On 9.14.13.4.17, a little more than a year before the erection of Stela 4, the first monument of Eighteen Jog, Two-legged Sky was afforded the manikin title, apparently not as king, but as "vulture," or military commander at Quirigua. This is not equivalent to royal accession, and there is no reason to think that Quirigua at that time was a capital city, as no stelae were erected in its Main Group until 9.16.0.0.0. It seems that it was founded as a second residence of the royal family of Copan, perhaps in anticipation of the disturbances that took place later.

The date that Kelley gives for the death of Eighteen Jog, 9.15.6.14.6 6 Cimi 4 Zec, is more than a year after the erection of Stela D at Copan, which I am inclined to think was his funerary monument, though it may mark the death of his wife. It is also the next-to-last date on the Hieroglyphic Stairway at Copan. The last known date here is 9.15.6.16.5, 6 Chicchan 3 Zec, which may mark the end of the funeral services for the king, or for his wife (?), the woman depicted on Stela H. Immediately after that we read of the "parrots," and until the problem of their identity is solved, this period of history at Copan and Quirigua will remain obscure. The glyph on which Kelley (1962) based his argument laying the blame for the death of Eighteen Jog on the shoulders of Two-legged Sky consists of a prefix composed of an axe and a comb element attached to the name Eighteen Jog, which constantly recurs with the date

6 Cimi 4 Zec (9.15.6.14.6). The prefix, unfortunately, is not common elsewhere, and its rare occurrences do not explain its meaning. I do not have an adequate interpretation for this glyph, but I think it may simply refer to the date as "after the reign of Eighteen Jog" or could read "successor to Eighteen Jog." Whatever the case, it is surely significant that the first stela erected in the main group at Quirigua, Stela H, has the date 9.16.0.0.0, which is not recorded at Copan. Earlier stelae in the vicinity were probably erected before the main group was built, and, to my knowledge, the Quirigua Emblem is not known outside the main group. In many respects, this monument resembles closely the stelae of Copan. The details of the portrait are extended on the sides of the stela, and on the back is an inscription arranged on a mat motif, such as is carved on Stela J at Copan. The only conspicuous difference is that the figure is shown standing on a mask, and this is probably due to the shape of the stone, which is narrow and tall. Unfortunately, the text is badly weathered, but in the next-to-last panel there is a clear record of a vulture glyph (a military title), another title, and the Emblem of Quirigua. Two-legged Sky, not yet king, may have returned to Copan to set up a new government under the aegis of Quirigua as the capital city. The situation at this time is not altogether clear. Both Copan and Quirigua erected stelae on 8 Ahau 8 Zotz' 9.16.5.0.0 and on 9.16.10.0.0 1 Ahau 3 Zip. The inscription of Stela M of Copan is interrupted in two places by a complete destruction of the glyphs. The stela stands in front of the Hieroglyphic Stairway of Copan, and may mark its completion. A name followed by the manikin-helmet title and the Copan Emblem Glyph appears after a destroyed portion of the text, but the compound that immediately precedes this name suggests to me that the reference may be to a former king and not to a living monarch. Another possibility is that the name is that of a priest, temporarily in charge after the death of the queen mother.

Stela N (9.16.10.0.0) is somewhat more informative, though it, also, confronts us with serious problems. The month position of its Initial Series, which should be 3 Zip, is given as 8 Uo, fifteen days earlier. Similar discrepancies occur on Stela E at Quirigua, erected 9.17.0.0.0, on which a priest from Copan may be mentioned, and it has been suggested that the apparent errors in month positions may be attempts to correct the solar year, but I am not concerned here with Maya astronomy. More relevant to history is the occurrence on Stela N of a glyph composed of a bearded head attached to the expression "sun-at-horizon." In later inscriptions of Copan "sun-at-horizon" is prefixed by *yax*. Some scholars have suggested that it is the name of the new ruler, but I prefer to read it as New Dawn, referring to a new regime—a new form of government instituted in Copan at this time, with a reference on Stela N to the "old" regime symbolized by the bearded-man prefix.

The inscription on the west side begins with a glorified *kin* sign, which may be followed by a name: a monster-head with an ik-sign

axe + comb + Eighteen Jog
(QRG St J, H3)

bearded head & sun-at-horizon
(CPN St N, A17)

T122.575:200
(CPN St N, B5)

katun variant
(CPN St N, B6)

eye. There is a "God C" glyph and what may be the same compound which introduces the name on Stela M. This compound consists of T122 (the scroll-and-flare prefix), T575 (the death-eye scroll), and the suffix T200 ("cloudless" *cauacs,* sometimes read as *cuc*), followed by what may be a verbal suffix. The next glyph on Stela N is the head variant of the katun, followed by a title glyph and finally by the Copan Emblem. The katun glyph here is probably not a calendrical sign but a symbol for war or the army. What seems to be hinted at here is the transfer of power to the military, probably backed by the clergy. Stela N presents a figure on each of its broad sides, and has, as such stelae usually do, both a historical and a prophetic text. Such stelae were usually erected at a time when a new reign began, and one of the figures is normally shown wearing a beard. In this instance, however, both figures are young, possibly implying a change in the priestly as well as in the royal office. Morley's reading of one of these dates on the pedestal of this stela as 6 Men 3 Yaxkin 9.16.13.4.15 may be incorrect. I prefer to read this date as 6 Chicchan 3 Yaxkin 9.15.6.16.5, a date recorded on the Hieroglyphic Stairway. Unfortunately, we have no definite statements of the death either of Eighteen Jog or of his wife (?), pictured on Stela H, but it is a fair assumption that both had died before the erection of Stela M in 9.16.5.0.0, and that the monarchical government of Copan was at an end. After 9.16.10.0.0, inscriptions continued to be made on altars and in buildings for at least two more katuns, but the erection of stelae was discontinued here, and we must turn to Quirigua for records of the royal family.

After 9.16.0.0.0, when Stela H was set up in Quirigua, the province was ruled from that city. Whether the jurisdiction extended to Copan is a debatable question, but at that time Two-legged Sky still held the title of vulture (military governor?), and the sky element was not included in his name. Just when he achieved the royal title is not clear. The second stela erected, Stela J, shows a different hieroglyphic and sculptural style, better adapted to the local type of stone, which was not as well suited to the carving of three-dimensional forms as was the trachyte used at Copan. A sort of compromise was reached by retaining the high, round relief of the head of the figure, while adapting the detail to the blocklike form of the stone. The style of the hieroglyphs also changed to more regular, rectangular forms. The texts are often repetitive, focused on the two events that support the legitimacy of the king, and stelae are erected on every hotun, instead of on the lahuntuns, as was the custom at Copan, except when a special event occurred.

The inscription on Stela J at Quirigua begins on the back of the monument with the Initial Series 9.16.5.0.0 8 Ahau 8 Zotz', hotun, and a divination sign. The next glyphs are somewhat damaged, but I suspect that the second glyph of the phrase may be the "*yax* sun-at-horizon" glyph that dominates the late period at Copan, and the following glyph may be the head variant for "katun" indicating the

army. At the top of the next two columns, 8 Ahau, haab (or tun) is repeated. I will not attempt an interpretation of the clause that follows. The next clause appears to begin with a somewhat eroded "jog" glyph followed by a personified *caban* glyph, and the name Two-legged Sky, though here, instead of the sky (T561) element, which usually stands under the superfix, is the sign T82.117. Three titles follow his name, then the glyph for South, another of unknown meaning, a bat glyph that may refer to Copan, and finally a vulture glyph. The meaning of this clause is by no means clear, but it may imply that he left Copan in charge of a military governor. Whether he was at that time already king of Quirigua remains in question.

On the sides of the stela are recorded the two events discussed by Kelley (1962). On the left, as one faces the inscription, is a Secondary Series leading back to the date 9.15.6.14.6, which Kelley then interpreted as the death of the king of Copan, Eighteen Jog. My version of this event is somewhat different. I think that Eighteen Jog had died more than a year before, and what is being said here is that the general of his army now succeeded him. On the other side of the stela is the date of his appointment as the "vulture" or army commander, 9.14.13.4.17 12 Caban 5 Kayab, accompanied by the fish-in-hand glyph, perhaps celebrating this event. The final clause on this monument begins with a "jog" glyph and names Two-legged Sky, for the first time adding to his name a sky glyph and another name beginning with a leaf element. The following glyph is a compound of the fire-fist glyph (T672), which I have noted elsewhere may refer to an ancestor, and which here is followed immediately by the Emblem Glyph of Quirigua, and may be read as "the founder of Quirigua." Thus it seems that he became king of Quirigua only after the death of his parents and the end of the dynasty at Copan.

The next stela erected at Quirigua was Stela F, one of the most elaborate and ambitious compositions that the Maya ever produced. Each of the broad sides of this stela is carved with a human figure standing on a mask which has the head and shoulders of a human figure above it. Both of the figures wear beards. They differ from each other only in minor details, but details that may be significant. The mask on which the figure on the north face of the monument is standing is a death mask. This figure holds a manikin scepter and a shield. His costume is extremely elaborate, and above his high headdress is the conventional bird of the sky. On the south side, the lower mask has shell earplugs and prominent tusks. His costume is perhaps even more elaborate than that on the north side. His arms are symmetrically bent as he holds a long chain hanging from the uppermost mask of his headdress to the level of his belt, where it ends in serpent heads.

The texts on the two sides of the monument both begin with Initial Series: that on the west side records the earliest date associated with Two-legged Sky: 9.14.13.4.17 12 Caban 5 Kayab, when he is said to have received the manikin helmet. The next phrase is not

Two-legged Sky
(QRG St J, C7)

bat glyph
(QRG St J, C10)

vulture glyph
(QRG St J, D10)

fire-fist glyph
(QRG St J, E8)

Quirigua Emblem Glyph
(QRG St J, F8)

clear. It contains the "torches" compound that was associated with the "parrots" at Copan and is followed by an eyeless head that later accompanies the name of Two-legged Sky. The reference here may be to his subjects or allies. Further a "jog" glyph introduces a record of 16 Zotz', possibly referring to the date 1 Lamat 16 Zotz' (9.14.16.11.8 ?) recorded on the step behind Stela D at Copan. The glyph with the coefficient 9 that follows it is somewhat damaged, and I suspect it may not be calendrical. Then a bat and a vulture glyph follow, and the clause ends with the Emblem Glyph of Quirigua. If the reference here is to the king of Quirigua, it would seem to me that at this time, in spite of having been given the rulership of Quirigua, he was still serving as general of the army.

A Secondary Series of 13.9.9 brings us from 12 Caban to 6 Cimi 4 Zec (9.15.6.14.6). Unfortunately the next glyph, with the "axe-and-comb" prefix, is badly effaced, though it is immediately followed by the name Eighteen Jog, the ruler of Copan. Other glyphs on this side of the monument are also obscured by erosion, but the dates are reasonably clear, though not especially informative. The date 3 Ahau 3 Mol is, of course, 9.15.10.0.0, and 4 Ahau 13 Yax, 9.15.0.0.0. Another Secondary Series, counted from the starting date 12 Caban 5 Kayab brings us to 1 Ahau 3 Zip, the lahuntun of 13 Ahau (9.16.10.0.0), recorded as an Initial Series on the other side of the stela. The meaning of the text here is obscure, and may be prophetic. Morley (1937–1938:4:123–131) gives no Long Count positions for the two dates, which he reads as 1 Ahau 13 Mol and 1 Ahau 13 Yaxkin, though the second date looks more like Men to me. Immediately after this date is a "jog" glyph with the axe-and-comb prefix that is often prefixed to Eighteen Jog at Quirigua, though the number 18 is not evident here.

After 9.16.10.0.0, no more stelae were erected at Copan, but Quirigua continued erecting stelae until 9.17.15.0.0, when here too erection of stelae was suspended for a time, and great zoomorphs took their place. Inscriptions on the stelae tend to be repetitive. They usually have two Initial Series, one dealing with history and referring again and again to the two dates 12 Caban 5 Kayab 9.14.13.4.17 and 6 Cimi 4 Zec 9.15.6.14.6, the other apparently prophetic and involving vast distances in time. These would make a fascinating study, but will not be dealt with here.

Thus the next stela erected, Stela D, features on its west side the second katun anniversary of the date 12 Caban 5 Kayab 9.16.13.4.17, recorded with elaborate full-figure glyphs. After the statement of the completion of two katuns, there is a mask glyph and what may be an affix cluster used with accession expressions, but the details of it are not clear and the "toothache" element of accession is missing. The statement refers to Two-legged Sky, though at the time of the event the sky element was not present in his name. It is nevertheless the best argument for Kelley's reconstruction of the events, which gives him the title of "ruler" or "king" of Quirigua two katuns earlier. A

Secondary Series, in part effaced, apparently leads to the contemporary date 9.16.15.0.0. After some obscure passages, the text concludes with the Emblem Glyph of Quirigua followed by a reference, I suspect, to the Copan origins of the matrilineage of the king.

Stela E, erected in 9.17.0.0.0, is the tallest monument in the Maya area. Like previous monuments, it records the dates 12 Caban 5 Kayab and 6 Cimi 4 Zec, but there appear to be errors in the tun coefficients both in the Initial Series and in two of the Secondary Series that follow. It is possible that these apparent errors were deliberate or were due to the senility of the person who composed this text. A third day mentioned is 11 Imix 19 Muan (9.16.11.13.1). The glyph of the event is eroded, but the passage seems to refer to the Jaguar Priest of Copan, perhaps the same priest who inscribed the unorthodox dates on Stela N there. A Secondary Series, 8.4.19, brings us to the date 9.17.0.0.0 13 Ahau 18 Cumku. The text ends with the name of Two-legged Sky, followed by three references to Ben-Ich Bat (Copan). It is conspicuous that the royal prefix of these references is missing, so that the Emblems seem to refer not to rulership, but rather to origins and family connections of the ruler.

The Initial Series on the east side of Stela E reads 9.17.0.0.0 13 Ahau 18 Cumku. It is followed immediately by a clause that includes an expression of death (the eye-scroll–*ahau-ik* expression), but it is not clear to me to whose death it refers, since it is immediately followed by 13 Ahau, haab. Two other 13 Ahau dates are mentioned: 13 Ahau 18 (Zac??), which seems to refer to "parrots," and 13 Ahau 13 Uo, followed by a *caban* compound and a Secondary Series of 10.0. I have no ready explanation of these dates and assume that they have either an astronomical or a prophetic meaning. At the end of the inscription, after a reference to Two-legged Sky, there is a divination glyph (?), 13 Ahau 18 Cumku (9.17.0.0.0), followed by a final statement that ends in *ah* (T12) *ben-ich* and the upright *kankin*.

In spite of the obscurity of this text, it seems clear that at this time, the king of Quirigua either had recently died or was about to die, for the next two monuments, Stelae A and C, both erected in 9.17.5.0.0, clearly present a mortuary motif. They are quite different from earlier stelae which depict a ruler. The carving on Stelae A and C is in low relief, and each pictures a masked dancing figure. Stela A is somewhat taller than Stela C, but the drawings of these monuments in Maudslay (1887–1902:2:Pls. 7, 19) exaggerate the difference. The masks of both monuments are essentially human, but both have large, squarish eyes. They differ principally in the treatment of the mouth and chin. The mask on Stela A has filed front teeth and wears an artificial beard; that on Stela C has a fleshless jaw and crossed diagonal bands in the mouth. The figure on Stela A has hands like the feet of some saurian monster with long claws, and his feet are encased in jaguar paws; the figure on Stela C is entirely human and dances in bare feet. There are other minor differences in the costumes of the two figures, but they are probably less significant.

Jaguar Priest
(QRG St E, A16)

of Copan
(QRG St E, B16a)

On or above their heads is a curious structure that upholds a rope forming a partial frame of the design, and on Stela C one can make out the figure of a bird perched on the frame. Both carvings are damaged here, but it is clear that this is a representation of the sky, the future abode of the deceased king. The inscriptions on these two stelae are analogous to those we find on stelae which present two figures, that on Stela A dealing with historical events, and that on Stela C with prophecy.

The Initial Series of Stela A records the contemporary date 9.17.5.0.0 6 Ahau 13 Kayab. Morley (1937–1938:4:152–156) does not suggest a Long Count position for the next date, 6 Ahau 13 Ch'en, but conceivably it could be 9.4.5.0.0, just thirteen katuns earlier. This does not explain, however, "completion of 19 tuns (?)" preceding the date. The passage that follows is of unknown meaning, but further we might read "prophecy or divination" (scattering-gesture glyph), 5 katun, fire-fist glyph, Two-legged Sky. If we count back five katuns from the Initial Series, we come to 9.12.5.0.0, the date of Stela I, which depicts a figure wearing the mask of God I of Palenque and a headdress with the Triadic Symbol of the Temple of the Cross. I have suggested elsewhere that the Palenque Triad may refer to matri-lineages, though I have not been able to substantiate this. It is the same symbol that appears on the back of Stela H at Copan, and it may be worth noting that the *kankin* on it side, which is the main element of the Quirigua Emblem, appears in a glyph on Stela I also. The precise meaning of the Triadic Symbol, which is usually at-tached to a *kin*-sign base, has yet to be worked out, and I mention it here only to show that the relation of Two-legged Sky to the royal family of Copan is not a casual one, and probably precedes the foun-dation of Quirigua itself.

In the remaining glyphs in this inscription, which are apparently intended to describe Two-legged Sky more fully, we can recognize a modified Emblem of Copan, and an emblem of Quirigua with a "God C" prefix. Farther on in the text is mentioned Eighteen U Jog, with his manikin title, an odd compound of the sky and a sun-eyed creature, and the conventional ending *imix*-comb-*imix*.

The text of Stela C is essentially prophetic. There are two Initial Series: 13.0.0.0.0 4 Ahau 8 Cumku and 9.1.0.0.0 6 Ahau 13 Yaxkin. There seems to be a backward count to the month of Ceh (9.0.0.0.0 8 Ahau 13 Ceh?) from which a Secondary Series of 17.5.0.0 leads forward to 6 Ahau 13 Kayab, the fifth tun (9.17.5.0.0). A divination glyph (scattering gesture) follows, and the name Two-legged Sky, 5 katun, and the fire-fist glyph, as on Stela A, but in reverse order. Below the vertical rows of the main inscription is a horizontal row of glyphs. It reads: 1 Eb 5 Yax (9.17.4.10.12 ?), 5 tuns, 6 Ahau (9.17.5.0.0 ?); then 8 days forward to 9 Ahau (9.17.4.11.0 ?). Nothing in this text indicates that either of these dates is that of the death of the king. He seems to have died some time before, possibly about the time of the erection of Stela E, and these monuments may have been set up to celebrate his ascent to the sky. Both these monuments stand at the far end of the Main Plaza of Quirigua, facing the main group of buildings, a position held at Copan by Stela D, which I have suggested may mark the tomb of Eighteen Jog. This conspicuous similarity in the layout of the two sites further suggests to me that Quirigua was at its beginning an offshoot, if not a dependency, of Copan, rather than a site of independent origin. The fact that the first stela at Quirigua (9.16.0.0.0) was set up at a time of a hiatus in stela erection at Copan tends to confirm the close relationship between the two sites. The two later stelae at Copan, Stelae M and N, may mark the apotheosis of Eighteen Jog of Copan and of his wife, leading to a reorganization of the government, making it subservient to Quirigua.

The date 9.16.12.5.17 6 Caban 10 Mol is the most frequently recorded date at Copan. It occurs on virtually every subsequently carved altar and is featured in Temple 11. It sometimes is recorded without a text, and in every text in which it does occur it is followed by a different expression. It is only by studying the carved figures on the monuments that we can get some intimation of what happened on that date. Perhaps the clearest scenic representation is on Altar Q. The first part of the inscription on this altar dealt with earlier events (see above). It included a reference to a "*yax* parrot," who again is mentioned after the record of 6 Ahau 13 Kayab (9.17.5.0.0). The parrot glyph is preceded here by a "*cauac* cluster" and the *kin*-bar prefix (T184). It is followed by an eroded sign and then by the expression *yax* sun-at-horizon. The sky title and another follow this expression, and then, on 5 Kan 12 Uo (written 13 Uo) 9.17.5.3.4, there is a hand glyph (thumb up, in receiving position?) holding an upside-down *ahau* sign and the "*cauac*-cluster" glyph. The expression "sun-at-horizon" occurs earlier on an altar associated with Stela E (9.9.5.0.0), but there it is prefixed by two superimposed *chuen*-like signs.

The illustration accompanying the date 6 Caban 10 Mol (9.16.12.5.17) on Altar Q is particularly revealing. It pictures sixteen figures seated on hieroglyphs, some of which are familiar and may constitute a text, though its meaning escapes me. One of the glyphs has a coefficient of 18, but is too badly damaged to be identified. It could be a reference to Eighteen Jog, and it is followed by "5 katun." There are other familiar forms, which I do not venture to interpret. The two principal figures face each other on the front of the altar with the date 6 Caban 10 Mol between them. They are distinguished from the others mainly by symbols on their turbanlike headdresses. The figure on the observer's right is followed by nine others facing in the same direction. The figure on the left has only five followers. His costume is of particular interest, for he wears a ring around his eye and a parrot with a long tail atop his turban. On his right arm is a small shield, and in his left hand he holds what may be a ceremonial

yax sun-at-horizon
(CPN Alt Q, F3)

bundle of darts. One is strongly reminded of the scene pictured on Lintel 2 of Piedras Negras many years before, in which the king presents a young man to six kneeling warriors. This youth also wears a ring around his eye, and a bird atop his tall headdress. One can hardly resist associating this figure with the "parrots" mentioned on top of Altar Q in connection with Katun 15.

A similar arrangement of two rows of turbaned figures seated on hieroglyphs facing each other with the 6 Caban date between them occurs on a step in Temple 11. In this case, there are ten individuals in each row. The principal figure on the right is again in part destroyed, but the bird on the turban of the figure on the left is clearly visible. Here the date 6 Caban 10 Mol is followed by a variant of the "toothache" expression and instead of the "_yax_ sun-at-horizon" by "_yax_ sky" (with two unknown signs prefixed). There are three more glyphs and the Emblem of Copan.

In the long inscription on Altar U, a partly damaged date, probably 6 Caban 10 Mol, is followed by a "seating to office" expression and "_yax_ sun-at-horizon," a sky title, a compound with a leaf prefix, and the Copan Emblem. This, however, is the only instance in which we can construe Yax Sun-at-Horizon as a person who became king of Copan on that day. My reluctance to accept this conclusion may be unfounded, but it is based on a number of other observations, among them the absence of stelae at Copan at this time, the fact that 6 Caban 10 Mol is a date elsewhere associated with animal symbolism, and that at Piedras Negras, "sun-at-horizon" usually takes as a prefix the number 1 or T679 and stands for a short, usually single-day, Secondary Series. It is for these reasons that I prefer to read the expression _yax_ sun-at-horizon" as New Dawn (not unlike the New Deal of the United States some years ago) referring to a "joint government" of this time.

Altar T, which celebrates the katun anniversary of the 6 Caban date, is also revealing in its group composition. The top of this altar represents an alligator or alligator skin, stretched, with human figures represented in the spaces between its limbs. On the south side of this altar are four figures seated on hieroglyphs, two on each side, facing a brief inscription between them. On each side of the altar, behind these figures, are four others facing in the same direction. Essentially, this composition is the same as those on Altar Q and on the step in Temple 11, but there are interesting differences. I am not certain whether the inscription should be read in the usual manner or whether each column, as I suspect, should be read separately. The left column begins with a compound of _ben-ich_ sky. It is followed by the glyph for South, a compound of "God C," and the Copan Emblem. The right-hand column is less clear. It ends with what could be the familiar _imix_-comb-_imix_ glyph, preceded by a sacrifice glyph. Neither of the two principals of this group wears a ring around his eye or a bird on the head. All four appear to be of equal rank.

Behind each pair of figures are four other figures carved on the sides of the altar. The first three figures on each side wear animal disguise, and the last, smaller figure, seated on an *imix*-like sign, is dressed in a beaded costume and appears to be a woman. The animal disguises suggest to me that they represent social groups such as clans or lineages. Most interesting of all are the two figures on the back wall of the altar. The figure on the left sits on a completion glyph and holds in his hand the month sign 10 Mol (presumably 6 Caban 10 Mol); that on the right sits on a katun sign and holds in his hand 10 Zip (9.17.12.5.17 4 Caban 10 Zip?). Between them are three hieroglyphs, of which the middle one is the sign for South. The figures are human, but their faces are covered with masks resembling the glyph for *caban,* and above their heads are cartouches containing the number 6 (according to Morley), the day coefficient of the first date, and the number 4, the day coefficient of the second. These figures, therefore, are nothing more than personified dates. There are, in all, ten undisguised male figures in this design, four of them shown seated in council. There are six animal impersonators, which I suspect may represent the six matrilineages of the six male figures on the top of the altar. We are still far from being able to substantiate such interpretations, but whatever mythical components are inherent in such compositions, I am convinced that they have a historical base, as the dates associated with them strongly suggest.

Altar T is the last of the "great" altars presenting a group composition, but there are two others that mention the 6 Caban date, and it is cited also on a jamb in Temple 11 and on a small all-glyphic stela, Stela 8. The front of Altar R is sculptured with a large skull. Its inscription begins with the 6 Caban 10 Mol date, but contains many unfamiliar glyphs, and I have no suggestions to offer concerning its meaning. Only at the very end is mentioned the "*yax* sun-at-horizon" in connection with a date 12 Ahau 3 Zip. This date is not connected with 6 Caban, and Morley reads the date 7 Ahau and gives it an earlier position, 9.15.9.13.0. The event glyph that follows this date is of unknown meaning, but it is followed by "*yax* sun-at-horizon," too early, for if our interpretation of this expression is correct, the new government did not exist at that time. Thus 12 Ahau 3 Zip (9.17.14.6.0) in my opinion would be a better reading. The death-head on the front is suggestive of death or human sacrifice, and since the preceding two glyphs are suggestive of the sacrifice of prisoners, it is possible that the altar was built for that purpose.

Altar Z is of similar, though much simpler design. Its front is sculptured with a grotesque mask, and there is an inscription on the sides and back. The only legible date on this altar is 13 Ahau 18 Cumku (9.17.0.0.0). Preceding this date is a Secondary Series of 1.8.1 or 1.8.0, and following it is a glyph with a "forward indicator" or *i* prefix. I am not prepared to give an interpretation of this inscription, but perhaps it is worth noting that the text ends with a reference to "*yax* sun-at-horizon" followed by the bird variant of the "katun" (army?), the usual glyph with a leaf prefix, and Ich-Ben Copan (lacking the "water-group" prefix of Emblem Glyphs).

Two other altars, made up of discrete blocks, Altars B' and C', are carved with skulls at each end, recalling the larger skull-altar R. For other altars and fragments at Copan and in its vicinity I refer the reader to Morley's monumental work on the site (1920) and to later studies by Berthold Riese (1971) and Michel Davoust (1979). It is to be hoped that final reports of the group now working at Copan will publish the sculptured material more fully. Here I merely want to point out that building and sculpture continued at Copan after what seems to have been the fall of the monarchy and a return to more secular rule, perhaps even one dominated by a merchant class, more suitable to a frontier town.

CHAPTER ELEVEN

Prelude to Disaster

9.17.10.0.0 — 10.0.0.0.0

A.D. 780 — 830

IN 9.17.10.0.0 THE MAJOR MAYA CITIES WERE STILL prospering, and more and more minor sites were erecting monuments. The relation of these smaller principalities to the larger, more ancient centers is not clear. It has been suggested that something in the nature of a feudal system was developing at this time, but our knowledge is still too scanty, exploration too incomplete, to permit anything more than speculation about the social and economic conditions of this period.

At Tikal, Stela 19 was erected in a twin pyramid enclosure to record the divination for Katun 9.18.0.0.0 on 9.17.18.3.1. Following this is a statement of the completion of one katun, but this date is not a katun anniversary of any known date at Tikal. Probably what is meant is that it is one katun later than the first katun divination performed by this ruler, the first being recorded on Stela 22. Although the first part of the inscription is virtually illegible, one can make out a thumb-up hand glyph that appears to indicate a status or an honor received, and later an *u ahaulil* expression and the name Dark Sky. This identifies the personage pictured as his successor, also pictured on the earlier Stela 22.

Stela 24, on the basis of a badly eroded inscription, has been assigned by Satterthwaite to Katun 19. It was found broken and buried in the debris of the stairway to Temple III, and recently published drawings by W. R. Coe (in C. Jones and Satterthwaite 1982:52–55) confirm this reading. The one surviving lintel in Temple III pictures a person dressed as a jaguar, with an elaborate mask on his back, with the jaws of death, and on his forehead the God C symbol, identical to the tail-mask of the sky-serpent depicted on Lintel 3 of Temple IV. The jaguar-man holds in his hands a simple staff and an eccentric flint, as do his two assistants. The inscription on this lintel is almost completely destroyed. The mortuary implications of the motif, however, suggest that Temple III may be the burial place of the successor to Dark Sky.

The almost total destruction of the inscription on Stela 24 is very unfortunate, for between Stela 19 (9.18.0.0.0) and Stela 11 (10.2.0.0.0) there is a period of eighty years for which we have no surviving documentation at Tikal. Possibly columnar altars were being set up during part of this period; possibly there are monuments yet undiscovered still buried in the debris of temples; but it is more likely that the king was absent on a military or diplomatic campaign and that the approaching disaster was already looming over the land.

In sites around Tikal, some inscriptions of this period survive, though they are not very informative. At Uaxactun, Stela 7 records 9.19.(0.0.0?) 9 Ahau (18 Mol), and a Secondary Series 14.6(?) may lead back to a date of birth or accession (9.18.19.3.14?) 9 (Ix 17 Ceh). This is a beautifully executed stela, in the exuberant style of this period, but we have only the top fragment of it. Other late monuments at Uaxactun are in such poor condition that it is difficult to tell whether there was an interruption in the erection of stelae here after the last katun of Baktun 9.

The sites of the Ixcan Valley in northern Peten almost surely have stelae of this period, but the stone in this region was of poor quality, and their eroded condition does not permit a confident reading of their dates. Morley's placement of Stelae 8, 4, and 5 at Xultun seems to me to be somewhat too early. The large tassels on the sandals of the figures suggest dates no earlier than 9.16.0.0.0, and the swaying position of the figures on Stelae 5 and 8 makes dates in 9.18.0.0.0 to 10.0.0.0.0 much more probable. On the other hand, figures at La Honradez, more rigid in pose and more restrained in detail, are in some cases placed too late by Morley. Stela 4 is the only monument that shows the exuberant detail one expects at this time, and Stela 5, with its relaxed pose, may also belong here, but the placing of Stelae 1, 2, and 9 I am inclined to question. Two of them are fragments, and Stela 1 is in very poor condition. None of these monuments has a legible text. La Honradez appears to be the principal city in its region and was probably occupied for a long time, as was Xultun, at the headwaters of the Río Azul. A stela from Chochkitam may also belong in this period, though it yielded no legible date. All three sites are described as large, with massive constructions, but none has been adequately mapped or explored.

At Nakum, there are only fragments of monuments that Morley (1937–1938 : 2 : 7–21) places in this period. One of them has a somewhat uncertain date, 9.19.10.1.0, but no other legible text. Thus, the texts of northeastern Peten provide us with little historical information, but the apparent clustering of the dates of their stelae in this and the preceding period suggests that they were rapidly achieving independence and gaining importance at this time.

Naranjo is somewhat better documented, but the distribution of well-dated monuments there is somewhat discontinuous, and on a number of stelae and fragments inscriptions are missing or illegible. Stela 6, like Stela 20 (see Chapter 9) records the accession of a new king, and the texts of these two monuments are suspiciously similar, but Stela 6 is undoubtedly the later monument of the two. Its date, however, is uncertain. Peter Mathews (in I. Graham 1978:111) reads the Calendar Round on the front as 9 Etz'nab 11 Muan (9.18.17.5.18), but I would prefer a date one Calendar Round earlier: 9.16.4.10.18. This date is followed by the bundle glyph of accession, so we must assume that the monument is the first of its group. The figure on the front is distinguished by a row of dots on its chin (a battle scar?), and this links the portrait with those of Stelae 13, 19, and 33. Stela 11 possibly also belongs in this group, for, though the chin marks are not clear, the king has a characteristically prominent nose.

If we restore the Secondary Series on Stela 6 as 1.5.7.2, we reach the date 9.17.10.0.0 12 Ahau 8 Pax, which is mentioned on all monuments of this group with the exception of Stela 11, which has no legible text. If the other four monuments were all erected on the same date, we might conclude that Naranjo was divided into four neighborhoods, or four ethnic groups, each paying homage separately to the king. A fifth stela with the date 9.17.10.0.0? has no figure and only two glyphs after the date (Stela 36). All these monuments are from Group B of Naranjo, but each is associated with a different structure. I have been unable to isolate personal names on these monuments, though titles such as *batab* occur, and there are subsidiary dates; but most of the texts are badly eroded. Stela 13, the tallest of these monuments, is over 3 meters high. It stands in front of Structure B-19, in the court of the main pyramid. Stela 33, in front of a long palace building of the same court, is less than 2 meters high; but Stela 19, though it is associated with a small, insignificant mound, B-21, is more than 2 meters high and is carved both on the front and on the back. All these monuments, if not carved by the same artist, were certainly carved by artists of one school and show a rigidity of pose and a simplicity of detail that are characteristic of this group. Stela 13 is the only monument of this group which has a well-preserved inscription on the back, but even on this monument I have not been able to isolate a personal name from the titles and other designations, as, for example, the glyphs in column A of Stela 13, 8 through 11. The glyph at A10 is a *batab* glyph and is followed by a sky sign and a mask. This expression also follows the Initial Series on the back. Most of the following text seems to concern a woman, or women, and leads to a Secondary Series, 5.13.10, followed by what may be a woman's name, a quincunx glyph, and a forward-count glyph, with which the inscription seems to end. I suspect that this refers to the death of a female relative of the king five years earlier (9.17.4.4.10?). On Stela 19 we read the same name as on Stela 13, and the subsidiary date is probably 9.17.5.8.12. The ruler wears no skirt, has exaggerated hips, and is standing over a kneeling captive. On the back of this stela is a bloodletting scene: the penitent is seated on a

batab
(NAR St 13, A10)

sky sign + mask
(NAR St 13, A11)

woman's name
(NAR St 13, H15)

quincunx glyph
(NAR St 13, G16)

name
(NAR St 19, C5)

bench or throne, and an attendant draws a long cord through his tongue. Above and below are rows of hieroglyphs beginning with a date, but they are so weathered that very little is legible. Stela 33 is a small, narrow shaft, showing a lord wearing a jaguar headdress and holding a staff decorated with triple knots. In his other hand is an eccentric flint. Like other figures of this group, he has a scar or tattoo on his chin, but the monument seems to have been carved by a less skillful artist, and facial features are somewhat distorted. The titles of the king do not appear in the brief inscription, which gives only the name which is given at C5 on the front of Stela 19. The final stela of this group, Stela 36, has only the Calendar Round date for 9.17.10.0.0 followed by two unknown glyphs.

In dress and accoutrement, the figures on this group of stelae closely parallel the figures of the previous group, though they were obviously carved by a different artist or group of artists. Stela 6 and Stela 20 are very much alike in design. Similarly we can pair Stela 13 with Stela 28, Stela 19 with Stela 2, and Stela 33 with Stela 30. It may pay to study such motifs and their sequences elsewhere and to try to determine their meanings, though such a study will not be attempted here. However, we might venture to add Stela 11 to this group to balance the earlier Stela 21. One might suspect that Naranjo was a capital of several semi-independent states, and the fact that it shares at least one date with Caracol suggests that it maintained close contact with other border cities. Moreover, Naranjo was not the only Maya city to erect several monuments on a given date. This was also done by Calakmul, on the northern border of the Maya area, and by Caracol to the south, just over the border in Belize.

After 9.18.0.0.0, the style of Naranjo monuments undergoes a radical change. Exuberantly rich, swirling forms fill the entire field around the figure. On Stela 14 (9.18.0.0.0 11 Ahau 18 Mac), the forms retain a certain rectangularity, which is not maintained on later monuments of its type. The inscription on the back begins with an Initial Series: 9.17.13.4.3 5 Akbal 11 Pop. The glyphs that follow are weathered, but the first two suggest a "toothache glyph" followed by an affix cluster of accession, and the name of the ruler, identified by a beaded-jewel prefix, appears at C12–D12. What may be the date of his birth is given on Stela 10 as 13 Eb 5 Zip (9.17.0.2.12), but on Stela 14, a Secondary Series before the final date leads to the preceding day, 12 Chuen. In any case, he seems to have been thirteen years old when he took the throne.

Stela 12 is a good example of the dynamic quality in art characteristic of this period: the long, swooping feathers of the headdress, with unusually long tassels; the sinuous swirl, not only of the scrolls that issue from the head of the manikin in the jaws of the serpent-bar, but of the serpent's snout itself; the projection of the frets of the apron beyond the figure's body. These features completely fill the ground, spilling over onto the border.

There are only four hieroglyphs on the front of this monument. They are somewhat weathered, but the first is probably the "jog" glyph, which often stands at the head of captions naming the individual portrayed. The second could be the name Jeweled Mirror (as I tentatively call this lord). Next is a title, perhaps the scroll-manikin cap, and the last is unknown, possibly a skull compound.

The principal text is on the back of this stela. It begins by giving the birthday of the lord: 13 Eb 5 Zip (9.17.0.2.12). A Secondary Series, 1.8.6.0, leads to 9.18.8.8.12, when the lord was twenty-eight years old. The statement that follows is obscure. Next there are seven dates connected by short Secondary Series. Statements with these dates are difficult to make out, but at least three begin with the glyph usually associated with the moon or with the number 20, but here with a hatchet protruding from its center. The hatchet occurs in the name or title of the previous ruler, but its significance in combination with the lunar (?) or 20 sign is not clear. However, the pattern of closely spaced dates apparently recording similar events suggests that the ruler was either reorganizing his reign by distributing honors or making new appointments, or aggrandizing it by bringing surrounding settlements into his orbit. The final date on the monument is probably 10 Ahau 8 Zac (9.18.10.0.0) at F12–G12.

Two other monuments at Naranjo bear the same date. They differ from Stelae 14 and 12 in style as well as in design, yet both exhibit late traits. Stela 8 presents the figure on an open ground with an inscription of twelve glyph-blocks. The lord holds an elaborately designed triplicate staff in six sections ending in a serpent head with a flint knife in its jaws, a typically late design. The design of the feathers on the headdress, with long beaded ends, is also late. In the left hand, the figure holds a small round fan, and his belt is curved around his body. He wears an artificial beard and a fillet under his eye that twists over his nose, suggesting the "God of the Number 7." The motif, therefore, may be a mortuary one, and the fact that in the inscription we find the name of a woman mentioned on Stela 13 suggests that the monument may have been erected in memory of the king's mother. The date on the front is best read as 11 Akbal 11 Yaxkin (9.18.9.14.3). There seems to be no Secondary Series, but the Initial Series on the back is 9.18.10.0.0. Stela 35, with the same date, is a small monument, comparable in size to Stela 33. It stood by itself in an open court near Structures C-4 and C-5. Its design is unique. The face of the figure is directed upward toward a huge double scroll that issues from a shaft that appears to be made of reeds, which he holds diagonally across his chest—perhaps a torch of some kind? It is rare to find the principal figure on a Maya stela representing someone other than the ruling lord or a royal woman, but this figure and that on Stela 33 may be exceptions. If the current ruler's name is mentioned on the inscription on the back, it is not now evident.

Stela 7 stands between Stelae 6 and 8 in front of Structure B-4. Its

beaded jewel + mask
(NAR St 14, D12)

Eighteen U Imix
(NAR St 32, X2)

manikin cap + T82
(NAR St 32, U3)

katun date is 9 Ahau 18 Mol (9.19.0.0.0), but a date below is 4 Ahau 18 Zac, which occurs three uinals later. The arrangement here is precisely opposite to that of Stelae 12, 13, and 14, where the earliest monument stands in the center. If Stela 6 is the accession monument of the lord who ruled in 9.17.10.0.0, then it is possible that Stela 8 may also represent him, though it was certainly carved later. Perhaps the false beard, the eye-fillet, and the jaguar ear of this monument all are not signs of mourning, but indicate a deceased person, and the portrait on Stela 8 is a posthumous portrait of the former king. The style of Stela 7 shows the typical sinuous curves of the period, though the serpent-bar is held horizontally as in earlier times, and the feathers appear to be without tassels. A new feature is introduced in the form of a small pointed beard which the ruler wears.

Stela 10, standing at the other end of the plaza next to Stela 11, in front of Structure B-23, has only an inscription. It begins with the birthday of the king on 13 Eb 5 Zip (9.17.0.2.12) and ends probably with the same date as on Stela 7 (9.19.0.3.0).

Stela 32 is probably one of the last monuments erected at Naranjo. It was found face down lying in front of Structure C-9, where many stelae pertaining to the woman from Tikal and to her son are grouped. A large area near the center of the stela was completely destroyed, whether by natural flaking away of the surface or by deliberate intent it is difficult to tell, and it is not clear whether a figure was depicted there or not, for the arrangement seems to have been asymmetrical. The lower part of the stela shows a construction consisting of three sky-bands with eagle heads on the ends, alternating with bands decorated with abstract forms. In the center appears to be a stairway with inscribed glyphs, and above, a curious bundle of reeds or feathers, apparently resembling some sort of saurian creature. On this is placed a padded seat. On the right of the destroyed area we see a monstrous serpent head with a manikin in its gaping mouth. The remains of another appear at the left. Sinuous curving tendrils and scrolls fill the entire background around the ruined center. The motif of this monument is somewhat ambiguous. On the one hand it resembles the accession motif of Piedras Negras, and that on Naranjo's Stela 22, which also has been interpreted as an accession monument, since it appears to be the earliest of the "Squirrel" series. On the other hand, the design of Stela 32 can be compared to the motif on Lintel 3 of Temple IV at Tikal, which apparently refers to the rise of a deceased ruler to the sky. In any case, however, the text appears to deal with accession, and the ruler is referred to as Eighteen U Imix followed by the manikin-cap title with suffix T82. This is a strange expression for a personal name, and one may wonder whether it does not refer to eighteen subject chiefs, rather than to an individual, but we have no way of knowing what it means at present; it may merely imply that he was the eighteenth ruler since the founding of the town, or one of eighteen chiefs in the province.

The text at the top of the monument, which may have revealed the subject matter of the rest, is unfortunately badly damaged. The first date is illegible, and the Secondary Series that leads to it is destroyed. The second date, however, is restored by Morley (1937–1938:2:153–158) as 9.19.3.3.3 8 Akbal 6 Zac, and the last in this section is 13 Ahau 18 Mol (9.19.4.1.0). The section at the left begins with the next day, 1 Imix 19 Mol, which appears to be a date of accession of Eighteen U Imix. This phrase justifies our treating the peculiar name as referring to an individual, though the fact that no portrait of his exists, as well as the suffix T82 of the manikin-cap title, leaves some room for doubt.

The left section begins with a Secondary Series and the date 13 Ahau 8 Zip (9.19.9.15.0), but the statement of the event referring to the ruler is not clear. Nor is the passage that follows, leading to the final date, 8 Ahau 8 Xul (9.19.10.0.0). The theme of this monument—death or accession—remains in doubt, since the crucial central part of the text in the upper portion is destroyed.

Another interesting problem is raised by the incised text on the steps leading to the platform. It begins with the date 8 Imix 14 Zotz' (9.19.4.15.1), a date that is recorded also on Stela 3 at Machaquila, far to the south of Naranjo. The two statements after the date, however, are not identical. That on the steps begins with a fist glyph and proceeds to a Secondary Series leading to 12 Eb 5 Kayab (9.19.5.9.12) and finally to 8 Ahau 8 Xul (9.19.10.0.0). At Machaquila, the 8 Imix date is followed by a hand glyph (T670) and a compound with the "jog" glyph, which may refer to a marriage or to succession within the family. It is possible, of course, that the occurrence of the same date at sites so distant from each other is merely coincidental, but circumstances suggest some relation between the end of the last great dynasty at Naranjo and the rise to prominence of Machaquila. These were troubled times. There are evidences of trouble on the Usumacinta, and I suspect that the mutilation of Naranjo's Stela 32 may have been deliberate. The last stela of this period at Tikal seems to have been erected on 9.19.0.0.0, and it is possible that an exodus of noble families from some cities was already beginning. The end of Cycle 9, which one would expect to be particularly important, actually seldom serves as a date of dedication on stelae.

Two sites on the eastern border of the Maya area, Xunantunich (formerly called Benque Viejo) and Chunhuitz, probably have stelae of this period, but no legible dates or texts are known. Although there may have been as many as nine stelae at Xunantunich, photographs of only three of them have been published. These three and an altar all had inscriptions, but they are now virtually illegible. There is little doubt, however, that all the stelae belong in this period or the next. I suspect that Stela 9 was the earliest of these monuments, for, although like the others it shows an ornament of feathers worn on the back of the figure, helping to fill background space, it

hand + "jog"
(MQL St 3, A2)

does not fill the background completely, as it does on Stela 1. It does not appear clearly on the photographs or on Ian Graham's drawings (1978: 117–127), but I suspect that the long streams of the feathers on the headdresses of Stelae 8 and 9 had beads that produced the effect of long tassels, which is a common feature after 9.18.0.0.0. The front of the stela from Chunhuitz is too eroded to give us even that much information.

In the general region of the Mopan River, south of Naranjo, are two more sites from which we know only late monuments: Ixkun and Ucanal. Only partial plans of these sites are available, and we do not know their full extent, or whether they contain earlier precincts. Ucanal is located on the Mopan River, at some distance south of an abandoned logging camp called Sal Si Puedes (Get Out If You Can). Six stelae are reported from this group, but only one has a legible date. Morley (1937–1938: 2: 186–201) had proposed six consecutive lahuntun dates for these monuments, but has not taken account of the frequent duplication of the same date in this region, and his judgment of styles is notoriously unreliable. Stela 2 seems to me to be earlier than the date 10.0.0.0.0 that he assigns to it, and Stela 3, which he places in the next lahuntun, I would judge to be no later than 9.19.0.0.0. Very probably here, as at Naranjo, the same final date is recorded on more than one stela. As elsewhere in the eastern section, the stelae are badly eroded. Most of them seem to portray a figure holding a staff or spear, but Stela 6 apparently shows a gesture of divination. The best-preserved stela, Stela 4, though broken, was in surprisingly good condition and was removed to the archaeological museum in Guatemala City by Ian Graham in 1972. It will be described in Chapter 12.

The ruins of Ixkun also present some difficulties in dating. The quality of the stone in this region is very poor, and most of the inscriptions are virtually illegible. At least five sculptured stelae are known from this site, but none can be dated except approximately by the style of carving, with the possible exception of Stela 1. This stela is rectangular, well over 3 meters high and about 2 meters wide. Like Stela 4 at Ucanal, it is made of finer stone and is better preserved than other monuments at the site. It portrays two standing figures facing each other, holding staffs and wearing small round shields. Below them are two bound prisoners. Long plumes above their heads are directed forward, and between them is a date (13 ? 18 ?) and a sign of divination. This date could be 13 Ahau 18 Cumku (9.17.0.0.0). Below the figures is recorded what seems to be an impossible Initial Series: 9.0.0.0.(0?) 11 Ahau 18 (Mac?). This date could be 9.18.0.0.0, but I suspect that the motif of this stela is legendary and may illustrate a tale like that of the "heavenly twins" or be symbolic of the change of the baktun at 10.0.0.0.0. There are some apparent discrepancies in the Lunar Series of this inscription that Morley (1937–1938: 2: 177–183) attempts to correct, but I suspect that this is somehow tied up with the legendary motif, or with an attempt to correct the lunar calendar. It may be well to note here the presence of the sun-at-horizon glyph, for it may account for the discrepancy between the day and month positions of the second date. There is also present the hand-scattering-grain glyph, which I suspect indicates divination, so that the apparent calendrical discrepancies in this text may be due to its reference to some ancient prophecy.

Stela 2 is an all-glyphic stela. It begins with an Initial Series: 9.17.9.0.13 3 Ben (6) Kayab. A Secondary Series leads to 9.17.9.3.3 1 (Akbal) 11 (written 12) Pop. This apparent addition of one day to the month position may have been purposeful, for it is possible that months and days were not always reckoned from the same hour. However, a sun-at-horizon glyph at D3 may in some way be related to the difficulty of calculating the rather eroded dates that follow. Other texts at Ixkun seem to be too eroded to yield legible dates. Stela 3, depicting a figure holding a manikin scepter, shows no very late traits, but Stelae 4 and 5 are undoubtedly very late monuments, with long streams of feathers projecting forward over their heads and with texts above and both texts and figures below. Stela 4 is 4 meters high and must have been a very impressive monument. The figure holds a manikin scepter with its handle ending in sinuous round scrolls. Prominent frets on the apron and large tassels on the sandals fill the lower background. Stela 5 portrays the grain-scattering gesture that I associate with divination. It is simpler in design, but shares some of the late traits associated with other monuments of this group. Three stelae from Ixtutz, also probably of this period, are too weathered to reveal detail, but Stela 4, now in the Archaeological Museum in Guatemala, has a text, well preserved except for the last few glyphs. It begins with the date 12 Ahau 8 Pax (9.17.10.0.0), and its text contains some rare glyphs of unknown meaning. At A5b is the Emblem Glyph of Petexbatun.

Further exploration may reveal earlier dates in this fringe area of the Peten, but at present it seems that sites in this area had suddenly achieved independence or had been conquered by Maya lords. Whether this had anything to do with the "Maya Collapse" that ultimately followed I would not venture to guess. It may be worth noting, however, that 9.17.0.0.0 fell on 13 Ahau, and that thirteen katuns earlier on 9.4.0.0.0 13 Ahau, there was another and even more dramatic expansion of the Maya area into the region of the Usumacinta.

In the lake region south of Tikal, Yaxha seems to have been a major site, but the inscriptions there provide us with virtually no data on its history. Morley (1937–1938:3:454–483) has distributed the monuments of Yaxha as belonging to the Early, Middle, and Great periods, but it seems to me that the monuments that have been published indicate a discontinuity between the Early Classic group and such late stelae as Stela 13. The only date recorded on the face of this monument is 12 Ahau, but its month position is missing. Since

sun-at-horizon
(IXK St 2, D3)

Petexbatun Emblem Glyph
(IXZ St 4, A5b)

the figure is shown with the gesture of divination (scattering grains), one might expect the Ahau date to record the end of a katun, but neither of the two possible katuns (9.11.0.0.0 and 10.4.0.0.0) seems altogether satisfactory. The lahuntun 9.17.10.0.0 12 Ahau 8 Pax is perhaps more in keeping with the style of the sculpture. Whatever the case, there seems to have been a long period of time when there were few or no stelae being erected at Yaxha. Thus Yaxha can be grouped with other peripheral cities that begin a new series of monuments in 9.17.0.0.0 or 9.17.10.0.0. The last known twin pyramid complex at Tikal seems to be dated 9.18.0.0.0. The next seems to have been erected at Yaxha. We have no date for it, but there is a possibility that the priesthood, if not the royalty, of Tikal was already fleeing southward to escape whatever disaster was overtaking Tikal at this time. Unfortunately, neither of the sites near Yaxha, Topoxte and San Clemente, has yielded any datable sculptures or texts.

In the vicinity of Lake Peten Itza, there are no known Early Classic sculptures, and all known fragments seem to be very late. Morley's reading (1937–1938:3:428–431) of a fragment of Lintel 1 at Tayasal is undoubtedly correct as 11 Ahau 18 Mac 9.18.0.0.0, but his other readings here are questionable, and, in any case, only Stela 1 shows any carving, and only a large base mask is fully preserved. Two stelae and a small fragment from a third found at Flores Morley places in the next baktun, as well as the stelae at Ixlu at the eastern end of the lake.

A short distance northwest of the shore of the lake is the site of Motul de San José. This site has never been surveyed, and the sketch maps made by Maler and Morley show a small group of long mounds and no temples or pyramids. The photograph in Maler's report on the site (1910) shows what is described as the back of a stela of large size and unusual proportions and what is probably the most ambitious carving known from the Maya area. It depicts two dancing figures dressed in regal costumes. Some of the detail is obscured, but both seem to hold manikin scepters, small shields, and bags, though only the manikin held by the figure on the left is clearly visible. Feathers attached to their backs blend with the mass of swirling featherwork above their headdresses composed of superimposed masks. The lifting of both feet in the depiction of the dancing pose is unique on this monument. Morley's (1937–1938:3:415–421) estimate of 10.0.0.0.0 for the erection of this stela appears to me to be too late. The peak of the dynamic and exuberant type of composition represented here had been reached by 9.18.10.0.0, but except for the extravagant featherwork, there is very little distortion or exaggeration of elements, and the fact that sandals are worn in the dance links the dancing figures with even earlier examples of the motif. If Morley's drawing of the text just below the central panel is accurate, the last glyph is an Emblem characterized by the sign Ik, one of the four Emblems that are noted on Stela 10 at Seibal (see Chapter 12). The central panel appears to be divided into two vertical panels of glyphs to be read separately rather than as a unit. The upper part of both panels is flaked away, but the next to last glyph of the left panel is the fish-in-hand, seemingly with a coefficient of 1, and the last glyph could be an abbreviated Emblem Glyph, lacking the normally attached prefixes and retaining only the element of the dots. The main sign of an Emblem (without its prefixes) is sometimes seen at sites other than its own, but usually it is then either preceded by a "God C" compound or other elements that can combine with it. Whatever the case here, it does not seem to be the Emblem of Motul de San José. The Ik-sign Emblem is more probable, though its unobtrusive position under the overhanging central panel throws some doubt on its affiliation with this site.

The known distribution of the dancing motif lies between 9.15.10.0.0 and 9.18.15.0.0, and I would hesitate to date this monument later than 9.19.0.0.0, as Morley suggests. Though much more elaborate, the figures on the Motul monument resemble the dancing figure on Stela 3 at Itzimte-Sacluk, which Morley believes was erected in 9.16.0.0.0.

In Chapter 10, I suggested that Stela 4 of Itzimte may belong in this period, on the basis of the square earplug, a placement strengthened by the treatment of the feathers and the strangely un-Maya profile. The date is very difficult to judge, for it seems to have been carved by an inferior artist and one not well trained in the Classic tradition. The rigid pose, the incongruity of the rounded outlines of the legs with the angularity of the arms, the imbalance of the background spaces, the disproportions of the body, and the inconsistent treatment of the detail are rarely encountered in Maya sculpture, and it is difficult to judge whether the stela is a deliberate attempt to break with the Classic tradition or simply the work of some provincial or foreign artist who was not sufficiently familiar with it.

It is strange to find, among the undistinguished monuments of this site, Altar 1, which, though broken and in places badly eroded, shows a detail which could only have been carved by an expert artist of the period between 9.18.0.0.0 and 9.19.10.0.0. It shows the head of a manikin, with the scroll issuing from its forehead ending in the sinuous tendrils so characteristic of this period. Morley's (1937–1938: 3:393–397) date for this altar is 9.17.5.0.0, but I suspect that it was carved in the next katun.

To the south of Itzimte are the ruins of Polol, a site which has not been fully explored. Except for one altar with an eroded Initial Series, which may or may not be Early Classic, the stelae of Polol record dates of this period. Morley (1937–1938:3:399–415) dates Stela 3 at 9.17.0.0.0, Stela 1 at 9.18.0.0.0, Stela 2 at 9.19.0.0.0, and Stela 4 at 9.19.10.0.0 or later. I have not been able to verify these tentative readings, since the inscriptions are badly eroded and the photographs are not clear. The details of Stela 2, published by Cyrus Lundell (1934: Pl.2 c,d), show a figure with sharp features, similar to those of stelae at Naranjo erected in 9.17.10.0.0, but other details

Emblem Glyph
(MTL St 1)

1 fish-in-hand
(MTL St 1)

abbreviated Emblem Glyph?
(MTL St 1)

seem to indicate that this monument is somewhat later. The superimposed masks on the headdress suggest a relation with the dancing figures of Motul de San José, and the angular sections of the triplicate staff he holds, as well as the forward-turning, tendril-like scrolls of the serpent-head's tongue, agree with Morley's late estimate of these stelae. The inscriptions, however, are too eroded and Lundell's photographs too indistinct to yield anything more of historic interest.

If the number of stelae erected at a site in any given period can be used as a measure of its prosperity, Calakmul, north of the Peten, had already been in decline for some thirty years before 9.17.10.0.0. After 9.10.0.0.0 and through 9.12.10.0.0, according to Morley (see Ruppert and Dennison 1943:153–154), eighteen monuments were erected at Calakmul and an equal number after this date and through 9.15.0.0.0. Comparable figures for the next two fifty-year periods are 9 and 6. Nevertheless, I suspect that even if Morley's dating of these monuments is correct (of which I am not at all certain), the decline in the number of monuments was not a decline in prosperity but is an indication of centralized rule over earlier scattered settlements. Whether this had anything to do with the apparent inactivity at Tikal in this period and the sudden burst of stela-erection on the eastern and southern frontiers of the Maya area remains in question.

Naachtun is a site that may have some monuments in this period, but the inscriptions are so eroded that none of the dates are certain. At the beginning of this period, artists of Piedras Negras were at the peak of their creativity. Their ascension motif, carved on the occasion of the inauguration of new rulers, with its combination of deep relief in the niche and the surrounding bas-relief, led gradually to greater interest in three-dimensional forms and culminated in the scene on Lintel 3, mentioned in Chapter 10. Although the scene portrayed deals with earlier events, this lintel may not have been carved until after 9.17.11.6.1 (if Thompson's (1944b) reading of the last date on this lintel is correct). We have no ascension stela at this time, but a fairly well preserved inscription of Throne 1, in the central palace of the acropolis, Structure J-6, gives us information about the new king. The back-screen of this throne is a huge mask, in whose hollow eyes are the busts of two figures facing each other. There are small glyphs that may one day identify them, but we do not know enough at present to offer a firm interpretation of them. The main inscription on this throne pertains to the life of the reigning king and is carved on the front and sides of the slab that form the seat of the throne and on its two supports.

This ruler was born on 12 Manik 5 Zotz' (9.15.18.16.7) and took the throne on 1 Kan 7 Yaxkin (9.17.10.9.4). He has an interesting name, which begins with a complex glyph with the prefix T12, suggesting a descriptive name or title rather than a personal name. This is followed by a numerical coefficient, 1, over glyph T563 (fire) with a superfix of T25 (*ca?*) flanking a smaller element. Next to this glyph is a *cauac* sign with superfix T25. Is it possible that this name implies

name
(PNG Thr 1, I'3–J'3)

that the ruler is the first high priest and prophet of the katun? The first glyph of his name varies. Essentially, it is an animal mask with a crossed-bands infix, but on Throne 1 and on Stelae 12 and 15 it has a prefix T74.184, and on Lintel 3, T126. Piedras Negras erected for the first time a divination stela at the end of a katun for Katun 13 Ahau, 9.17.0.0.0 (if our dating is correct). Whether this has any significance in regard to the abandonment of the traditional ascension motif of new rulers is not easy to determine, but on Stela 15, erected in 9.17.15.0.0 and recording the accession of the new king, he is shown standing, and holding in his hand the bag that is traditionally associated with the accession of kings at Piedras Negras as well as with the motif of divination. This stela is carved in three-quarters relief, but unlike the stelae at Copan, where such relief is common in the previous period, it is not complicated by extraneous detail, and the effect is almost that of a free-standing statue.

It is possible that since the monument apparently once stood on a high level of Structure O-13 the detail of the accession scene was carried out in the surrounding architecture or on a central stela that stood between Stelae 15 and 12. Unfortunately the failure of one of the lower terraces caused the entire front of this building to be destroyed in a downward slide of more than a meter. As a result of the destruction of stelae below, the only other monument we can attribute to this reign is Stela 12, erected in 9.18.5.0.0. This monument was found near the opposite end of the building, balancing Stela 15.

Stela 12 is carved in low but well-modulated relief. It has perhaps the most ambitious composition ever presented on a stela. The ruler is shown seated at the top of the monument, the plumes of his headdress swirling above, in the typical manner of this period. He holds a spear in his hand and leans forward in an attitude of attention. On either side, but at a lower level, stands a well-dressed figure, and between them is seated a figure divested of his finery, which is shown behind the figure at the right. The seated figure holds his hand on his shoulder in token of submission. At a still lower level are eight figures of captives bound with ropes. Morley (1037–1938 : 3 : 262–271) describes the figure seated before the king as a captive of especially high rank, but it may be worthwhile, in view of the imminent destruction of Piedras Negras, to consider a somewhat different set of circumstances. Although the finery and accoutrement of the seated figure appears to be in custody of the guard at the right, it does not include anything suggesting military arms. The figure on the right holds a small rectangle, apparently a document of some sort. It is possible that the seated figure is either a messenger or a ruler of a minor province come to plead before the king for protection from an invading foe, bringing with him prisoners taken in battle or a gift of slaves for sacrifice from various threatened settlements.

Almost an entire column of the main inscription on this monument is destroyed, and it would be difficult if not impossible to reconstruct the text. The small glyphs on the face of the monument are

T74.184.animal name
(PNG Thr 1, G'4–H'4)

fairly well preserved, and every individual portrayed is apparently named or given a designation of some sort, but our knowledge of Maya writing is still too scanty to give us even a hint of the direction from which the threat was coming, or of its nature. We know only that within the lifetime of this ruler of Piedras Negras, his throne in Structure J-6 was broken and the fragments scattered in a way that precludes its destruction being the result of a later collapse of the vault. Fragments of a throne from another palace that showed no trace of a masonry roof were found outside the building, though a number of pottery vessels inside one of the rooms suffered comparatively little damage. The deliberate mutilation of the throne suggests either a foreign foe or a violent revolt by the lower class rather than a conflict among the established cities of the Maya. In the latter case, the figure on Stela 12 shown seated before the throne may be an agent of the king, sent to round up rebellious chiefs of subject towns. Whatever the case, the end seems to have come quite suddenly and at a high point of prosperity indicated by the splendid art of the time.

Yaxchilan did not survive much longer. Here, as at Piedras Negras, we find evidence of intensified conflict during this period. Whether its militarism at this time was defensive or was due to the aggressive character of the ruler whom I have named Shield Jaguar's Descendant, it is not easy to determine. As noted in Chapter 10, we have no certain record of his birth or of his accession to power. He first appears on Lintel 2 (9.16.6.0.0) as a boy with Bird Jaguar, both holding crosses surmounted by birds, recalling the crosses of the Palenque shrines. What they signify is still a matter of speculation. Possibly they indicate the boy's initiation into membership of a clan, or his eligibility for the first rung of the ladder leading to rulership. Nine years later, on Lintel 52, we see him again with Bird Jaguar, both holding at this time manikin scepters, suggesting that he then became eligible to rule.

Unlike the art style of Piedras Negras, which seems to have been cut off abruptly at the height of its development, the style of Yaxchilan was gradually developing characteristics that I have called "decadent": overelaboration of costumes with overlapping elements and unduly exaggerated forms, the virtual elimination of space in the design, etc. Unfortunately the stelae documenting this change are not well dated by the inscriptions. Some are badly broken, perhaps deliberately destroyed. The one intact monument, Stela 16 (see Chapter 10), does not have a securely read date, although I believe it can be no earlier than 9.16.7.6.11. Stela 7 names Shield Jaguar's Descendant, apparently as the ruling lord. It is probably the earliest of his monuments. If we accept the date 9.17.5.0.0 for Stela 4, we could tentatively place Stela 7 in 9.17.10.0.0. Stelae 5 and 17 are even more typical of his reign. On both sides of Stela 5 he is shown as a warrior with two seated or kneeling figures at his feet. The better-preserved back of this monument clearly shows the long-tasseled plumes characteristic of this period, multiple ornaments on the chest, and a low-

Shield Jaguar's Descendant
(YAX St 7, pD2b)

hanging ornament suspended from his neck. Normally this ornament includes three trophy heads hung upside down, though here there is only one large upright head. The staff or spear that the figure holds ends in a serpent head with a flint knife projecting upward from its open jaws. Although the figure is badly eroded, its strongly directed pose is also characteristic of the times. Stela 17 shows a similar asymmetry, and there is little doubt that it too is of this final period of Yaxchilan. Morley (1937–1938:2:460–461) places this monument in 9.13.0.0.0, apparently on the basis of its association with Structure 44, which celebrates the victories of Shield Jaguar, but if I am right in placing it in the reign of his descendant, this may be sufficient justification for its location.

The only clear record we have concerning this ruler is on two small fragments from Stela 21, which was also associated with Structure 44. Here, the descendant is described as the captor of four persons or peoples. Of course our translation of the term may be inaccurate; he may be described merely as an overlord of certain tribes of territories. The second "name" in particular is rather suggestive of this, for it consists of the numeral 9 followed by an *ich-ben* compound suspiciously like the affix cluster of accession, as if he were being described as the ruler of "many realms." It would be a mistake to treat any of the terms here as verbatim translations, since that is not how they are intended.

captor of
(YAX St 21, G7)

9 affix cluster
(YAX St 21, H7)

Since lintels usually carry no dedicatory dates, and since their representations are not always limited to events in a single reign, we can date them only by style and association in a single building. Even this is not always possible, as in the case of the central lintel on Structure 13, Lintel 32, which names Shield Jaguar, whose representation is completely consistent with the style of his reign, although the other two lintels cannot be earlier than the last years of Bird Jaguar and were even more probably carved in the reign of his successor. Lintel 32 itself could have been copied from an earlier manuscript. The figures on Lintels 50 and 33 flank Lintel 32 on either side, both facing to the right and showing the left profile. Although Lintel 33 depicts Bird Jaguar, and the ensemble is discussed in Chapter 10, the inscription on Lintel 50 is too badly eroded to yield a reading, and these two lintels, if not all three, may well have been carved in the reign of Shield Jaguar's Descendant.

There is assuredly no question that the lintels of Structure 20 are no earlier than his reign, though none of the three lintels of this structure clearly records his name. These lintels are analogous to those of Structures 23 and 21, which were built during the two previous reigns. One lintel in each of these structures features the ruler as a warrior, though in each case the lintel occupies a different position in its building, and the motif is presented somewhat differently. In Structure 21 it is the central lintel, in Structure 23 it is on the right of the central lintel as one faces the building, and in Structure 20 it is on the left. Shield Jaguar is shown with a woman who holds his jaguar helmet and shield while he holds a knife in his hand. Bird Jaguar is shown with a spear before a crouching figure. Shield Jaguar's Descendant, if it is he, is also shown with a spear, and stands with an attendant and four bound captives. In his temple, the bloodletting scene is omitted and another invocation scene is substituted. In these scenes, the woman holds a vessel with sacrificial objects, and both she and her companion hold pointed objects implying bloodletting. I have assumed that in the martial scene the protagonist is Shield Jaguar's Descendant though the text is completely illegible. Nor does either of the men pictured in the invocation scene bear his name.

In the earlier invocation scenes, it will be recalled that no men were present. In the scenes of Structure 20, the woman stands facing the ancestral figure in the jaws of the serpent which rests on the hand of the man. Although almost identical in composition, the two lintels differ in the quality of relief as well as in the composition of the text, suggesting that they were carved by different sculptors. Of the two, Lintel 14, over the doorway on the right, has the stronger relief and a much clearer text. The headdress of the woman on this lintel is essentially a mask with the *kin* sign on its forehead and the Triadic Symbol above. This probably indicates that she is a queen in her own right. The ancestor in the jaws of the serpent is apparently also a woman. Since on the earlier Lintel 15, the clause beginning with the fish-in-hand glyph does not contain a woman's name, which is in a separate cartouche and is introduced by the "jog" glyph, we may conclude that, on Lintel 14, the penitent's name is in the upper panel, which also begins with the "jog." A woman's head attached to the "spot" Emblem of Yaxchilan suggests that she may be from another district or maybe a descendant of Shield Jaguar. The second glyph of her name is a *yax*–moon-sign with infixed upside-down *ahau*, suggesting something in the nature of the new moon, or the first day of the calendar, Imix, which occurs in the cartouche below the serpent. This day, 4 Imix 4 Mol, followed by the fish-in-hand glyph, can be 9.15.10.0.1 if it refers to something in the past or 9.18.2.13.1 if it is more or less contemporary. The same date is also inscribed on the central lintel of Structure 16, Lintel 39, which depicts a male figure in a reclining pose, holding the flaccid body of a two-headed serpent on his arms. This lintel, however, is carved in a style that appears to be much earlier, and it is difficult to reconcile either of these dates with the two quite different styles of the two lintels. It should be noted, however, that the "jog" glyph on Lintel 39 refers to a woman with a *kin* title, while on Lintel 14 this title does not appear after the "jog" glyph, but after the statement that follows the fish-in-hand glyph. The interpretation of such scenes as these and of the fish-in-hand glyph requires more study than I have afforded it in the present work, but we might speculate that in spite of the identity of dates, Lintel 39 refers to Bird Jaguar soon after his death, and Lintel 14 depicts mourning for the death of the woman shown on Lintel 1,

"jog"
(YAX L 14, A)

Lady of Yaxchilan
(YAX L 14, B)

Lady Yax Moon Inverted-Ahau
(YAX L 14, C)

where she is designated as the "daughter (?) of Skull," here simply Lady X Skull. It is interesting to note that the last hieroglyph of her name appears to be the bat which also accompanies her name on Lintel 1 and that the next-to-last is also the last that appears in the name of the man shown with Bird Jaguar on Lintel 3 as well as with the man pictured on Lintel 42 (see Chapter 10).

Lintel 13 shows in its design a certain imprecision that was not noticeable on Lintel 14. Perhaps it was designed by a less able artist or was deliberately sketched to give the effect of freedom from the dominant tradition—a quality that I have elsewhere called "decadence." The hieroglyphs are irregular in form and crowded together in panels that are not strictly perpendicular, and whose lines are not strictly straight. Ian Graham gives 1 ? 13 ? as the numbers for the date recorded (Graham and von Euw 1977:35), and his drawing of the event glyph looks somewhat like the usual birth notation, followed by the first glyph of Shield Jaguar's Descendant's name. I can neither confirm nor refute this reading from the photograph published in Morley (1937–1938), but I think a redating of 1 ? 11 Pop is also possible. If we accept Graham's reading and assume that Shield Jaguar's Descendant is still very young when he appears on Lintel 2 (9.16.6.0.0), four dates are possible for his birth: 9.16.1.9.5 1 Chicchan 13 Kankin, 9.16.0.14.5 1 Chicchan 13 Pop, 9.15.8.6.0 1 Ahau 13 Kankin, and 9.15.7.11.0 1 Ahau 13 Pop. The first two, however, leave him too young, at four or five years old; the second pair, at seventeen or eighteen, are better, but I would prefer a date between. This can be done by changing the coefficient of the month to 11 or 12, but this would not be justified without a careful examination of both the month coefficient and the day sign. Moreover, I suspect that what looks like a birth notation may in fact be the fish-in-hand glyph that goes with such scenes, though in that case, the mention of Bird Jaguar would have to be explained. To create further confusion, on Lintel 57, the first glyph of Shield Jaguar's Descendant without the mention of Shield Jaguar, but with a sky title and main Emblem Glyph of Yaxchilan appears over the figure of a woman seated on a throne. Preceding, however, are four glyphs giving a woman's name which contains a skull glyph and ends with what is often the last glyph of both women's and men's names (see Lintels 54, 6, 8, 16, etc.). It is not clear, however, whether the two parts of the inscription should be read as one, or whether the name on the left belongs to the younger woman standing in front, wearing on her head an enormous bird with a fish in its mouth.

We know in fact very little about the reign of Shield Jaguar's Descendant, and I suspect that he did not reign very long and either was killed in battle or was caught up in the disaster that soon overtook Yaxchilan. There is a fourth invocation scene shown on Lintel 55 in Structure 88, but it apparently had no inscription at all, or had one that was painted. On this lintel, both the man and the woman are seated, and the visage of the ancestor in the mouth of a serpent

Lady X Skull
(YAX L 14, F2)

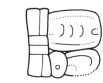

Shield Jaguar's Descendant
(YAX L 57, D1)

sky title
(YAX L 57, D2)

Yaxchilan Emblem Glyph
(YAX L 57, D3)

looms over the woman's head. The date of this carving is difficult to judge, but I suspect that it might be quite late, and may refer to an unknown last ruler of Yaxchilan.

What seems to be the last record we have from Yaxchilan is on Lintel 10 from Structure 3, on the lowest terrace overlooking the river. It is an all-glyphic lintel, and the glyph-blocks are poorly defined, especially at the end, where four are crowded into one block. The sculptor did not plan his work well, and the script is cursive and irregular. Certain aspects of this inscription are suggestive of the character of the events with which it deals. The entire inscription covers a period of twenty eight days—the length of one moon. The only personal name that we can clearly recognize is that of the woman named in the principal panel of Lintel 13. Three dates separate the inscription into three parts, and the first, longest part is further subdivided into four segments by the presence of the "jog" glyph. What is most notable in this inscription is that although both Emblems used at Yaxchilan are present here, they do not occur together.

The text begins with the date 7 Cimi G3(?) F 14 Zip (9.18.17.12.6?) followed by a hand glyph (T670), with an infixed inverted *ahau,* and *u*-2 plus a cartouche with circlets in a vertical row, which I have not found in Thompson's catalog. The two seem to form an introductory statement to the statement introduced by the "jog," which names someone as a captor of Ah (T12) ? Parrot from, or belonging to, the "spot" Emblem of Yaxchilan, first used by Shield Jaguar. Another clause closes with a *kin* compound, an *ahau* compound (evidently a name), and the statement that he is "captor of Torch Parrot, Ah Sixteen Bone" and the original Yaxchilan Emblem Glyph. Nowhere in this inscription are the two Emblems used together, and considering the number of "captor" expressions used, I suspect that what is implied is an internal conflict between two factions or terri-

hand with inverted *ahau*
(YAX L 10, A2b)

cartouche with circlets
(YAX L 10, B2a)

captor of
(YAX L 10, A3b)

Ah ? Parrot + Yaxchilan "spot"
Emblem Glyph
(YAX L 10, B3)

Captor of Torch Parrot
(YAX L 10, B6)

Ah Sixteen Bone + Yaxchilan
Emblem Glyph
(YAX L 10, A7)

tories of the Yaxchilan state: the original city and the followers of Shield Jaguar, whose territory may have been united with it, or whose people may have immigrated there.

The final statement in the first pair of columns declares the capture of still another "parrot." The first and the last parrots mentioned are both prefixed with T12, a prefix which sometimes appears before expressions that may designate groups as in the Yucatec "Ah Itza," and in this case the parrot names may well be generic, referring to the tribe or clan. The second parrot mentioned, however, does not have this prefix but one that looks like a torch, and this may designate the chief of the parrots.

The middle pair of columns begins again with the introductory expression and the "jog" glyph. It contains a skull glyph, a quincunx glyph, an *imix* compound, and again a captor expression, but whether in this case the parrot is the captive or the captor is not entirely clear. The next "jog" glyph is followed by signs with numbers 1 and 5, for which I have no explanation, and the name of a woman who almost certainly is the same one who is mentioned in the central glyphic panel on Lintel 13, or possibly her daughter. The first glyph of her name on Lintel 13 is not clear, but could conceivably be the *kin*-on-pedestal sign which on Lintel 10 is shown lying on its side. On both lintels it is followed by a woman's head with a necklace, a common combination used as a title (possibly designating a queen). The identifying sign of a woman's head with encircled crossed bands is present in both inscriptions, though on Lintel 10 it is preceded by another head glyph which may indicate a daughter, and the two are followed by a third head, also with the crossed-bands sign, and by an *ich-ben* expression that usually indicates the Emblem of her origin. Next is mentioned the captor of Torch Parrot, and a Secondary Series of 1.4 leads to the date 5 Oc 19 Zotz' (9.18.17.13.10).

I am at a loss to interpret the passage that follows, though it might be worth mentioning that it contains a half-spotted *ahau* and a sky glyph that vaguely links it with the inscription on the main panel of Lintel 14. It contains a curious set of three consecutive compounds, two containing the *ich-ben* and the third the *ben-ich* compound. The next phrase can be read: *u caban,* the captor of (the sacrificed?) Parrot, (original) Emblem of Yaxchilan. Four days later, on 9 Ix 2 Zec, the same hand glyph as before introduces a passage that I do not venture to interpret, except to note that the inscription ends by naming the captor and sacrificer of Parrot, and concludes with the main (original) Emblem of Yaxchilan.

This inscription deserves more detailed study than I have devoted to it in this work. Thompson lists all the "parrots" that I have mentioned as "turtles" (T743), but the forms at B6 and C7 have suffixes that suggest a feather, as somewhat less clearly do those at D3 and F8. The parrots at A8 and F4 do not have a feather, but have a ring of dots around the eye. F2 and E3, on the other hand, have a large eye with a pupil, and the latter shows the curl that distinguishes the

kin on pedestal + woman's head with necklace (YAX L 10 C5)

turtle from the bird. The rather ambiguous "turtles" with circles attached to the eye on the back of their heads on Lintels 1 and 2, I believe to be animated forms of T516b, for they function with affixes that suggest verbal rather than substantive forms. However, I do not intend to pursue these matters here. What is more important is whether this cursive and unrestrained style of Yaxchilan is properly dated, and whether its date is consistent with the disciplined and sophisticated style that we see in Piedras Negras only two years earlier.

Although both Bowditch (1903) and Morley (1937–1938:2:393–394) judged the character of the script on Lintel 10 to be early, I have elected to place it at the very end of the sequence of known dates here, in a period of decline in a last struggle against a foe that finally destroyed the city. I base this conclusion on two considerations: the presence of the name of a woman who is mentioned also on Lintel 13 of Structure 20, a lintel carved in the exuberant style that followed the rule of the great Bird Jaguar, and on a comparison with the script on this lintel, which also exhibits some degenerative qualities. However, lintels occasionally refer to events in the past, and since there are two lintels in Structure 20 which present the same motif, it is possible that the date on Lintel 13 is earlier than that which I have suggested. The text of the lintel may refer to a birth, perhaps the birth of Shield Jaguar's Descendant, though Shield Jaguar's name is omitted, and farther on appears the name Bird Jaguar.

Considering the ambiguity of this text, one should allow for the possibility that the reference is to a past occurrence, to an event in the life of an earlier Bird Jaguar or to the time of his death, celebrated by his descendants. The values 9.10.19.9.6, 9.10.19.10.10, and 9.10.19.10.14 for the dates on Lintel 10 would place the conflict with the "parrots" closer to the time when Lightning Sky of Tikal subdued the "parrots" at Dos Pilas in 9.11.11.9.17. This would mean that the conflict at Yaxchilan preceded that at Dos Pilas and that the crude script of Lintel 10 was due to the disruption of the court, either by the absence of the king or by his death in battle. It could account also for the destruction of the monuments pertaining to the earlier Bird Jaguar and their later recarving. Shield Jaguar, in such a case, would appear to have been the rescuer of Yaxchilan from a bad situation, rather than its conqueror. The matter can only be resolved if we can determine the identity of the "parrots." There are two promising possibilities: the parrot glyph may represent the local aristocracy because of its gaudy attire; or it may be an ancient term for highlanders, with whom the Maya of the lowlands traded to obtain feathers for their headdresses: the long green tail feathers of the quetzal, the national bird of Guatemala, and the brilliant red plumage of the macaw. Several different varieties of parrots can be distinguished, including one that has a prefix that looks like a bundle of sticks, who may have been their leader (Fire-parrot, the Macaw?).

Bonampak is best known for its magnificent murals, discovered by Giles Healey in 1946, photographed by him, and drawn and painted by Carlos Villagra and Antonio Tejeda (Ruppert, Thompson, and Proskouriakoff 1955). The region between the Jatate and the Usumacinta rivers, where the ruins are located, is heavily forested and has been only sketchily explored. Even the location of Bonampak in relation to other sites in the vicinity, such as Lacanha and Kuna, is only approximately known. Until recently the only inhabitants of the region were Lacandon Indians taking refuge from civilization, and perhaps in ancient times, too, it served as a retreat in times of invasion or other catastrophes in the cities on the Usumacinta.

Bonampak is a small site, but among its sculptured remains we find a strange discontinuity in style. Of its eight stelae, only three show sculpture, and all are in a late style very like that of Yaxchilan. The three lintels of Structure 1, on which Stela 1 is centered, are also of this period. The lintel of Structure 6 (Lintel 1), however, appears to be in an earlier style. The date suggested by J. E. S. Thompson (Ruppert, Thompson, and Proskouriakoff 1955), 9.8.9.15.11 7 Chuen 4 Zotz', would place it near the date of Lacanha Stela 1 (see Chapter 7), and in view of some early elements in its design, such as the position of the hands holding a serpent-bar and the form of the snout of the serpent, it seems an appropriate date for it, though unlike the stela at Lacanha it is, in general conception, more like motifs of Yaxchilan than of Piedras Negras. This was still a period of unrest when the frontiers of the larger sites were probably not clearly drawn and the dynasties not firmly fixed, and defeated factions may have chosen to emigrate. Thus the earlier sculptures of Bonampak show divergent styles and techniques.

Sculptured Stone 2 shows a figure seated in a lunar cartouche, an arrangement that recalls the sky motifs of later stelae at Yaxchilan, but at Yaxchilan the lunar cartouche encloses the figure of a woman, while here the figure appears to be that of a man. Moreover, the figure here is shown in full-face view, and holds in his arms a creature that looks somewhat like a rabbit, though I am not certain of this identification. Unfortunately the text on this piece is inscribed, and is so worn and faint that it is virtually illegible.

Sculptured Stone 1 is carved in a different technique and a completely different style. The figures are deeply inscribed, with only touches here and there of modeling, giving the impression of intaglio relief. This stone depicts a man seated on a bench, leaning forward toward three figures seated on the ground before him. The foremost man holds up to him the head of the so-called Jester God, like that held by the main figure in the sanctuary of the Temple of the Cross at Palenque. The slender figure of the man on the bench, his simple costume, the marked deformation of his head, and the way he leans stiffly forward without bending his body all recall Palenque reliefs. However, a similar pose can be seen also at Piedras Negras, on Lintel 7, which has an Initial Series in Katun 9. The dates of the inscription of the Bonampak stone are written with head numerals which are difficult to identify. Thompson (Ruppert, Thompson, and Proskouriakoff 1955) has suggested the date 9.10.0.0.0 for this stone, but Peter Mathews (1980:72) has proposed the date 9.13.0.0.0 as the final date of this inscription, which accords better with my judgment of its style. On the subject matter of the inscription and on the interpretation of the scene we differ somewhat, but since Mathews' article is unpublished at the time of writing of this chapter, I do not wish to argue the matter here. To me, the scene seems to imply an offering by a delegation to the man on the bench of some office of honor, perhaps a rulership of a town or people, perhaps merely the submission of a neighboring group or clan.

Sculptured Stone 3, which Ruppert describes as a figure of a crouching jaguar (Ruppert, Thompson, and Proskouriakoff 1955), is very similar to the "alligator" pictured in Morley's (1937-1938) Plate 178A-c, which is said to have been near Stela 1 of Yaxchilan. It is a pity these sculptures cannot be dated. On the photograph in Ruppert, Thompson, and Proskouriakoff 1955, the creature looks to me more like an alligator than like a jaguar. I have no suggestions about its significance, except as another link between Yaxchilan and Bonampak.

The intriguing aspect of these sculptures is that their differences cannot be readily explained by reference only to a developing local tradition. The presence of plain stelae does not permit us to conclude that the occupation of this small site was discontinuous, but it does suggest that originally Bonampak was a dependency of a larger site in the vicinity, and may even have been unoccupied for a time before it was conquered or resettled by a group from Yaxchilan.

It is unfortunate that Stela 2, which appears to be the earliest of the three sculptured stelae, has no period-ending date. It is carved in much lower relief than the other two monuments, and is much more static and conventional in style. I would be inclined to put it earlier rather than later than the two other stelae or to assume that it was copied from an earlier document, therefore placing the dates one Calendar Round earlier. This does not result, however, in a viable solution to the problem of the two names that are repeatedly mentioned on these monuments. I therefore tentatively accept Thompson's reading, 9.17.5.8.9 6 Muluc 17 Yaxkin and 9.17.18.15.18 12 Etz'nab 1 Ceh. The first date records an accession to rulership, followed by a compound of a sky glyph and a *moan* bird, which normally would be read as the name of the new king, pictured on the stela, but I have some hesitation in doing so, since this name is never, so far as we know, associated with the Emblem Glyph. Several reasons may come to mind: that the reference here is not to a person, but to the seizing of power by an invading army; that the reference is to a person who ruled without a royal title, this title being held by a woman whose husband had died in battle; and finally, that the person pictured is not the *moan* bird, but the king who is mentioned at the end of the

sky + *moan* compound
(BPK St 2, D1)

inscription. Other interpretations of this text can be proposed, and it is a sad reminder of how little we know of what is actually said in Maya texts.

The second date refers to the woman standing before the main figure, holding a sharp point associated with bloodletting rites. The meaning of the statement about her is unknown. Her name ends with one of two glyphs that occur with various names of men and women at Yaxchilan. This glyph is a head with a sign covering the mouth, and a lunar postfix. The other such glyph has the same postfix attached to a comb element. These two glyphs apparently distinguish two royal clans or lineages at Yaxchilan, and an interesting study could be made of them if other such pairs could be found elsewhere. It may be worth noting here that the comb-moon element occurs four times on the lintel from Kuna, dated 9.15.15.0.0, where it is associated with a quincunx and fire-fist glyph, both of which are strongly linked to mortuary motifs. The problem of family structure among the aristocratic Maya is much too intricate and complex to be discussed here. The results of my own research on the subject have been inconclusive so far, as, it appears to me, have been those of others.

The next two columns repeat the name *Moan* Bird, expanding it into three glyphs. The first is a bat glyph with prefix T126, the second, the sky element with the same prefix, and the third the *moan* bird, who is then characterized as the captor of Five Skull (?). I am uncertain how to read the final passage. Some scholars interpret the first glyph of this passage as indicating that the name that follows is that of the father of the king, but I do not see on what evidence they base this conclusion. This compound of the sign *ahau* does, usually, refer to a previous reign, but to assume that it implies paternity is a gratuitous conclusion, since we do not know the rules that governed the succession of Maya kings. I prefer to read it as "in the reign of." Another question arises in regard to the Emblem Glyph at the end of the passage. Does it refer to the name of a former ruler, which is a compound of Thompson's (ocelot?) glyph T742, or does it refer to the *moan* bird? I think the former is the case. Whether we assume that the *moan* bird is a person or that it stands for an invading group, the composition, which makes reference to a bloodletting ceremony, is not unlike that which is depicted on such lintels as Lintel 17 and Lintel 24 at Yaxchilan. If the widow of the "ocelot" king inherited the rule, as apparently happened in the case of Shield Jaguar's wife (see Chapter 10), then it would be understandable why the *moan* bird figure does not lay claim to the rulership, though he may be actually in control. The feminine figure behind him is apparently from Yaxchilan, since she has the Yaxchilan Emblem Glyph, though without the prefix of royalty.

Peter Mathews (1980:61–64) has restored the almost completely effaced Initial Series on Stela 1 to read 9.17.10.0.0. The date is followed by two glyphs of unknown meaning, and then by the hand-

head with sign over mouth
(BPK St 2, E8)

? + ocelot?
(BPK St 2, G4)

Lady of Yaxchilan
(BPK St 2, H3)

face with black mask + death mask
(BPK St 1, J)

Bonampak Emblem Glyph
(BPK St 1, M)

bat Emblem Glyph
(BPK St 1, N)

scattering-grains glyph that apparently signifies divination. The first glyphs of the lower frame, which probably names the portrait on this stela, end with the *moan* bird, and again there is no indication of an Emblem. Thus the status of the *moan* bird remains ambiguous. The horizontal row of glyphs above the base mask of this monument is of some interest, though its meaning escapes me. It begins with the expression of a hand glyph, with thumb pointing upward, and an infixed upside-down *ahau*. This seems to be followed by a woman's head and a glyph of unknown meaning. The second glyph-block, however, is composed of a face covered by a black mask with a suffix, and then a death mask. The identical black mask and its suffix followed by a death expression follow the capture glyph on Lintel 44 of Yaxchilan, which depicts the capture of a prisoner by Shield Jaguar on 13 Ahau 3 Muan (9.12.17.12.0?). Immediately following the death glyph on Stela 1 is the *ahau* compound followed by a skull compound and the "ocelot" name. The next glyphs are an incomplete Emblem Glyph of Bonampak attached to a young head and a bat Emblem Glyph with all its components. This bat glyph, with infixed spots on its cheek, is clearly not the "sky bat" of Copan, but perhaps a cave bat of the earth. A number of possible interpretations of this passage come to mind, but all involve one or another unjustified assumption. Although it appears that the *moan* bird may have been an intruder from Yaxchilan of less than royal status, the resolution of the problems must be put off until we know the meaning of the hand glyph and of the *ahau* compound, which has not been determined to my satisfaction.

Stela 3, dated 9.17.15.0.0, is even more flamboyant than Stela 1 in its use of sweeping feathers and the principal figure's enormous mask headdress. Above a kneeling figure wearing armor, he holds an *atlatl* in the form of a serpent, as well as a bag in his left hand. The text after the hotun date begins with the divination glyph and ends with the sky-and-*moan* glyph and two *ich-ben* expressions, the first the Bonampak Emblem Glyph, the second possibly the bat. Below is a column of smaller glyphs which seems to begin with a Secondary Series to be counted forward to a date that is indistinct on the published photographs.

The presence here and at this time of the Mexican *atlatl* is unexpected. Possibly it was taken from the enemy kneeling at the figure's feet. If Stela 2 is correctly dated, its more conservative style also deserves an explanation. One may wonder if Stelae 1 and 3 were not carved later than their dates indicate, to commemorate the takeover of this small site by some group from Yaxchilan in the course of the wars that ultimately destroyed the larger city.

Lintels 1, 2, and 3, which span the doorways of Structure 1, the building with the famous murals, are remarkably like the lintels of Structure 44 at Yaxchilan that record the conquests of Shield Jaguar. From the dynamic poses of the figures and the flamboyant use of featherwork, we judge them to have been executed much later. Since they do not record Initial Series, we cannot place them in time with any certainty, but, relying on the names mentioned, we can assume that the dates must fall near those that we find on stelae associated with the same individuals. In the case of Lintels 1 and 2, this poses no problem. The date of Lintel 3, however, remains problematical. The inscriptions on all the lintels are somewhat damaged and appear to be encrusted with lime. Mathews has kindly provided me with drawings that are more legible.

Lintel 1 begins with a date 8 Eb 10 (probably Cumku) that can be read as 9.17.16.3.12, recording the capture of (Ah?) Five Skull. Three more glyphs follow. Another column begins with a damaged glyph and names Moan Bird. As before, there is no associated Emblem Glyph, and the last two glyphs are of unknown meaning. The illustration shows a warrior with a spear grasping a recumbent figure by the hair. The figure is scantily dressed, but carries a flexible shield, which suggests that he, too, may be a warrior. Such figures, however, may be symbolic of conquered peoples, rather than portraits of specific individuals.

The date on Lintel 2 is very probably 9.17.16.3.8 4 Lamat 6 Cumku, four days before the date on Lintel 1. One may wonder if it is mere coincidence that two of the captures recorded on Lintel 10 of Yaxchilan were also just four days apart. The hieroglyphs on this lintel are not at all clear and their meaning is enigmatic. Mathews suggests that the protagonist of this scene is the ruler of Yaxchilan to whom I have referred as Shield Jaguar's Descendant. His name, unfortunately, is variable and his dates uncertain, and although a "parrot" is mentioned among his captures, it is not the Torch Parrot who is credited to a king of Yaxchilan at the feet of the main figure on Lintel 2. The main capture reported on the lintel appears to be that of Bat, but his other designations are not clear. Nor is the column over the head of the captive clear, though the last two glyphs refer to a parrot, and record the Emblem Glyph of Yaxchilan without the royal prefix. I would prefer, for the present, to leave the identity of these individuals open.

Lintel 3, like Lintels 1 and 2, is a capture scene, and its inscription also presents problems that are not easily solved. Its date, moreover, is written in the manner that was prevalent in the reign of Shield Jaguar, with the coefficient of the month one less than expected: 3 Ix 1 Yax. This is a capture date, but who is the captor and who the captured is not clear. The date itself, if it is indeed 3 Ix 2 Yax, is probably 9.17.9.11.14, but if the month is Ceh, it could be 9.18.1.16.14, a value that I prefer, since it brings it nearer to the probable date of the paintings within the building.

It is interesting to note here the Trophy Jaguar glyph that accompanied a conquest made by Shield Jaguar in 9.12.0.0.0. This name is mentioned on very early lintels at Yaxchilan, apparently as one of the earliest settlers of the region. This throws some doubt on my suggestion that Shield Jaguar came from the north, where the aberrant

Trophy Jaguar
(BPK L 3, A6)

numbering of the days of the month is more common; however, we have no early inscriptions anywhere of this type of notation, and its late occurrence here does not help to solve the problem of its origin. Presumably the name of the captor is given in the column of glyphs in front of him, but strangely enough, the "jog" glyph, which usually introduces a name, is here directly followed by a *ben-ich* bat glyph and what is probably the Emblem Glyph of Bonampak. There are still so many aspects of these inscriptions that are obscure that it is hazardous to try to reconstruct the events, and in particular to identify the conquered, but I have little doubt that the conquerors came from Yaxchilan and, though not themselves of royal family, were perhaps rewarded with a marriage which gave to their sons the privileges of royalty.

There seems to be no strict rule at Yaxchilan for the arrangement of lintels. Two structures there, Structure 10 and Structure 12, have all-glyphic lintels, so that the order of reading is known. In Structure 10, the text apparently starts in the central doorway and proceeds left to right as one faces the building. If one views Structure 12 from outside, however, the text, starting with an Initial Series, runs from right to left, though from the inside of the building, it would start just to the left of the central doorway, run left to right to the end wall, and then continue from the extreme right wall back to the central lintel. Although the lintels at Bonampak do not form a continuous text, the murals inside the three rooms may show an order similar to that of these Yaxchilan examples.

The murals of Bonampak are too well known to deserve a detailed description here. I would surmise that the central room depicting the taking of captives should be considered first. The aggressors are dressed in full battle array, wearing headdresses, often in the form of animal heads, and carrying spears and shields, but though the spears are brandished menacingly, the object apparently is not to kill, but to grasp by the hair or otherwise subdue the unarmed and scantily dressed victims. On the end wall on the left, there is a blowing of trumpets and a waving of huge fans, and on the back wall at the top we see the leaders of this fray, two dressed in jaguar skins and others wearing huge feather headdresses. Over the front doorway is a scene usually alluded to as "the arraignment of prisoners." It takes place on a platform approached by six steps. Here four figures are dressed in jaguar skins. At the left, the leader of a group of six men is presenting a seated prisoner to the central figure. On the left of the central figure are two more dressed in jaguar costume, and behind them are two women, very probably the women portrayed on Stela 2. Behind them stands a fat servant dressed in a white loincloth and cap. Each individual is seemingly identified by two or more glyphs, but the script is cursive and damaged, and from Tejeda's drawings I have not been able to identify more than three or four characters. On the two steps just below sit six more captives and another who is sprawling as if wounded, with a severed head placed on leaves at his feet. Red drops fall from the hands of the four captives on the left, and a warrior is holding up the hand of one of these captives. It has been suggested that fingernails were being torn from the hands by this warrior, but perhaps the prisoners are merely being marked with paint or tattooed to identify their captors. Sixteen other figures are grouped on the ground below the steps.

The room at the left end of the building contains a long inscription, but one which is badly damaged. It begins with an Initial Series in Katun 16 or 18. The latter seems more likely, and I am inclined to accept Thompson's reading of 9.18.0.3.4 (Ruppert, Thompson, and Proskouriakoff 1955), though I am somewhat skeptical of the second date he proposes. The principal scene in this room is an interior, as indicated by the reddish background. At the left we see a company of dignitaries wearing white capes decorated with shells. All have their heads turned toward a couple in their midst, a man and a woman, who seem to be explaining to them the significance of the occasion. On a raised dais is a family group, and from the edge of this dais a man is presenting an infant to the assembled dignitaries, who, however, are not looking at him, but conferring among themselves. The man holding the infant is looking back toward the family group. This group includes five persons: a man in the center, on his left two women, probably the same two that appeared in the arraignment scene and also on Stela 2. The younger woman stands on the floor with a bundle behind her. The man and the older woman are seated on a throne, with another individual seated to the man's right, and what appears to be a servant on the floor in front of him. I will not attempt to suggest the family relationships of this group, except to conjecture that the young lady at the right, who, from the inscription on Stela 2, appears to be from Yaxchilan, may be the mother of the future king. The remainder of this room is apparently devoted to a pageant or dance performed for the entertainment of the guests. In the upper register, over the doorway, we see the preparation for the performance. Three men wearing jaguar-skin skirts apparently are being dressed for the outdoor performance shown below. On a lower level, the servants are preparing jaguar skins, dyeing cloth, and so forth. One servant apparently reaches to the higher level to adjust a tassel worn by one of the performers. In the outdoor scene below, we see five performers dressed like aquatic animals surrounding the hero of the piece, who is a young man. There is a full orchestra that includes trumpets, turtle carapaces stroked with a forked stick, a drum, and rattles. In the center stand three dancers with enormous feather back ornaments, such as were being tried on in the dressing scene. At the right are thirteen other performers, two of them carrying large feather fans or parasols, such as appear in the battle scene also.

The scene in the third room is a veritable extravaganza. It takes place on an open platform approached by a stairway. In the upper register on the left, the royal family is seen performing a blood sacrifice. The younger woman stands behind the throne, and seated on the floor in front is apparently a servant holding the infant. At the right kneels the fat man who presents the child to the audience in the interior scene of the room at the other end of the building. Over the front doorway is an assemblage of ten dignitaries standing in a row and conversing, and below them are seated nine persons apparently of lesser rank. The upper register of the outer wall is mostly destroyed, but it seems once to have shown a crowd of people carrying on their shoulders something like a litter raising aloft an individual with an enormous nose and unidentifiable objects in his hands. It may be that he is directing the performance, but I rather suspect that he is a dressed wooden image of some sort, designed for the amusement of the audience. There are ten dancers in all, wearing enormous feather headdresses, with long red and green swirling plumes. Great triangular projections at hip level are painted with various devices and trimmed with clipped feathers. Three of these dancers are ranged on the top two steps at the center. They carry fans and small hatchets. A red hand is painted on one of the fans. The other dancers are standing below, on the ground. The focus of the entire design appears to be a nude figure apparently sprawled on the steps or tumbling down, while two attendants are tying his wrists and ankles. Above them stands a small individual, possibly the executioner. This has been interpreted as a scene of human sacrifice: but if the man has been killed and is being thrown down the steps of the pyramid, why tie his hands and feet?

There are still many questions more serious than these that have not been answered. Even the order of the events presented here is uncertain. The pomp and triumph displayed in these scenes is out of character with the undistinguished architectural remains of this small site, and if this was an attempt to remove the court of Yaxchilan to a new location or to establish a satellite dynasty, the attempt probably failed, for there are no later monuments to tell us of later events. This could have been, however, a temporary expedient to remove the heir to the throne from Yaxchilan if the city was under siege and its king had been killed. Soon after the events recorded at Bonampak, Yaxchilan Lintel 10 was inscribed to commemorate the battles that took place there, but at that time, Yaxchilan may already have been in ruins, or about to fall to the enemy. At Piedras Negras, Satterthwaite (1937:20) has noted deliberate destruction of thrones, which could not be ascribed to natural causes. Elsewhere, the breaking up of older monuments and their reuse in later construction has been noted, but these finds are incidental, and I know of no instance where there has been observed large-scale destruction prior to final abandonment of a site.

We have very little information on other minor sites on the Usumacinta and in the region between this river and the Jatate. Two wall panels from El Cayo, on the left bank of the river between Piedras Negras and Yaxchilan, have been mentioned in Chapter 10. There are at least two stelae there pertaining to this period. They stand on one of the platforms of a large palace-like building. Both are carved only on one face, and neither has a legible text, but both are very clearly of this general period. Stela 1 presents a divination motif. The swaying position of the figure as he leans forward to scatter grains, the rounded contour of his belt, and especially the long tasseled plumes that fall forward from his headdress are clear indications of its late date. Stela 2 shows two figures at different elevations. One figure stands at ground level holding a feathered object in his hand; the other is seated on high, above the level of his shoulders. The design is obscure, and the brief inscriptions on both the monuments are not legible in Maler's (1901–1903:2: Pl. 34) photographs. Nor do we know the extent of this site or whether there are other monuments in the vicinity.

While at El Cayo, Maler was told of magnificent sculptures and paintings to be found at Budsilha, where the stream of that name enters the Usumacinta. He went there but found only an insignificant temple. One can't help wondering whether the rumor originated at Bonampak, or if there is another site like Bonampak still undiscovered on that stream.

At a short distance from El Cayo, near the Laguna Petha, is the site of La Mar. Here there are three known stelae, two broken but with carving fairly well preserved, though the glyphs of the inscriptions are difficult to make out. On one of the stelae, we see a scene comparable to that of Stela 2 at El Cayo. The principal figure sits on high, and on a lower level are two kneeling figures, one of which may be a woman. The inscription begins with a date 2 Muluc (?) 2 Uo (9.17.12.4.9), and a Secondary Series, 2.13.11, leads to 5 Ahau 3 Muan (9.17.15.0.0). Stela 2 of La Mar was probably erected one katun later on 3 Ahau 3 Yax (9.18.15.0.0). It, too, shows figures on two levels, and above them seems to have been some carving which was later trimmed off. There are two figures on the upper level, one of them in dancing pose, very common, especially in minor sites, at this time. All the figures carry in one hand small rectangular objects with two projecting strings at one end, possible scrolls of paper, and all wear elaborate mask headdresses. Each personage is identified by a small group of glyphs. For the most part, the glyphs are badly damaged, though one may note that the group pertaining to the personage at the upper left ends with a face glyph with covered mouth and lunar postfix, somewhat like Thompson's 1004a, a glyph often seen with names at Yaxchilan. Maler (1901–1903:2:95–96) describes this monument as having been painted with red, green, and blue pigment, and I have noted faint traces of these colors also on some of the stelae from Piedras Negras now in the National Museum of Guatemala, though the actual pigments had disappeared, and only a faint stain on the stone was discernible.

The third stela from La Mar dated from 9.18.5.0.0 and mentions two earlier dates: 9.18.1.8.18 3 Etz'nab 6 Zotz' and probably 9.18.3.2.19 6 Cauac 2 Pax, if the Distance Number, 1.12.1, is a forward count.

Maler (1901–1903:2:100–104) describes El Chicozapote as a large site, but illustrates only four lintels from a minor building, which he describes as "archaic." I suspect, however, that they may be very late. Only two of these lintels have inscriptions, and they are poorly executed, more in the manner of Yaxchilan's Lintel 10 than of any early style with which I am familiar. The other two show seated figures dressed very simply and wearing high, plain, almost cylindrical headdresses. This site might be worth exploring more thoroughly, but being in a heavily wooded area, and not readily accessible, little seems to be known about it.

Better known is the site of Altar de Sacrificios, at the confluence of the rivers Chixoy and Pasión, whose inscriptions were studied by John A. Graham (1972). Here, there is a gap in the epigraphic record after 9.17.0.0.0, which is not resumed until after the turn of the cycle. There had been a previous such gap in stela erection between 9.11.10.0.0 and 9.14.0.0.0, at a time when Shield Jaguar took over the reign of Yaxchilan, and when the presence of a king of Tikal was noted at Dos Pilas. Uninterrupted erection of stelae is the best indication of stable and peaceful conditions. Unfortunately, the absence of stelae is not necessarily significant. Excavation of a site is never so complete that they may not be found beneath the surface. Nevertheless, it is worth noting such gaps in the sequence of recorded dates and correlating them with events at other sites.

Altar de Sacrificios must have been an important commercial center, commanding as it did riverine traffic between the towns on the Usumacinta and the highland regions of Guatemala. Our failure to find an Emblem Glyph on its stelae, however, may indicate that it was not the capital city of its province, though it was ruled by a local aristocracy. There is a small cluster of sites in the vicinity from each of which we have one or two stelae. Below Altar de Sacrificios on the Usumacinta is the site of El Pabellón, sometimes considered to be a part of the Altar series. From here an early Late Classic stela has been reported, but most of these smaller sites have yielded only late monuments. Morley (1937–1938:2:289–294) illustrates one monument from Aguas Calientes, said to be a small site on the Pasión River, at some distance above Altar de Sacrificios. It shows some very unusual elements of costume and equipment, such as a hatchet with a bone handle, held in the left hand of the single figure presented, enormous pads projecting from the knees and similarly designed wristlets, a serpent-bar across the chest, with flint points at either end, and curiously designed plumes decorated with beads and long tassels. Morley's reading of the dates as 9.17.16.6.1, 9.17.19.7.4, 9.18.0.13.18, and 9.18.0.0.0 is altogether consistent with the originality of the design and the strongly directed pose of the figure. The back of this monument appears to be badly damaged, but though only fragments of the design can be made out on the published photograph, it is evident that the carving here was even more unconventional.

South of Aguas Calientes, which is in the northeast corner of the Petexbatun area, are two other minor sites, El Caribe and La Amelia. From El Caribe, Morley (1937–1938:2:294–301) shows drawings of two monuments, each only about 1.5 meters above the plain butt and only 19 centimeters in thickness. They are designated as stelae, but they seem to have been set into the steps and the foundation of a building and perhaps are better considered as panels. Each major figure carries a spear and a sun-shield of standard design. In front of each of these warriors sits a figure of a captive, apparently not bound, but with a tight rope collar on the neck. Although these panels were set on different levels, one above the other, the figures face in opposite directions. The brief inscriptions on these monuments are ambiguous, but I am inclined to accept Morley's dating of both as 9.17.10.0.0, on stylistic grounds, for although the dress of the figures is undistinguished, they have elaborate and original head-dresses, one of them in the form of an animal skull with enormously long tasseled plumes, the other with a small cap which is surrounded with a huge mass of short feathers arranged to simulate a turban. A similar headdress is worn by a figure on Lintel 4 at Piedras Negras (see Chapter 8), and they are not uncommon elsewhere.

A short distance south-southwest is the site known as La Amelia. Two excellently designed stelae from this site undoubtedly belong in this period. Each presents a figure in "dancing" pose, above a panel showing a recumbent jaguar. The headdresses are very elaborate, with long swirling plumes, but the pad that the dancers wear on one knee shows that they are ballplayers, and their feet are bare. With each player there are two raised columns of glyphs, and probably also two in the background. Morley (1937–1938:2:308) states that on Stela 1, each of the three columns of glyphs that can be seen starts with the same Calendar Round date—2 Ben 6 Zac (9.18.17.1.13??). On Stela 2, this does not seem to be the case, but in both inscriptions, the use of crosses for fillers in writing the day coefficient seems to suggest an even later date. On Stela 2, the day, with coefficient 1, must be Imix, Cimi, Chuen, or Cib, for the month coefficient seems to be 9. The portrayal of ballplayers on stelae appears to be characteristic of this late period in the Petexbatun area. Stela 1 (and probably also Stela 2) is associated with a hieroglyphic stairway, and I suspect that both stelae should be designated as panels, and that they may have been actually set into masonry and were not free-standing monuments. This may also be true of the stela from Aguas Calientes, in view of the very rough appearance of its back and the peculiarly disassociated motifs of its carving. The inscriptions on these monuments are far from clear, but both those of La Amelia and that of Aguas Calientes use the Emblem of Petexbatun.

Seibal, however, has its own Emblem, though, as in other sites in the region, its Stelae 5 and 7 seem to be large panels portraying ball-players, and Stela 7 seems to have been definitely associated with a hieroglyphic stairway. Stela 6 is a glyphic panel that may have been part of the arrangement. Stela 7 records the dates 9.17.0.0.0 and 9.18.10.0.0, and the others probably also fall in this range.

It may be well to note here that 9.17.0.0.0 is 13 Ahau. The previous Katun 13 Ahau was 9.4.0.0.0. At that time the Classic Maya area was expanding westward. On the eastern frontier, several new sites begin their inscriptions with the date 9.17.0.0.0. At Seibal and elsewhere, such monuments are often associated with hieroglyphic stairways and, being square at the top, were often not stelae, but hieroglyphic panels set into masonry. This important distinction, unfortunately, is often overlooked.

The last monument we have from Aguateca, its Stela 7, records the date 9.18.0.0.0 11 Ahau 18 Mac. The name of the person portrayed may be recorded at C1-D1, which is followed by a record of 3 *ich-ben* katun, still uncertain in meaning. Nor am I inclined to speculate about the meaning of the phrase that follows, which I suspect may refer to his clan or to his marriage. The difficult problem of Maya kinship and clan structure is yet to be solved and I do not feel competent to undertake it—I can only point out such phrases as this that may be relevant.

A number of other sites in this general region have been visited, but published reports on the inscriptions are not yet available. Gair Tourtellot III, Norman Hammond, and Richard M. Rose (1978) made a brief visit to Itzan, on a tributary of the Pasión north of Altar de Sacrificios, where they observed sculptured stelae, but most of them were in fragments, and the published photographs of inscriptions do not reveal legible texts. It is worth noting, however, that here too were hieroglyphic stairways with panels depicting ballplayers.

The inscriptions in the region of Petexbatun also offer intriguing opportunities for speculation about intersite relations and the precise meaning of "captor" expressions. It is encouraging that linguists are becoming interested in the grammatical structure of glyphic statements, but unfortunate that they are sometimes misled by unwarranted speculations about the meaning of texts, and the temptation to accept literally the tentative names we give to certain expressions that may not reflect accurately their actual meanings. Yet the circumstances in the Petexbatun area and surrounding sites are intriguing. Two late sites to the east and south are undoubtedly related to what went on earlier in the Petexbatun region. To the south on the Pasión River is the site of Cancuen. It has a number of plain stelae, as well as two that were carved. Both are of peculiar shape with a central projection at the top that also occurs on Stela 13 of Machaquila. At Cancuen, Stela 1 has two large round holes near the top, possibly functional, but more likely caused by the removal of round inclusions in the rock. The front of this monument is badly eroded, but shows a conventional figure, holding a manikin scepter and a round shield. He wears a helmet, not unlike that worn by the figure on Aguateca Stela 3, the first stela of its group. The Cancuen stela is, however, undoubtedly later. The figure of a seated woman on the back is better preserved. And the beautifully executed detail with its sinuous curves almost certainly dates this monument in the neighborhood of 9.18.0.0.0. The serpents in the sky above both figures confirm this estimate. There is some suggestion that the portrait of the woman is posthumous, for she seems to hold in her arms a ceremonial bar which at Yaxchilan is held by women only in sky motifs. The panel below the main carving shows a bird mask also suggesting that the lady is pictured here in heaven. Her relationship to the figure on the front is not clear, but I venture to suggest that, if no earlier stelae are found here, she may be, as seems to happen at other sites, the originator of a new dynasty, perhaps a royal lady from Aguateca, who married a local lord, and whose son became the ruler of Cancuen. Stela 2, probably the earlier of the two and dated 9.18.0.0.0 by Morley, depicts this ruler seated on a throne, but with his feet hanging down above a bound captive. His dress and accoutrement are very similar to those shown on Aguateca Stela 2 and on Dos Pilas Stela 16. He holds a rectangular shield carved with what I believe is a bat mask and trimmed with short feathers. With it is a bundle of short darts. Goggle eyes decorate the ankle guards of his sandals, and the flaps hanging from his belt and garters remind one of Piedras Negras. He wears a helmetlike headdress of a soldier, but its construction is more like the huge scroll-headdresses of the Yaxchilan Bird Jaguar than like the quilted helmets one sees at Piedras Negras and Lacanha. These costume elements have never been observed in central Peten, though they occur at different times in peripheral sites such as Calakmul and Piedras Negras and do not seem to be limited to any particular area and any particular time.

Cancuen apparently has a hieroglyphic stairway, but no large sculptures of ballplayers. Its Altar 1, depicting a ballgame, is dated 9.18.5.0.0 and is very probably a ballcourt marker.

Stelae 10 and 17 at Machaquila show the figure with the left knee bent, raising the heel off the ground. Though is is not very clear on Ian Graham's (1967) photographs, I believe these figures wear a pad on the left knee which identifies them as ballplayers. Each figure holds a manikin scepter in one hand, and both are dressed in royal finery. The figure on Stela 10 holds what is probably an eccentric flint in his left hand, suggesting that he is a prophet or diviner besides. Although both these monuments are shaped like stelae, the peculiar state of their back surfaces, noted by Graham (1967), suggests that they, too, like the ballplayers of the region between the Pasión and the Chixoy, were once set into masonry. The presence here of scattered blocks from a hieroglyphic stairway confirms the impression that they were part of the same tradition. For this reason, I suspect that the date 9.15.0.0.0, tentatively ascribed by Graham to

Ah Five Death(?)
(MQL St 2, C1)

Machaquila Emblem Glyph
(MQL St 2, C2)

Stela 10, may be too early, and I prefer to place them no earlier than 9.17.0.0.0, and no later than 9.18.0.0.0 in the interval between the earlier and later groups of this site.

With Stela 2, erected in 9.18.10.0.0 or in 9.19.0.0.0, begins a new series of monuments, different in conception and in style. This first monument, however, is uniquely designed. A unique feature of the elaborate headdress of its figure is a hand holding a curious object that suggests a torch, though an eccentric form set in its handle may indicate a hatchet. A characteristic feature of this group of monuments is the long nose of a dragon forming a mask in front of the face, combined with an artificial beard on the face and long strands of hair hanging below the earplug. Very high beaded wristlets and ankle guards are also typical of the style introduced at this time. Long, flowing feathers on the headdress, a huge beaded pectoral of Classic design, and forward-curling scrolls are unmistakable features of this period, but the owl-like bird head suspended by beads from the belt and hanging low behind the legs of the figure is an original touch. Aside from these details the figure is typical. It holds a manikin scepter in its right hand, and a round shield with the jaguar mask of the "midnight sun" worn on the left wrist. A kneeling figure in front, with a long-beaked bird on its headdress, holds up before the ruler a device composed of a compound of the *kan* cross and the number 7. The name of the main personage appears to be Ah Five Death(?) and is followed by the Emblem of Machaquila.

The remaining six stelae apparently marked consecutive hotuns. Graham, however, suggests that there were originally eight, and restores one at the beginning and one at the end of the series. The series is divided into two groups. In the first group (Stelae 3, 4, and 8), the hotun date is followed by the next occurring 1 Ahau date, forming a series at intervals of 5.1.0 from each other, and regressing by five days in the position of the year each time. The first date of this series is 1 Ahau 13 Cumku, and it is fifteen years later than the date recorded on Stela 2: 12 Chicchan 13 Cumku. The last date, 1 Ahau 3 Cumku, is thirteen uinals later than the preceding hotun, which is also 1 Ahau. In the second half of the series, it is the year position, rather than the Tzolkin position, of the odd dates that is preserved, and this position is the same as that of the odd date on Stela 2, and on Stela 3, which is the first of this series: 13 Cumku.

The portraits of the ruler of Machaquila on Stelae 3, 4, and 8 are remarkably similar. The only significant difference is that Stela 3 lacks a panel at the base. Nor does it change significantly on Stela 7, erected in 10.0.0.0.0, though a different individual is represented, and it is better considered with the second group of this series. The long, sweeping plumes on these monuments are not trimmed with beads, as we usually find in the Peten. The long hair, trimmed straight across the forehead, and the long nose of a mask worn in front of the face are the same on all of them. A huge and elaborate headdress has a waterflower on the front, with a fish nibbling at it.

Machaquila Stela 4, front: Portrait of
the ruler holding the manikin scepter.
(Drawing courtesy of Ian Graham.)

Above it is a sort of bar, somewhat variable in form, on which sits a snail-like creature, very like the creatures in the inscriptions of Dos Pilas.

It is impossible to say how long after 9.17.10.0.0 building activities continued in the two southern courts of Copan. Although on Stela 8 there is a reference to Cycle 10, it may be a calendrical rather than a historical reference. More probably major construction and sculpture was halted by 9.18.0.0.0 or 9.18.10.0.0, though occupation of the site may have continued for an indefinite time. The latest definite date we now have is 9.17.12.5.17, the katun anniversary of the important 6 Caban date, discussed in Chapter 10.

After the mourning period for the king of Quirigua was over, erection of stelae was suspended, and in their stead were carved huge "zoomorphs" and flat "altars." As yet, no one has given an adequate interpretation of these carvings or explained the nature of their elaborate symbolism; nor will I attempt to do so here. I would like to suggest, however, that this symbolism probably operates on at least two different levels: it may make reference to myth and cosmology at the same time as it speaks of mundane events and of persons and functional groups within the society. In any case, the zoomorphs do not merely substitute for stelae, and there is reason to think that they are postmortem monuments, referring principally to the foundation of the state and its subsequent history.

Two-legged Sky apparently had no immediate successor. If I am right in thinking that Stelae A and C represent mortuary rites, he must have died before 9.17.5.0.0, though his name continues to be mentioned on zoomorphs and their altars for another katun. These fantastic monuments were set up at hotun intervals, as were the stelae before them. Zoomorph B (9.17.10.0.0) represents an amphibian monster, with the Initial Series shown in full-figure glyphs on its body. Zoomorph G (9.17.15.0.0) has a longer and much more difficult text. It makes reference to Two-legged Sky and to the two dates associated with his reign: 9.14.13.4.17 12 Caban 5 Kayab and 9.15.6.14.6 6 Cimi 4 Zec. However, the Secondary Series associated with these dates do not lead to other recorded dates, and Morley (1937–1938:4:169–180) has to make some adjustments to give values to other dates in the text. The values he gives them are all close to the Initial Series date, but the statements accompanying them are badly eroded and what they record is obscure. The end of Baktun 10 is mentioned twice, and this is curious, since there were still nine hotuns lacking to the conclusion of the current baktun.

Although we have no definite statement of the death of Two-legged Sky, and it is possible that he was still living, it seems highly improbable, for if he was given the important title of "vulture" and commissioned to found Quirigua when he was about twenty years old, he must have been at least eighty-two years old at the time when Zoomorph G was carved. It seems more probable that the text on

Zoomorph G, although it mentions his name and the two dates associated with his career, is concerned primarily not with his life, but with the circumstances of the founding of Quirigua itself. I will not attempt to improve on Morley's reading of the series of dates on the zoomorphs or on their altars, for this would constitute a major study in itself, with a dubious chance of any substantial improvement unless we can determine the meaning and intention of these complex sets of dates.

The Initial Series on Zoomorph O reads 9.18.0.0.0 11 Ahau (18 Mac). Other glyphs on this zoomorph seem to be too badly eroded to be read. The altar associated with Zoomorph O, however, has a very long inscription beginning with an Initial Series that Morley reads 9.17.14.16.18 9 Etz'nab (1 Kankin), the last date mentioned on Zoomorph G before its dedication date of 9.17.15.0.0. Up to this point Morley (1937–1938) and J. E. S. Thompson (1945) agree in their reading of the dates on this altar. Then they diverge sharply. In Morley's scheme, the count abruptly jumps back to a date that precedes 4 Ahau 8 Cumku, the start of the calendar, and continues forward, meandering here and there until it reaches 9.18.0.0.0. In Thompson's scheme the text follows a meandering course starting at 9.17.14.16.18, generally retreating until it reaches the neighborhood of 9.17.8.0.0, from where it proceeds with small steps until it reaches 9.17.15.0.0 and finally 9.18.0.0.0. In spite of the fact that Thompson put four question marks after each of the last ten dates he proposes, I am inclined to favor his scheme over Morley's. At least one date in Thompson's scheme, 9.15.6.14.6 6 Cimi 4 Zec, is a very important date in the history of Quirigua, though its reading here is not altogether certain. We do, however, find in its vicinity the name of Two-legged Sky, indicating its historical allusion, and the possibility that a thorough study of this inscription may suggest a reason for the change from stelae to zoomorphic sculptures.

Zoomorph P is the last, and the most elaborate, of these monuments. It is difficult for us to understand its intricate symbolism, but one may conjecture that zoomorphs represent the land and its people, and that the various grotesque forms refer not to mythological beings, but to various divisions of society—families or clans, or perhaps lineages. In the wide-open jaws of the zoomorph sits a human figure with a shield and manikin scepter indicating his royal status, probably the deceased founder of Quirigua, Two-legged Sky. His name is mentioned in the inscription contained in panels on the jaw of the monster. The inscription begins with the Initial Series 9.18.5.0.0 4 Ahau 13 Ceh. In the following passage is a glyph signifying divination (the scattering gesture), and farther on we read the name of the king followed by 5 katun over a fist compound (since the founding?). A backward count then seems to be indicated, then a glyph with the coefficient 18 (but seemingly not Eighteen Jog); a title: Lord of or from Copan; and a reference to thirteen baktuns

(13.0.0.0.0). Too many glyphs in the long inscription that follows are damaged, and many of those that are preserved are of unknown meaning. As in the case of the dates for the altar of Zoomorph O, Morley suggests for Zoomorph P and its altars a range of dates that seems to me excessive. I doubt that these inscriptions reach back beyond the time of the arrival of Two-legged Sky in the region, but until we can determine the nature of at least some of the events that are recorded here, it will be profitless to seek other solutions. It may be worth noting, however, that Zoomorph P, the last of the zoomorphs, was set up on the katun anniversary of the two stelae, C and D, which seem to pertain to the end of the mourning period after the death of Two-legged Sky, and that his name is constantly mentioned on the zoomorphs. Unlike the late altars of Copan, the zoomorphs do not suggest a change in the structure of government, but rather the continuation of the reign in the absence of the king. Perhaps only after he emerges from his tomb to take his permanent abode in the sky (as shown on Zoomorph P?) can another take his place.

The erection of stelae is resumed in 9.18.10.0.0, with Stela I. In proportion, it is lower and wider than earlier stelae. It depicts a king holding the manikin scepter and shield. On the back, we see a figure seated on high in a niche under a sky-serpent. It is not clear whether this is a coronation scene, or whether the figure is that of the former king, now resident in the sky. Only the face and the headdress of the figure on the front are sculptured in the round. The body is carved in high but squarish relief. The inscription is presented in double columns on the sides. It begins with the Initial Series 9.18.10.0.0 10 Ahau 8 Zac. There are two more dates, to which Morley (1937–1938: 4: 215–223) gives the values 9.17.13.0.0 10 Ahau 8 Ch'en and 9.17.19.9.0 13 Ahau 18 Zotz'. Thompson, however, places them earlier: 9.15.5.0.0 and 9.15.6.14.0. I am inclined to concur with this reading because the later date is only six days before the very important date that marks the establishment of a royal court at Quirigua, making it the capital of its province. I have not been able to identify the name of the king pictured on this monument.

Stela K, the last monument erected here, is clearly dated 9.18.15.0.0 3 Ahau 3 Yax. In size and proportion it is comparable to Stela I, and it is similar also in its style of carving. It displays a standing figure on each of its broad sides, one holding a manikin scepter, the other a ceremonial bar. After glyphs G and F of the Initial Series is interpolated a Secondary Series of 10.10, which, counted back, reaches the date 1 Oc 18 Kayab, one of the series of dates identified by Thompson (1943) as occurring at intervals of 819 days. The usual "explanatory clause" follows, beginning with a glyph with a Pax-like prefix and ending with a rodent glyph with coefficient of 1. The Lunar Series is then continued, and after Glyph A the date of the Initial Series, 3 Ahau(?) 3 Yax(?), is repeated, as well as the first glyph of the

"explanatory clause." Some of the following glyphs are eroded, but the day 3 Ahau occurs once more. The final glyphs record a divination glyph followed by a mask with the squarish eye of the sun, possibly designating Ah Kin, the high priest, a sky glyph, and the Emblem of Quirigua preceded by its usual glyph. This appears to be a record of a prophecy made by the high priest of Quirigua, but the "explanatory clause" seems to be the same in all such interpolations, whose meaning still remains obscure. Since this is the last date recorded at Quirigua, with the exception of casual references to Cycle 10 on earlier monuments, one wonders if this prophet was foretelling the eventual abandonment of the city.

CHAPTER TWELVE

The Final Years

10.0.0.0.0 — 10.2.10.0.0

A.D. 831 — 909

REMARKABLY FEW MONUMENTS WERE ERECTED AT the completion of the two baktuns that fall within the scope of the Maya Classic Era, 9.0.0.0.0 and 10.0.0.0.0. Both dates are occasionally mentioned on later monuments, and more rarely as prophetic dates on earlier ones, as on Altar 1 at Piedras Negras. Morley dates this altar at 10.0.0.0.0, but I follow here J. E. S. Thompson (1944b), who considered the date to be a projection into the future. This calls to mind the refusal of the Itza of Tayasal to surrender to the Spaniards until 8 Ahau, which had been prophesied by their priests. As a dedicatory date I have noted Baktun 9 only on Stela 5 at El Zapote, and Baktun 10 on only four monuments: Uaxactun Stela 13, an all-glyphic stela with a beautiful script; Oxpemul Stela 7, which, except for its date, is very badly eroded; Tila Stela A; and Machaquila Stela 7. All but the Uaxactun stela are peripheral to central Peten.

It may be that at the close of a baktun major attention was given to the renovation of buildings, but the destruction of the cities along the Usumacinta in the previous period certainly impoverished the cities of the Peten, if it did not pose a direct threat of invasion from the west. The lack of stelae before the second katun of Baktun 10 at Tikal suggests that the king was not in residence, and may have been absent on military or diplomatic missions elsewhere. With the exception of Uaxactun, all the other monuments erected in the first katun of Baktun 10 are on the fringes of the central area. In addition to those mentioned, there is only Altar 1 at Tzimin Kax in Belize, with the date 10.0.5.0.0, and Stela 1 at Chinkultik in the Chiapas highlands, with the date 10.0.15.0.0. Machaquila is the only site known to me where a continuous record of consecutive hotuns spanning the change of the baktuns is preserved. The dates run from 9.19.0.0.0 to 10.0.10.0.0. Although there is no radical change in the style of the monuments at the turn of the cycle, there is a subtle decline in the artistry of the later monuments. On earlier monuments the pose of the figure is slightly swayed and directed toward the right. Later, the body of the figure is rigidly frontal, and its proportions tend to be somewhat distorted. On Stela 2, erected in 9.19.0.0.0, the figure wears a mask in the form of a serpent's jaw hanging down from the headdress. In 9.19.10.0.0, the mask is abbreviated to a jaw projecting from behind the nose of the figure, without any visible support. By 10.0.5.0.0, it is replaced by a bar noseplug. The main element of the headdress here is a simple jaguar head. The figure on Stela 5, the final stela of the series, erected in 10.0.10.0.0, diverges even more from the Classic style. The body is shown in frontal position, standing with its feet far apart, and the figure is holding a baton in its right hand, similar to that held by one of the figures on Stela 3 at Seibal (see Chapter 13). The headdress is in the form of a strange animal with a long, pointed nose. In most other details of costume, however, the figure conforms to others of this group. Corresponding to the change in the overrun of dates beyond the period endings, there is a change in certain glyphs that appear to be the names of rulers. Stelae set up before Baktun 10 show a head glyph prefixed by a flaming *kin* glyph; those of Baktun 10 show an expression that can be read as Captor of Double Chuen (see I. Graham 1967).

Machaquila is located in a strategic position in hilly country overlooking the river of the same name that flows from southern Belize, joining the Pasión not far below Tres Islas. The city seems to have been well protected from direct attack, and may have served as a trading center for merchants, linking the Peten with the east coast of the Yucatan Peninsula. This is suggested by the fact that the most prosperous period of the city began after the destruction of the cities along the Usumacinta. One may wonder if the experimentation with the calendar at Machaquila was not an attempt to correlate the Maya tun count with a year count used by some alien group with which they were in contact. It was not long, however, that this period of prosperity lasted, and there is some reason to think that even before the turn of the baktun, its best artists were emigrating to southern Peten, for there is little doubt that the style of the five monuments associated with Structure A-3 at Seibal, all with the date 10.1.0.0.0, clearly derives from that of the late Baktun 9 monuments of Machaquila.

Seibal is located on the west bank of the Pasión River, in the northeastern corner of the Petexbatun region. Structure A-3 is a small pyramid facing east toward a causeway connecting Group A with Group D. Stela 21, found buried in the debris of the small temple on the summit of the pyramid (Willey et al. 1975) was broken and in poor condition, but it is very similar in style to the four stelae standing below, in front of the four stairways of the pyramid. The figure on Stela 21 is shown holding a manikin scepter in his right hand and a shield in his left. He faces east, overlooking through a doorway Stela 11 below.

In the lower assemblage, two distinct physical types are represented. Figures in front of the southern and western stairways (Stelae 8 and 9) have typically Maya face profiles, with sharply sloping foreheads and prominent noses. The figure in the temple, as well as the two in front of the east and north stairways (Stelae 11 and 10) have short, broad noses and more prominent chins. Their hair is cut straight across the forehead just above the eyes, and there is a suggestion of a moustache on the upper lip. Whether this connotes a foreign admixture in the population, a lower social status, or merely a changing style I am not prepared to say. In costume these figures do not differ from other Maya figures of this period, and all four figures wear their hair hanging down in back to the level of their shoulders.

The man shown on the east side, on Stela 11, performs the gesture of divination (scattering grains). He is masked, and in his elaborate headdress is a bar on which sits a little creature resembling a snail, a feature apparently derived from Machaquila. The headdress is similar to that of Stela 8, on the south side. The figures on Stela 10 (north) and on Stela 9 (west) both carry serpent-bars with tails ending in upside-down masks. Stela 8 and Stela 11, like Stelae 10 and 9, appear to be different in their facial features but alike in status and function. Though the man on Stela 8 does not wear a mask, he has a ring around the eye and wears an artificial beard. Moreover, though he is not a diviner, his hands and feet are covered with jaguar paws, so he appears as a priest rather than as a secular potentate. Thus we seem to have here two ethnic types, each represented by two functionaries. One might be tempted to infer from this an alliance between the Classic Maya and an aberrant group, or between the aristocracy and representatives of the commoners. Whatever the case, it seems to be altogether in keeping with the tendency of the Maya to adapt their statements about mundane events to the structure of their calendar and their philosophical notions of time and space. Thus we find on Stela 10, on the north side of the temple, a mention of four Emblem Glyphs: that of Seibal, that of Tikal, a third site identified by Marcus (1973) as Calakmul, and a fourth, with Ik as the main sign, as yet not surely identified. Marcus has suggested that it is the Emblem of Motul de San José, but it is doubtful that Emblems are names of towns, since a number of sites have more than one. They may refer to provinces, or to clans or tribal names of their occupants, or even to lineages.

Morley's (1937–1938:2:282–284) date 10.2.0.0.0 3 Ahau 3 Ceh for Stela 1 is probably correct. This monument and another, Stela 14, are essentially Classic in conception, but in both the feet are shown in side view, one behind the other, while the torso is turned in three-quarters view, a pose not entirely successful, since the elaborate ornaments worn on the body had to be turned to the front to be properly displayed. Stela 1 stood near the entrance to the main plaza, and Stela 14 stood with two other monuments at the intersection of two

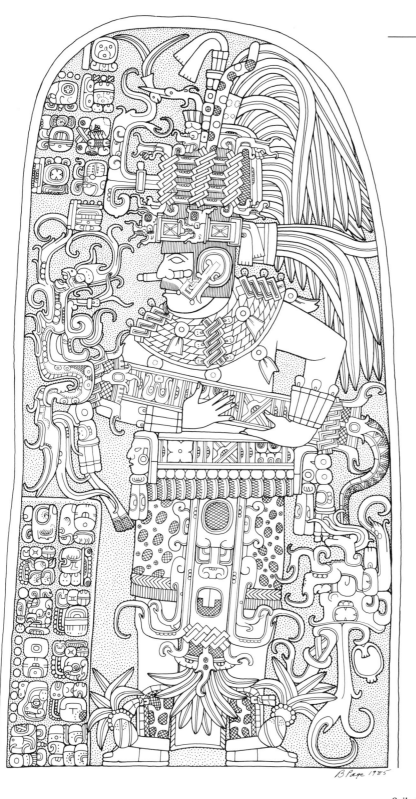

Seibal Stela 10, front: Non-Classic depiction of figure on north side of Structure A-3. (Drawing by Barbara Page.)

sacbes. Stela 14 has no date and is difficult to place in time. The pose of the figure is essentially that shown on Stela 1, but the execution of the fine detail that fills the entire field argues that it was designed by a different sculptor.

The meeting at Seibal in 10.1.0.0.0 may have been occasioned by the closing of a profitable trade route, leading to Belize by way of Machaquila. Naranjo had fallen some years before, but there remained two towns in its vicinity, both of which had access to the east coast, and both of which erected stelae in 10.1.0.0.0. Nakum was quite a large town, with at least fifteen stelae, but only three of them were sculptured, and all three are in poor condition. Stela D, however, shows clearly parts of a typical Classic Maya figure of Cycle 10 and the date 10.1.0.0.0. Xunantunich (formerly Benque Viejo), in Belize, is a much smaller site, set on a hill, perhaps for purposes of defense. It has only one carved monument of this period, also dated 10.1.0.0.0. Naranjo, no longer active, lies between these two towns, which once may have been within its province.

The site of Caracol in Belize seems to have at least three stelae erected in Cycle 10, but only one, Stela 17, has a legible date (10.1.0.0.0). There is another date on this monument, a day Ix in the month Zec, the position of which I have not been able to calculate from the drawing available to me. The form of this stela is irregular, and below the inscription are shown two seated figures, apparently in simple dress, though one of them is wearing a turban. The other two stelae that I attribute to Cycle 10 have no legible dates, but they are also of irregular shape and peculiar design. On Stela 18, only scrolls can be seen and a rectangle possibly containing two glyphs. Stela 20 shows only a column of illegible glyphs at the top, and some distance below four large cartouches that evidently contained multiple glyphs that are now entirely eroded. I suspect that these two monuments are considerably later than Stela 17.

Stelae 3 and 4 at Xmakabatun I would also place in Baktun 10, though Morley proposes an earlier date for them. The exaggeration of the frets on the aprons on these two monuments is extreme, and the quality of the draftsmanship on Stela 4 is poor. On the other hand, the strongly directed pose of this figure and its partial concealment behind the border suggest a certain relaxation of the Classic tradition that is evident on a number of monuments at this time.

It should be noted that at this time Initial Series are rare, and most stelae are dated by period endings, preponderantly lahuntuns. It is only at peripheral sites, as in the highlands of Chiapas and in the north, that we find hotuns being recorded, and Initial Series dating. Stelae 3 and 10 at Xultun appear to be exceptions. Xultun, northeast of Uaxactun, is located near the headwaters of the Río Azul, which joins the Río Hondo to form the boundary between Belize and Quintana Roo. Twenty-two stelae are reported from this site, but most of them are so broken and eroded that their dates are illegible. Such great destruction of the monuments is unusual, and one wonders if it may have been in part deliberate. Morley (1937–1938:1:419) has arranged all the monuments in chronological order, but unfortunately his judgment of style was not always reliable, and his placement of Stelae 7 and 8 in 9.8.10.0.0 and 9.7.10.0.0 is surely too early. The fact that both these monuments have only period-ending dates, and that they are both lahuntuns, argues strongly for dates in Cycle 10. Stela 7 is too badly eroded to be judged by its style, but the off-vertical position of the body of the figure on Stela 8, the projecting frets of his costume, and the roughly incised prone figure beneath him all suggest a much later date for this monument, and one probably in Cycle 10. In these respects it is not unlike Stela 3, erected in 10.1.10.0.0, and may have been carved in the previous lahuntun. Stela 3 also records an earlier date: 10.0.3.3.8 11 Lamat 11 Xul, which seems to be a birth date, probably of the king portrayed, who would then have been about twenty-six years old.

After 10.1.0.0.0, hotun markers are extremely rare, but are occasionally found in peripheral areas. Thus we find Stela 1 at Comitan in the Chiapas highlands with the date 10.2.5.0.0 and Stela 1 at Quen Santo in the northwest corner of Guatemala with the same date. Moreover, the Quen Santo date is an Initial Series, and these are rare in the central area at this time.

An especially interesting motif which occurs at different times in different sites, but which is limited to this period, is one that I call the "cloud-rider" motif. The monuments on which it occurs tend to be wider at the top than at the base. Like other Maya stelae, they feature a principal figure, in some cases accompanied by a minor one, while above these figures are shown large scrolls with dotted borders, giving the suggestion of clouds, perched on which ride one, two, or four smaller figures in various recumbent or crouching poses. This motif originates with Stela 4 at Ucanal, at the time of the meeting of chiefs at Seibal. In addition, the group includes Stela 11 of Tikal, Stela 1 of Jimbal, and Stelae 1 and 2 at Ixlu. The dates of these monuments range from 10.1.0.0.0 to 10.2.10.0.0. The fact that this motif occurs so near the end of all monumental activity in the region invites speculation about its meaning and brings us to the brink of the "Maya Collapse," which has recently engaged the attention of Maya archaeologists. Unfortunately, the motif can be variously interpreted. Some may regard the cloud-riders as representing natural forces, spirits of the rains, in which case we must assume some natural disaster that led to the eventual abandonment of the region, perhaps a drought or, on the contrary, several seasons of torrential rains, washing away the soil denuded of forest protection, disasters that required an appeal to heaven for intervention. Others may see the cloud-riders as symbolic of the people of the highlands, perhaps even the Toltec, who were soon to settle at Chichen Itza. Whatever the case, the motif was a prelude to foreseen disaster, which was foreshadowed by the decreasing number of stelae being erected at formerly prosperous towns.

Stela 4 at Ucanal is the best-preserved monument of this group. It was erected in 10.1.0.0.0, at the same time as the group at Seibal. The site is to the southeast of Tikal, between two rivers that join to form the Belize River. The shape of this monument is somewhat asymmetrical, projecting at the upper left to make room for its single cloud-rider, who holds in his right hand something like a decorated dart-thrower and in his left, a dart. Below him is the main figure, shown performing the rite of divination, and another, smaller figure. They are dressed alike, and each holds a manikin scepter. Beneath their feet is a prone captive. It is possible that the main figure is the king of Tikal, who is not at this time represented in his native city, and who has come to the aid of a minor ruler. The hieroglyphs of the text are arranged in three groups on the face of the monument, and the first glyphs record 5 Ahau 3 Kayab (10.1.0.0.0). The inscription is somewhat worn, and the arrangement of the glyphs in three columns makes the order of reading somewhat uncertain. At B2 there is a hand-scattering glyph, suggesting divination, and at C2 are two numbered glyphs in rectangular cartouches. The number of the first is not clear but could conceivably be 12, and the glyph itself is illegible. The second glyph, however, clearly reads 13 Vulture. These appear to be calendrical glyphs, but the structure of the calendar to which they belong is not known. Although Vulture is a day in the Aztec calendar (corresponding to the day Cib in that of the Maya), the Aztec did not enclose their day names in cartouches. The rectangular cartouche is very ancient. We see it as early as 9.0.0.0.0 on Stela 5 at El Zapote, where it is held by a woman. It encloses the glyph of an infant and is combined with the numeral 12 and what has been called the Mexican Year Sign, often worn by Piedras Negras warriors and later at Dos Pilas and at Calakmul. In the case of El Zapote, it may be that the number refers to the year sign, possibly indicating the woman's age.

The next stela of this group to be erected is Stela 1 at Ixlu, a site very near the eastern end of Lake Peten Itza. Like other stelae of the cloud-rider group it does not record an Initial Series, but its period-ending date is fairly clear as 4 Ahau 13 Kankin (10.1.10.0.0). It is very much broader at the top than at the base, and originally accommodated four cloud-riders. One of the upper riders seems to be missing, and the other is masked. His mask has a long down-curved beak and a large round eye. The two lower riders are human. The principal figure is shown in profile, performing the "scattering" gesture of divination, the glyph for which appears below. The ornament on the back of the main figure projects strongly to the right margin, and below it is a small seated figure. Detail is badly eroded. Morley (1937–1938:3:447–448) has shown that the monuments of Ixlu alternate with those of Flores, which record ends of katuns, but they are badly eroded, and only Stela 1, which he assigns to 10.2.0.0.0, retains some of its design. It features a serpent rising upward with a small figure in its jaws and another below. The design is obscure, but here, too, is an implication of recourse to heavenly powers.

At this same time, Tikal erected its last known monument, Stela 11. It is more conservative in design than the Ixlu monument. It is not wedge-shaped and has only two cloud-riders at the top. The figure, in frontal position, is scattering grains, a gesture of divination, but details of the text are obscure. An innovation is the decorated border of this stela. This decorated border is used again on Stela 1 at Jimbal, erected on 10.2.10.0.0. Jimbal is halfway between Uaxactun and Tikal, and it may be that Tikal at this time was under siege, or was suffering from some other disaster that prompted the court, or some of its members, to move to an outlying region. On the other hand, it may be a victorious invader that is pictured here. Unlike other monuments with the cloud-rider motif, this stela does not picture divination, but shows the figure holding a manikin scepter and a round shield. That he wears a short cape and a bar noseplug suggests, however, that he is not the king of Tikal, and may even be a usurper. It is the cloud-rider on his right, a strange creature with clawed feet, that seems to be performing the rite of divination. With each rider, there is an identical group of four glyphs. The double column of glyphs of the main inscription begins with the date 2 Ahau 13 Ch'en. Two rows down is a lahuntun sign. The date is almost certainly 10.2.10.0.0. After the lahuntun sign are three signs in square cartouches with coefficients 12, 13, and 1. They could indicate three consecutive days in some unknown calendar, perhaps days corresponding to the Aztec days Serpent, Death, and Deer, equivalent to the Maya days Chicchan, Cimi, and Manik. In artistry this stela is far inferior to Stela 11 of Tikal. The figure is very tall, poorly proportioned, stiff in pose, and lacking in bodily curvatures. Apparently it was executed by a local artist, or one not schooled in the style of the royal court.

At Ixlu, Stela 2, also executed in 10.2.10.0.0, is almost a replica of its earlier Stela 1, and preserves the Maya tradition of draftsmanship. The only significant difference between the two stelae is that the smaller figure now stands in front of the ruler or priest. As before, there are four cloud-riders. The one at the upper left, as one faces the monument, wears the mask of Tlaloc; that on the right may portray the Mexican god of wind, Ehecatl. The two lower cloud-riders are human.

This group of monuments presenting a single motif links Tikal, first of all, by way of Ucanal to the Belize River, and the east coast of Belize, and later to the lake region by the two stelae at Ixlu. Since the Tikal Emblem occurs in connection with the four stelae around Structure A-3 at Seibal, at the time when this motif originated, the cloud-rider motif may have been the result of the meeting held there. However, I would not venture to speculate further about its meaning.

CHAPTER THIRTEEN

The Last Survivals

10.2.10.0.0 – 10.4.0.0.0

A.D. 909 – 938

IN ADDITION TO STELA 2 OF IXLU AND STELA 1 AT Jimbal, both covered in Chapter 12, two other stelae were erected on the date 10.2.10.0.0: Stela 7 at Xamantun, northeast of Calakmul in southern Campeche, and Stela 2 at Quen Santo in Guatemala, not far from Chinkultik. In 10.2.15.0.0, El Palmar erected the latest monument we know that was dedicated on a hotun. Slightly south of Calakmul, and in the state of Quintana Roo, it too is on the fringes of the distribution of known Classic Maya sites.

Xultun seems to be the only city in the Peten that was still erecting stelae in the Classic style in 10.3.0.0.0. Stela 10 repeats the motif earlier presented on Stelae 19 (undated) and 3. It is interesting to compare the style of Stela 10 with that of Stela 3. The technique of carving on Stela 10 appears to be crisper and less modulated, and though this may be due in part to its better preservation, there is a decided stress on angular forms, expressed in such details as the angular earplugs and the squared ends of the belt. The pose, too, is rigidly vertical in contrast to the swaying pose of the figure on Stela 3. The abbreviated squared glyphs in the band below repeat a single, apparently meaningless form. Under the right elbow is a Secondary Series, 1.6.10.3, leading from 6 Caban 10 Zip to 10.3.0.0.0, recorded on the sides of this stela. Although no statement follows the Caban date, as on Stela 3, it is probably the birth date of the ruler portrayed.

Uaxactun and Jimbal erected one stela each in 10.3.0.0.0. Both monuments are small, and both are sculptured only with glyphs. The indifferent quality of carving on Stela 13 at Uaxactun contrasts strongly with the script of Stela 12. The inscription on Jimbal Stela 2 is somewhat damaged, and the order of reading of the Initial Series appears to be from right to left. Whether this is true of the rest of the text is somewhat uncertain, for the last four glyphs, if they follow

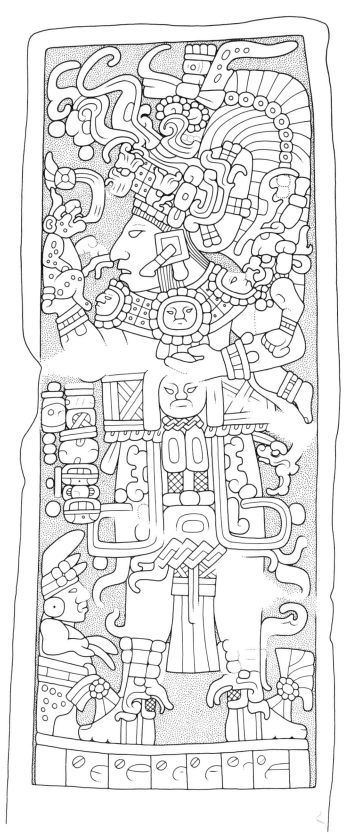

Xultun Stela 10, front: Angular forms and vertical pose in a late portrait of a ruler. (Eric von Euw, *Corpus of Maya Hieroglyphic Inscriptions, Volume 5, Part I: Xultun,* Peabody Museum of Archaeology and Ethnology. Copyright 1978 by the President and Fellows of Harvard College.)

the usual order, would be read first from left to right, then from right to left. Whatever the case, the Initial Series is on the right side of the text, and Satterthwaite's reading of it (C. Jones and Satterthwaite 1982: 111–113) is probably correct. Continuing in this fashion, the first glyph following the date is a hand-scattering-grains glyph, which I read as "divination." Three head or mask glyphs follow, and the Emblem of Tikal. Either the king of Tikal now resided in this minor site or it was in possession of the former province. The last four glyphs of these two columns, however, if they are to be read in the order we find elsewhere, should be read first from left to right, then from right to left. The three final glyphs are those in square cartouches also shown on Jimbal Stela 1: 12 Serpent, 13 Death(?), 1 Deer. Like the earlier stela, Stela 2 has a decorated border and is wider at the top than at the base, though this is a shape not well adapted to an all-glyphic monument.

At Seibal, Stela 20, standing at the foot of the stairway to Temple A-24, one of the most imposing pyramid temples at the site, has a Calendar Round date that reads best as 1 Ahau 3 Yaxkin, very probably 10.3.0.0.0. The position of the figure recalls that on Stela 1, but here, instead of the long serrated spear, the figure holds a staff with a crook on the end, possibly signifying that he comes from somewhere else, and in his left hand he holds two darts. His headdress is essentially Classic, as is his heavy pectoral and the abbreviation of a mask in front of his face, but his costume is rather unusual. He wears a close-fitting belt of a figured material and a short fringed skirt. A long knotted tail trails behind him. The crook he holds and the fringed skirt link this figure with one of the two figures on "Stela 17" at the base of the temple above. This figure, however, has long, shaggy hair and peculiar proportions. The face is somewhat eroded, but there is a suggestion that he wears a moustache. He is facing a figure in what apparently is intended as Classic Maya attire, though it is even more distorted in proportions than the other.

In the middle of the broad low platform in front of the temple is Stela 13, one of the strangest monuments at Seibal. At the top is a text consisting of twelve glyphs. It begins with a large glyph in a rectangular cartouche with the number 7. The glyph itself looks like a jar with a large, flat lid. Although some of the signs in the inscription are recognizable, its meaning is obscure. The eighth glyph is a fist with the coefficient 3 and the ninth a zoomorphic mask. Conceivably this may record the completion of the third katun. The figure below is shown in full-front view, with his head in profile. He wears no headdress. His hair streams down over his shoulder, and a death mask is fastened behind. He wears a bar noseplug and a necklace and armbands of round beads. From his mouth issues a huge speech-scroll, encircled with nine large dots. In his right hand he holds up a glyph, the nature of which is not clear. The left hand is encased in a glove from which issues an elaborate scroll, perhaps an indication that his hand had been severed. Around his waist is tied a huge serpent. From his apron, which seems to have had glyphs on it, now erased, issue four more serpents, and two more from behind the anklets of his bare feet. In spite of the peculiarity of the motif, the sinuous curves of the scrolls pictured on this stela suggest a Maya artist schooled in the Classic Maya tradition of draftsmanship, far superior to those who carved the monuments above.

The same elaborate scrollwork can be seen on Stela 18 at the base of a stairway leading to a pyramid that faces on the Central Plaza and is adjacent to the ballcourt. It is only partially preserved, and its one Calendar Round date is damaged. The lower part of the monument shows only two serpent heads framing a design that is completely effaced. Above is a serpent head facing upward supporting a seated figure holding in the right hand a hooked stick and in the left a nondescript object which may or may not be an *atlatl*. He wears a square earplug and a helmet topped with plumes. His face is not clear. He may be wearing a mask.

There remain three stelae at Seibal, all three distinct in style, but all impossible to date even approximately, for they are quite unlike each other or any other sculpture at Seibal. Stela 2 is described by John Graham (Greene Robertson, Rands, and Graham 1972) as columnar in form, and is without borders. It shows an individual in full-front view, with feet pointing outward. He is wearing a mask with projecting shell earplugs, a wide collar projecting beyond the shoulders, a tight belt showing above the more usual belt of his skirt, which has a bat mask in front, and sandals with a low strap of an archaic type that came into fashion in Cycle 10. Stela 3 is of some interest because it is designed in three superimposed panels, not unlike some stelae at the site of Oxkintok in northern Yucatan (see Pollock 1980: Fig. 547). The upper register of the Seibal stela shows two apparently identical glyphs in square cartouches with coefficients 7 and 9. Below are two masked figures with shaggy hair, apparently conversing and gesticulating. The face of the figure on the right is that of Tlaloc. In the central register, a figure, simply dressed and without sandals, stands in an elaborate frame that suggests a gateway. He wears a bar noseplug and holds up a hieroglyph in his right hand. In the lowest register are two more figures conversing. The one on the right wears a long-beaked mask, probably representing Ehecatl, the Mexican god of wind. Stelae 2 and 3 stand in front of a small building next to the entrance to the *sacbe* leading to Group D, and facing Pyramid A-24 across the South Plaza.

Also on the east side of the South Plaza, in front of a low platform supporting a small building, is Stela 19. John Graham (Greene Robertson, Rands, and Graham 1972: 244) writes about this sculpture that it "clearly shows the work of a sophisticated, masterful hand." My impression is quite different. It is a singularly fragmented composition. The rigid, straight-line rendering of the figure gives no emphasis to the motif suggested by the scattering gesture, and contrasts strangely with the sinuous Classic scrolls of the serpent motif concentrated in a small area on top of the headdress. The sharp, long beak of the mask the figure wears and the large round speech-scroll only fragment the design further. I would surmise that it was a scribe and not a sculptor who designed this strange monument, and a foreign scribe at that. The inscription below, however, is in Maya script. It is badly damaged, but one can see that it began with four Maya day names beginning with 1 Ben. The other days also have the coefficient 1. Possibly they divide the Tzolkin into four parts: 1 Ben, 1 Etz'nab, 1 Akbal, 1 Lamat. If the intervals were only thirteen days, they would read: 1 Ben, 1 Cimi, 1 Cauac, 1 Eb. Reading the text in double columns, the third day looks more like Akbal than Cauac, and I believe that the first series proposed is more probably correct. On the other hand there is some advantage to the second series, for 1 Ben is only thirteen days after 1 Ahau, and 10.3.0.0.0 was 1 Ahau, which would give this stela a possible dedicatory date. Other solutions to the series are possible, but unless we can read at least two days in the series with certainty, speculation is hardly worthwhile. If 10.3.0.0.0 is the correct date for this monument, then it is contemporary to Stela 20, and probably roughly contemporary also to Stela 13, which has a similar speech-scroll. Stela 13, in my opinion, shows a more practiced hand than Stela 19, and it is also associated with a much more important building. It is unfortunate that we have no date for Stela 13.

Archaeologists have long been concerned with what they term as the Maya Collapse, and excavations recently concluded at Seibal have provided important data on the subject. Here I can only remark that the evidence of the stelae suggests a long period of infiltration of new elements, probably from border towns and surrounding regions, rather than a single invasion. Thus in 10.1.0.0.0 can be noted a strong influence from Machaquila, the sequence of whose stelae ends in the previous lahuntun. The gap in the sequence of dates at Tikal before 10.2.0.0.0, perhaps filled by the cloud-rider stelae at various sites and the pitiful final stelae at Jimbal and Uaxactun, suggests that the conquest of Chichen Itza by the Toltec was only the culmination of previous incursions that left Seibal for a time as a refuge for immigrants of other, conquered towns.

Although the latest-known date in central Peten is 10.3.0.0.0, Peter Mathews has recently reported a stela from Tonina with the date 10.4.0.0.0. Tonina had begun to erect stelae at the beginning of the Late Classic period and from the begining had a statuesque style uniquely its own. Its apparent isolation and independence of established lowland centers was probably due to its location in a valley at the foothills of the cordillera. This does not mean, of course, that the Peten region was already completely abandoned and reverting to forest. Chichen Itza had probably been conquered by the Toltec even before the end of the third katun, but whether the history of northern Yucatan can ever be correlated with that of the southern Maya remains a problem that is beyond the scope of this book.

Bibliography

(Including sources cited by Willey, Graham, and Joyce, as well as a compilation by John G. Fox of those cited by Proskouriakoff)

Andrews, E. Wyllys IV
1943   *The Archeology of Southwestern Campeche*. Carnegie Institution of Washington Publication 546. Washington, D.C.

Ashmore, Wendy
1986   Peten Cosmology in the Maya Southeast: An Analysis of Architecture and Settlement Patterns at Classic Quirigua. In *The Southeast Maya Periphery*, edited by Patricia A. Urban and Edward M. Schortman, pp. 35–49. Austin: University of Texas Press.

Aveni, Anthony
1980   *Skywatchers of Ancient Mexico*. Austin: University of Texas Press.

Bailey, Joyce Waddell
1972   A Preliminary Investigation of the Formal and Interpretive Histories of Monumental Relief Sculpture from Tikal, Guatemala: Pre-, Early and Middle Classic Periods. Ph.D. dissertation, Yale University.

Ball, Joseph
1979   Ceramics, Culture History, and the Puuc Tradition: Some Alternative Possibilities. In *The Puuc: New Perspectives; Papers presented at the Puuc Symposium, Central College, May 1977,* edited by Lawrence Mills, pp. 18–35. Scholarly Studies in the Liberal Arts, Publication No. 1. Pella, Iowa: Central College.
1983   Teotihuacan, the Maya, and Ceramic Interchange: A Contextual Perspective. In *Highland-Lowland Interaction in Mesoamerica: Interdisciplinary Approaches,* edited by Arthur Miller, pp. 125–146. Washington, D.C.: Dumbarton Oaks.

Barthel, Thomas S.
1968   El complejo 'Emblema.' *Estudios de Cultura Maya* 7 : 159–193.

Baudez, Claude F.
1986   Iconography and History at Copan. In *The Southeast Maya*

Periphery, edited by Patricia A. Urban and Edward M. Schortman, pp. 16–26. Austin: University of Texas Press.

Baudez, Claude F., and Peter Mathews
1979   Capture and Sacrifice at Palenque. In *Tercera Mesa Redonda de Palenque, Vol. IV,* edited by Merle Greene Robertson and Donnan Call Jeffers, pp. 31–40. Palenque: Pre-Columbian Art Research Center.

Becquelin, Pierre, and Claude Baudez
1979–1982   *Toniná, une cité Maya du Chiapas.* Mexico City: Mission Archéologique et Ethnologique Française au Mexique.

Beetz, Carl, and Linton Satterthwaite
1981   *The Monuments and Inscriptions of Caracol, Belize.* University Museum Monograph 45. Philadelphia: University of Pennsylvania.

Berlin, Heinrich
1968   *Estudios epigráficos II.* Antropología e Historia de Guatemala 20, no. 1. Guatemala City.
1973   Beiträge zum Verständnis der Inschriften von Naranjo. Société Suisse des Américanistes, *Bulletin* no. 37, pp. 7–14. Geneva.
1977   *Signos y significados en las inscripciones maya.* Guatemala City: Instituto Nacional del Patrimonio Cultural, Ministerio de Educación Pública.

Beyer, Hermann
1939   Elucidation of a Series on Lintel 2 of Piedras Negras. *El México Antiguo,* vol. 4. Mexico City.

Bishop, Ronald L., Marilyn P. Beaudry, Richard M. Leventhal and Robert J. Sharer
1986   Compositional Analysis of Copador and Related Pottery in the Southeast Maya Area. In *The Southeast Maya Periphery,* edited by Patricia A. Urban and Edward M. Schortman, pp. 143–167. Austin: University of Texas Press.

Bowditch, Charles P.
1903   *Notes on the Report of Teobert Maler in Memoirs of the Peabody Museum, vol. II. no. 2.* Cambridge, Mass.: Peabody Museum of Archaeology and Ethnology, Harvard University.

Brack-Bernsen, Lis
1977   Die Basler Mayatafeln: Astronomische Deutung der Inschriften auf den Türstürzen 2 und 3 aus Temple IV in Tikal. *Verhandlungen der Naturforschenden Gesellschaft in Basel,* vol. 86, nos. 1–2. Basel.

Bricker, Victoria R.
1986   *A Grammar of Mayan Hieroglyphs.* Middle American Research Institute Publication 56. New Orleans: Tulane University.

Bruhns, Karen O.
1988   Yesterday the Queen Wore . . . an Analysis of Women and Costume in Public Art of the Late Classic Maya. In *The Role of Gender in Pre-columbian Art and Architecture,* edited by Virginia Miller, pp. 105–134. Lanham, Md.: University Press of America.

Butler, Mary
1931   Dress and Decoration of the Maya Old Empire. University of Pennsylvania, *Museum Journal* 22(2): 155–183.

Chase, Arlen, and Diane Z. Chase
1987   *Investigations at the Classic Maya City of Caracol, Belize: 1985–1987.*

Pre-Columbian Art Research Institute Monograph 3. San Francisco.

Cheek, Charles

1986 Construction Activity as a Measurement of Change at Copan, Honduras. In *The Southeast Maya Periphery,* edited by Patricia A. Urban and Edward M. Schortman, pp. 50–71. Austin: University of Texas Press.

Closs, Michael

1984 The Dynastic History of Naranjo: The Early Period. *Estudios de Cultura Maya* 15:77–96.

1985 The Dynastic History of Naranjo: The Middle Period. In *Fifth Palenque Round Table, 1983, Vol. VII,* edited by Merle Greene Robertson and Virginia Fields, pp. 65–78. San Francisco: Pre-Columbian Art Research Institute.

1988 The hieroglyphic text of Stela 9, Lamanai, Belize. *Research Reports on Ancient Maya Writing* No. 20. Washington, D.C.

Coe, Michael D., and Elizabeth Benson

1966 *Three Maya Relief Panels at Dumbarton Oaks.* Studies in Pre-Columbian Art and Archaeology, no. 2. Washington, D.C.: Dumbarton Oaks.

Coe, William R.

1959 *Piedras Negras Archeology: Artifacts, Caches, and Burials.* Philadelphia: University Museum, University of Pennsylvania.

Coggins, Clemency Chase

1975 *Painting and Drawing Styles at Tikal: An Historical and Iconographic Reconstruction.* Ph.D. dissertation, Harvard University. Ann Arbor: University Microfilms.

1979 A New Order and the Role of the Calendar: Some Characteristics of the Middle Classic Period at Tikal. In *Maya Archaeology and Ethnohistory,* edited by Norman Hammond and Gordon R. Willey, pp. 38–50. Austin: University of Texas Press.

1983 An Instrument of Expansion: Monte Alban, Teotihuacan and Tikal. In *Highland-Lowland Interaction in Mesoamerica: Interdisciplinary Approaches,* edited by Arthur Miller, pp. 49–68. Washington, D.C.: Dumbarton Oaks.

Davoust, Michel

1979 Les Chefs mayas de Copan. In *Acts of the 42nd International Congress of Americanists* 7:221–237. Paris.

Edmonson, Munro S.

1982 *The Ancient Future of the Itza: The Book of Chilam Balam of Tizimin.* Austin: University of Texas Press.

Fahsen, Federico

1984 Notes for a Sequence of Rulers of Machaquila. *American Antiquity* 49:94–104.

1987 Los personajes de Tikal en el Clásico Temprano, la evidencia epigráfica. In *Primer Simposio Mundial sobre Epigrafía Maya, Agosto 19–21, 1986,* pp. 47–60. Guatemala City: Asociación Tikal.

1988 A New Early Classic Text from Tikal. *Research Reports on Ancient Maya Writing* 17. Washington, D.C.

Fialko C., Vilma

1987 El marcador de juego de pelota de Tikal: Nuevas referencias epigráficas para el Clásico Temprano. In *Primer Simposio Mundial sobre Epigrafía Maya, Agosto 19–21, 1986*, pp. 61–80. Guatemala City: Asociación Tikal.

1988   El marcador de juego de pelota de Tikal: Nuevas referencias epigráficas para el Clásico Temprano. *Mesoamérica* 15:117–135.

Fox, James A., and John S. Justeson

1986   Classic Maya Dynastic Alliance and Succession. In *Handbook of Middle American Indians, Supplement Volume 4, Ethnohistory,* edited by Victoria Reifler Bricker and Ronald Spores, pp. 7–34. Austin: University of Texas Press.

Friedel, David

1985   Polychrome Façades of the Lowland Maya Preclassic. In *Painted Architecture and Polychrome Monumental Sculpture in Mesoamerica,* edited by Elizabeth H. Boone, pp. 5–30. Washington, D.C.: Dumbarton Oaks.

Graham, Ian

1967   *Archaeological Explorations in El Peten, Guatemala.* Middle American Research Institute Publication 33. New Orleans: Tulane University.

1978   *Corpus of Maya Hieroglyphic Inscriptions, Volume 2, Part 2: Naranjo, Chunhuitz, Xunantunich.* Cambridge, Mass.: Peabody Museum of Archaeology and Ethnology, Harvard University.

1979   *Corpus of Maya Hieroglyphic Inscriptions, Volume 3, Part 2: Yaxchilan.* Cambridge, Mass.: Peabody Museum of Archaeology and Ethnology, Harvard University.

Graham, Ian, and Eric von Euw

1975   *Corpus of Maya Hieroglyphic Inscriptions, Volume 2, Part 1: Naranjo.* Cambridge: Mass.: Peabody Museum of Archaeology and Ethnology, Harvard University.

1977   *Corpus of Maya Hieroglyphic Inscriptions, Volume 3, Part 1: Yaxchilan.* Cambridge, Mass.: Peabody Museum of Archaeology and Ethnology, Harvard University.

Graham, John Allen

1972   *The Hieroglyphic Inscriptions and Monumental Art of Altar de Sacrificios.* Peabody Museum of Archaeology and Ethnology, Harvard University, Papers, vol. 64, no. 2. Cambridge, Mass.

Greene Robertson, Merle, Robert L. Rands, and John A. Graham

1972   *Maya Sculptures from the Southern Lowlands, Highlands and Pacific Piedmont.* Berkeley: Lederer, Street and Zeus.

Houston, Stephen D.

1989   *Reading Maya Glyphs.* Stanford: Stanford University Press.

Houston, Stephen D., and Peter Mathews

1985   *The Dynastic Sequence of Dos Pilas, Guatemala.* San Francisco: Pre-Columbian Art Research Institute Monograph 1.

Johnston, Kevin

1985   Maya Dynastic Territorial Expansion: Glyphic Evidence from Classic Centers of the Pasion River, Guatemala. In *Fifth Palenque Round Table, 1983, Vol. VII,* edited by Merle Greene Robertson and Virginia Fields, pp. 49–56. San Francisco: Pre-Columbian Art Research Institute.

Jones, Christopher

1977   Inauguration Dates of Three Late Classic Rulers of Tikal, Guatemala. *American Antiquity* 42:28–60.

1983   Monument 26, Quirigua. In *Quirigua Reports II,* edited by Edward
           M. Schortman and Patricia A. Urban, pp. 118–128. University
           Museum Monograph 49. Philadelphia: University of Pennsylvania.

Jones, Christopher, William R. Coe, and William A. Haviland

1981   Tikal: An Outline of Its Field Study (1956–1970) and a Project
           Bibliography. In *Handbook of Middle American Indians, Supplement
           Volume 1, Archaeology,* edited by Victoria Reifler Bricker and
           Jeremy A. Sabloff, pp. 296–312. Austin: University of Texas Press.

Jones, Christopher, and Linton Satterthwaite

1982   *The Monuments and Inscriptions at Tikal: The Carved Monuments.*
           Tikal Report vol. 33(A); University Museum Monograph 44.
           Philadelphia: University of Pennsylvania.

Jones, Christopher, and Robert J. Sharer

1986   Archaeological Investigations in the Site Core of Quirigua, Guate-
           mala. In *The Southeast Maya Periphery,* edited by Patricia A. Urban
           and Edward M. Schortman, pp. 27–34. Austin: University of Texas
           Press.

Justeson, John S.

1975   The Identification of the Emblem Glyph of Yaxha, El Peten.
           Archaeological Research Facility Contributions, no. 27, pp. 123–129.
           Berkeley: University of California.

Justeson, John S. and Lyle Campbell, eds.

1984   *Phoneticism in Mayan Hieroglyphic Writing.* Institute for Mesoamer-
           ican Studies, State University of New York at Albany, Publication
           No. 9. Albany.

Kelley, David Humiston

1962   Glyphic Evidence for a Dynastic Sequence at Quirigua, Guatemala.
           American Antiquity 27:323–335.

1976   *Deciphering the Maya Script.* Austin: University of Texas Press.

1982   Notes on Puuc Inscriptions. In *The Puuc: New Perspectives. Papers
           presented at the Puuc Symposium, Central College, May 1977,* edited by
           Lawrence Mills. Scholarly Studies in the Liberal Arts, Publication
           No. 1, Supplement. Pella, Iowa: Central College.

Knorosov, Yurii

1967   *Selected Chapters from the Writing of the Maya Indians.* Translated by
           Sophie Coe. Russian Translation Series No. 4. Cambridge, Mass.:
           Peabody Museum of Archaeology and Ethnology, Harvard
           University.

Korbjuhn, Kornelia, comp.

1989   *Maya: The Complete Catalog of Glyph Readings.* Kassel, Germany:
           Schneider und Weber.

Kowalski, Jeffrey

1985   A Historical Interpretation of the Inscriptions of Uxmal. In *Fourth
           Palenque Round Table, 1980, Vol. VI,* edited by Merle Greene
           Robertson and Elizabeth P. Benson, pp. 235–247. San Francisco:
           Pre-Columbian Art Research Institute.

Laporte, Juan Pedro, and Lilian Vega de Zea

1987   Aspectos dinásticos para el Clásico Temprano de Mundo Perdido,
           Tikal. In *Primer Simposio Mundial sobre Epigrafía Maya, Agosto
           19–21, 1986,* pp. 127–140. Guatemala City: Asociación Tikal.

Lincoln, Charles

1986   The Chronology of Chichen Itza: A Review of the Literature. In
           Late Lowland Maya Civilization: Classic to Postclassic, edited by

Jeremy A. Sabloff and E. Wyllys Andrews V, pp. 141–196. Albuquerque: University of New Mexico Press.

Lounsbury, Floyd G.

1974　The Inscription of the Sarcophagus Lid at Palenque. In *Primera Mesa Redonda de Palenque, Part II,* edited by Merle Greene Robertson, pp. 5–19. Pebble Beach, Calif.: Robert Louis Stevenson School.

1982　Astronomical Knowledge and Its Uses at Bonampak, Mexico. In *Archaeoastronomy in the New World,* edited by Anthony F. Aveni, pp. 143–168. Cambridge: The University Press.

1985　The Identities of the Mythological Figures in the Cross Group Inscriptions of Palenque. In *Fourth Palenque Round Table, 1980, Vol. VI,* edited by Merle Greene Robertson and Elizabeth P. Benson, pp. 45–58. San Francisco: Pre-Columbian Art Research Institute.

1988　A Palenque King and the Planet Jupiter. In *World Archaeoastronomy,* edited by Anthony F. Aveni, pp. 246–249. Cambridge: University Press.

Love, Bruce

1989　The Hieroglyphic Lintels of Yula, Yucatan, Mexico. *Research Reports in Ancient Maya Writing* 24:15–22. Washington, D.C.

Lundell, Cyrus Longworth

1934　Ruins of Polol and Other Archaeological Discoveries in the Department of Peten, Guatemala. In *Carnegie Institution of Washington, Contributions to American Archaeology* 2(8):173–186. Carnegie Institute of Washington Publication 436. Washington, D.C.

Maler, Teobert

1901–1903　*Researches in the Central Portion of the Usumatsintla Valley.* Peabody Museum of Archaeology and Ethnology, Harvard University, Memoirs, vol. 2, nos. 1–2. Cambridge, Mass.

1908　*Explorations in the Department of Peten, Guatemala, and Adjacent Region: Topoxte; Yaxha; Benque Viejo; Naranjo.* Peabody Museum of Archaeology and Ethnology, Harvard University, Memoirs, vol. 4, no. 2. Cambridge, Mass.

1910　*Explorations in the Department of Peten, Guatemala, and Adjacent Region: Motul de San José; Peten Itza.* Peabody Museum of Archaeology and Ethnology, Harvard University, Memoirs, vol. 4, no. 3. Cambridge, Mass.

Marcus, Joyce

1973　Territorial Organization of the Lowland Classic Maya. *Science* 180:911–916.

1976　*Emblem and State in the Classic Maya Lowlands: An Epigraphic Approach to Territorial Organization.* Washington, D.C.: Dumbarton Oaks.

1987　*The Inscriptions of Calakmul: Royal Marriage at a Maya City in Campeche, Mexico.* University of Michigan Museum of Anthropology, Technical Report 21. Ann Arbor.

Mathews, Peter

1980　Notes on the Dynastic Sequence of Bonampak, Part 1. In *Third Palenque Round Table, 1978, Part 2,* edited by Merle Greene Robertson, pp. 60–73. Austin: University of Texas Press.

1983　*Corpus of Maya Hieroglyphic Inscriptions, Volume 6, Part 1: Tonina.* Cambridge, Mass.: Peabody Museum of Archaeology and Ethnology, Harvard University.

1985   Maya Early Classic Monuments and Inscriptions. In *A Consid-eration of the Early Classic Period in the Maya Lowlands,* edited by Gordon R. Willey and Peter Mathews, pp. 5–54. Institute for Mesoamerican Studies, State University of New York at Albany, Publication No. 10. Albany.

Mathews, Peter, and Linda Schele

1974   Lords of Palenque—The Glyphic Evidence. In *Primera Mesa Redonda de Palenque, Part I,* edited by Merle Greene Robertson, pp. 63–75. Pebble Beach, Calif.: Robert Louis Stephenson School.

Maudslay, A. P.

1889–1902   *Biologia Centrali-Americana: Archaeology.* 5 vols. London: R. H. Porter and Dulau and Co.

Miller, Arthur, ed.

1983   *Highland-Lowland Interaction in Mesoamerica: Interdisciplinary Approaches.* Washington, D.C.: Dumbarton Oaks.

Miller, Mary Ellen

1986   *The Murals of Bonampak.* Princeton: Princeton University Press.

Miller, Mary Ellen, and Stephen D. Houston

1987   The Classic Maya Ballgame and Its Architectural Setting: A Study of Relations between Text and Image. *Res* 14:47–66.

Molloy, John P., and William L. Rathje

1974   Sexploitation among the Late Classic Maya. In *Mesoamerican Archaeology: New Approaches,* edited by Norman Hammond, pp. 431–444. Austin: University of Texas Press.

Morley, Sylvanus G.

1920   *The Inscriptions at Copan.* Carnegie Institution of Washington Publication 219. Washington, D.C.

1937–1938   *The Inscriptions of Peten.* 5 vols. Carnegie Institution of Washington Publication 437. Washington, D.C.

Pahl, Gary

1977   The Inscriptions of Rio Amarillo and Los Higos: Secondary Centers of the Southeastern Maya Frontier. *Journal of Latin American Lore* 3(1):133–154.

Pollock, H. E. D.

1980   *The Puuc: An Architectural Survey of the Hill Country of Yucatan and Northern Campeche, Mexico.* Peabody Museum of Archaeology and Ethnology, Harvard University, Memoirs, vol. 19. Cambridge, Mass.

Proskouriakoff, Tatiana

1944   An Inscription on a Jade Probably Carved at Piedras Negras. *Notes on Middle American Archaeology and Ethnology* 2:142–147. Cambridge, Mass.: Carnegie Institution of Washington, Division of Historical Research.

1950   *A Study of Classic Maya Sculpture.* Carnegie Institution of Washington Publication 593. Washington, D.C.

1960   Historical Implications of a Pattern of Dates at Piedras Negras, Guatemala. *American Antiquity* 25:454–475.

1961a   The Lords of the Maya Realm. *Expedition* 4(1):14–21.

1961b   Portraits of Women in Maya Art. In *Essays in Pre-Columbian Art and Archaeology,* by Samuel K. Lothrop et al., pp. 81–99. Cambridge, Mass.: Harvard University Press.

1963   Historical Data in the Inscriptions of Yaxchilan (Part I). *Estudios de Cultura Maya* 3:149–167.

1964   Historical Data in the Inscriptions of Yaxchilan (Part II). *Estudios de Cultura Maya* 4:177–202.

1968   The Jog and Jaguar Signs in Maya Writing. *American Antiquity* 33(2):247–251.

1973   The 'Hand-grasping-fish' and Associated Glyphs on Classic Maya Monuments. In *Mesoamerican Writing Systems,* edited by Elizabeth P. Benson, pp. 165–178. Washington, D.C.: Dumbarton Oaks.

1974   *Jades from the Cenote of Sacrifice, Chichen Itza, Yucatan.* Peabody Museum of Archaeology and Ethnology, Harvard University, Memoirs, vol. 10, no. 1. Cambridge, Mass.

1978   Olmec Gods and Maya God-Glyphs. In *Codex Wauchope: A Tribute Roll,* edited by M. Giardino, B. Edmonson, and W. Crenier, pp. 113–117. *Human Mosaic,* vol. 12. New Orleans: Tulane University.

Reents, Dorie

1986   Inter-site Dynastic Relations Recorded on a Plate from Holmul, Guatemala. *Estudios de Cultura Maya* 16:149–166.

Riese, Berthold

1971   *Grundlagen zur Entzifferung der Maya-hieroglyphen: Dargestellt an den Inschriften von Copan.* Beiträge zur Mittelamerikanischen Volkerkunde, vol. 11. Hamburg.

1983   Esculturas de las Estructuras 10L-2 y -4: Estudio epigráfico. In *Introducción a la arqueología de Copán, Honduras, Tomo II,* edited by Claude F. Baudez, pp. 147–185. Tegucigalpa: Proyecto Arqueológico Copán, Instituto Hondureño de Antropología e Historia, Secretaría de Estado en Despacho de Cultura y Turismo.

1986   Late Classic Relationship between Copan and Quirigua: Some Epigraphic Evidence. In *The Southeast Maya Periphery,* edited by Patricia A. Urban and Edward M. Schortman, pp. 94–101. Austin: University of Texas Press.

1988   Epigraphy of the Southeast Zone in Relation to Other Parts of the Maya Realm. In *The Southeast Classic Maya Zone,* edited by Elizabeth H. Boone and Gordon R. Willey, pp. 67–94. Washington, D.C.: Dumbarton Oaks.

Roys, Ralph L., trans.

1933   *The Book of Chilam Balam of Chumayel.* Carnegie Institution of Washington Publication 438. Washington, D.C.

Ruppert, Karl, and John H. Dennison

1943   *Archeological Reconnaissance in Campeche, Quintana Roo, and Peten.* Carnegie Institution of Washington Publication 543. Washington, D.C.

Ruppert, Karl, J. Eric S. Thompson, and Tatiana Proskouriakoff

1955   *Bonampak, Chiapas Mexico.* Carnegie Institution of Washington Publication 602. Washington, D.C.

Satterthwaite, Linton

1937   Thrones at Piedras Negras. *University Museum Bulletin* 7(1):18–23. Philadelphia.

Schele, Linda

1979   Genealogical Documentation on the Tri-figure Panels at Palenque. In *Tercera Mesa Redonda de Palenque, Vol. IV,* edited by Merle Greene Robertson and Donnan Call Jeffers, pp. 41–70. Palenque: Pre-Columbian Art Research Center.

1982   *Maya Glyphs: The Verbs.* Austin: University of Texas Press.

1984a Human Sacrifice among the Classic Maya. In *Ritual Sacrifice in Meso-america,* edited by Elizabeth H. Boone, pp. 7–48. Washington, D.C.: Dumbarton Oaks.

1984b Some Suggested Readings for the Event and Office of Heir-designate at Palenque. In *Phoneticism in Mayan Hieroglyphic Writing,* edited by John S. Justeson and Lyle Campbell, pp. 287–305. Institute for Mesoamerican Studies, State University of New York at Albany, Publication No. 9. Albany.

Schele, Linda, Peter Mathews, and Floyd G. Lounsbury

1977   Parentage Expressions in Classic Maya Inscriptions. Paper presented at the International Conference on Maya Iconography and Hieroglyphic Writing, Guatemala City.

Sharer, Robert H.

1978   Archaeology and History at Quirigua, Guatemala. *Journal of Field Archaeology* 5:51–70.

Simpson, Jon Erik

1972   *The Iconology and Epigraphy of Sacred Kingship at Yaxchilan.* Philadelphia.

1976   The New York Relief Panel—and Some Associations with Reliefs at Palenque and Elsewhere, Part I. In *Segunda Mesa Redonda de Palenque, Part III,* edited by Merle Greene Robertson, pp. 95–105. Pebble Beach, Calif.: Robert Louis Stevenson School.

Smith, A. Ledyard

1950   *Uaxactun, Guatemala: Excavations of 1931–1937.* Carnegie Institution of Washington Publication 588. Washington, D.C.

Smith, Robert Eliot

1955   *Ceramic Sequence at Uaxactun, Guatemala.* 2 vols. Middle American Research Institute Publication 20. New Orleans: Tulane University.

Spinden, Herbert Joseph

1913   *A Study of Maya Art: Its Subject Matter and Historical Development.* Peabody Museum of Archaeology and Ethnology, Harvard University, Memoirs, vol. 6. Cambridge, Mass.

Stone, Andrea

1985   Variety and Transformations in the Cosmic Monster Theme at Quirigua, Guatemala. In *Fifth Palenque Round Table, 1983, Vol. VII,* edited by Merle Greene Robertson and Virginia M. Fields, pp. 39–48. San Francisco: Pre-Columbian Art Research Institute.

1988   Sacrifice and Sexuality: Some Structural Relationships in Classic Maya Art. In *The Role of Gender in Precolumbian Art and Architecture,* edited by Virginia Miller, pp. 75–104. Lanham, Md.: University Press of America.

1991   Aspects of Impersonation in Classic Maya Art. In *Sixth Palenque Round Table, 1986,* edited by Merle Greene Robertson and Virginia M. Fields, pp. 194–202. Norman: University of Oklahoma Press.

Stone, Andrea, Dorie Reents, and Robert Coffman

1985   Genealogical Documentation of the Middle Classic Dynasty of Caracol, El Cayo, Belize. In *Fourth Palenque Round Table, 1980, vol. VI,* edited by Merle Greene Robertson and Elizabeth P. Benson, pp. 267–276. San Francisco: Pre-Columbian Art Research Institute.

Stromsvik, Gustav

1952 *The Ballcourts at Copan, with Notes on Courts at La Union, Quirigua, San Pedro Pinula, and Asuncion Mita.* Carnegie Institution of Washington Publication 596. Washington, D.C.

Stuart, David

1984 Royal Auto-sacrifice among the Maya: A Study of Image and Meaning. *Res* 7/8:6–20.

1985 The Inscriptions on Four Shell Plaques from Piedras Negras. In *Fourth Palenque Round Table, 1980, Vol. VI,* edited by Merle Greene Robertson and Elizabeth P. Benson, pp. 175–183. San Francisco: Pre-Columbian Art Research Institute.

1986 Subsidiaries and Scribes: New Epigraphic Light on Classic Maya Political and Social Organization. Paper presented in the symposium "The New Dynamics" May 1986, at the Kimball Art Museum, Fort Worth.

Stuart, George

1989 City of Kings and Commoners: Copan. *National Geographic* 176(4): 488–505.

Tate, Carolyn

1992 *Yaxchilan: The Design of a Maya Ceremonial City.* Austin: University of Texas Press.

Thompson, J. Eric S.

1943 Maya Epigraphy: A Cycle of 819 Days. *Notes on Middle American Archaeology and Ethnology* 1:137–151. Cambridge, Mass.: Carnegie Institution of Washington, Division of Historical Research.

1944a Jottings on Inscriptions at Copan. *Notes on Middle American Archaeology and Ethnology* 2:48–64. Cambridge, Mass.: Carnegie Institution of Washington, Division of Historical Research.

1944b The Dating of Seven Monuments at Piedras Negras. *Notes on Middle American Archaeology and Ethnology* 2:65–82. Cambridge, Mass.: Carnegie Institution of Washington, Division of Historical Research.

1945 The Inscription on the Altar of Zoomorph O, Quirigua. *Notes on Middle American Archaeology and Ethnology* 2:189–199. Cambridge, Mass.: Carnegie Institution of Washington, Division of Historical Research.

1946 The Dating of Structure 44, Yaxchilan, and Its Bearing on the Sequence of Texts at the Site. *Notes on Middle American Archaeology and Ethnology* 3:62–74. Cambridge, Mass.: Carnegie Institution of Washington, Division of Historical Research.

1950 *Maya Hieroglyphic Writing: Introduction.* Carnegie Institution of Washington Publication 589. Washington, D.C.

1952 The Introduction of Puuc Style of Dating at Yaxchilan. *Notes on Middle American Archaeology and Ethnology,* no. 110, pp. 196–202. Cambridge, Mass.: Carnegie Institution of Washington, Division of Historical Research.

1962 *A Catalog of Maya Hieroglyphs.* Norman: University of Oklahoma Press.

Thompson, J. Eric S., Harry E. D. Pollock, and Jean Charlot

1932 *A Preliminary Study of the Ruins of Coba, Quintana Roo, Mexico.* Carnegie Institution of Washington Publication 424. Washington, D.C.

Thompson, Philip C.
1982   Dynastic Marriage and Succession at Tikal. *Estudios de Cultura Maya* 14:261–287.

Tourtellot, Gair III, Norman Hammond, and Richard M. Rose
1978   *A Brief Reconnaissance of Itzan*. Peabody Museum of Archaeology and Ethnology, Harvard University, Memoirs, no. 14, pp. 241–250. Cambridge, Mass.

Tozzer, A. M., trans.
1941   *Landa's 'Relación de las cosas de Yucatán'*. Cambridge, Mass.: Peabody Museum of Archaeology and Ethnology, Harvard University, Papers, vol. 18.

von Euw, Eric
1978   *Corpus of Maya Hieroglyphic Inscriptions, Volume 5, Part 1: Xultun*. Cambridge, Mass.: Peabody Museum of Archaeology and Ethnology, Harvard University.

Webster, David, ed.
1989   *The House of the Bacabs, Copan, Honduras*. Dumbarton Oaks, Studies in Pre-Columbian Art and Archaeology, No. 29. Washington, D.C.

Willey, Gordon R., A. Ledyard Smith, Gair Tourtellot III, and Ian Graham
1975   *Excavations at Seibal, Department of Peten, Guatemala*. 3 vols. Peabody Museum of Archaeology and Ethnology, Harvard University, Memoirs, vol. 13. Cambridge, Mass.

Wren, Linnea, Peter Schmidt, and Ruth Krochok
1989   The Great Ball Court Stone of Chichen Itza. *Research Reports on Ancient Maya Writing*, no. 25, pp. 23–27. Washington, D.C.

Index